Arguments and Actions in Social Theory

Arguments and Actions in Social Theory

Peter Preston
University of Birmingham, UK

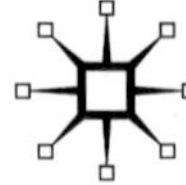

First published 2009 by
PALGRAVE MACMILLAN

Palgrave Macmillan in the UK is an imprint of Macmillan Publishers Limited, registered in England, company number 785998, of Houndmills, Basingstoke, Hampshire RG21 6XS.

Palgrave Macmillan in the US is a division of St Martin's Press LLC, 175 Fifth Avenue, New York, NY 10010.

Palgrave Macmillan is the global academic imprint of the above companies and has companies and representatives throughout the world.

Palgrave® and Macmillan® are registered trademarks in the United States, the United Kingdom, Europe and other countries.

ISBN-13: 978–0–230–57600–1 hardback
ISBN-10: 0–230–57600–1   hardback

This book is printed on paper suitable for recycling and made from fully managed and sustained forest sources. Logging, pulping and manufacturing processes are expected to conform to the environmental regulations of the country of origin.

A catalogue record for this book is available from the British Library.

A catalogue record for this book is available from the Library of Congress.

10   9   8   7   6   5   4   3   2   1
18 17 16 15 14 13 12 11 10 09

Printed and bound in Great Britain by
CPI Antony Rowe, Chippenham and Eastbourne

Contents

Preface

This text argues that making sense of the social world is an activity generic to humankind; that such activities are diverse; and that they are present in the informal routines of family, everyday social life and the mundane procedures of familiar voluntary, commercial and state organisations. The business of making sense is also evident in more distinctive, self-conscious forms; thus the work of witch doctors, shamans, novelists, politicians, media commentators and so on. Self-conscious exercises in making sense are also the province of social theorists, those who look to the resources of the disciplines of the social sciences.

Social theorists are firmly located within the social world; exercises in social theorizing are both bounded and creative; the former enables the latter; imagination and creativity build upon the resources of the given context. Social theorists make arguments for audiences; the process of social theorizing is an exchange between context, theorist and audience; the context is both practical, the unfolding dynamics of structures, agents and events, and intellectual, the epistemic and ethical resources of the tradition which the theorist inhabits; social theorists, as noted, are diverse, their exchanges with contexts and audiences will be subtle, idiosyncratic and creative; and audiences, the addressees of exercises in social theorizing, perhaps formal, as required by the logic of argument, or substantive, in the form of particular social groups or organisations, will be diverse in their make up and their requirements; thus there is no simple, single model of social theorizing.

Acknowledgements

This manuscript runs together some familiar materials from the philosophy of social science with ideas taken from development theory plus some reflections from my own experience of living and working in mainland Europe and various parts of East Asia in order to argue for a particular view of the social sciences as diverse, practical and carried in tradition.

The issues addressed here have been considered in the company of earlier enquiries in respect of development theory; this work looked at the arguments presented and against the familiar claims of practitioners to clarity in respect of analytical procedures and practical goals, a multiplicity of lines of argument were evident, each serving a particular agenda; the context-bound and engaged nature of such argument was mapped in a preliminary fashion using the resources of the sociology of knowledge and the philosophy of social science. The present text – *Arguments and Actions in Social Theory* – is a synthesis of all this earlier material; it runs together the lessons of development theory (the business of social science is practical) with the lessons of the philosophy of social science (the task of making arguments is both crucial and non-obvious) in order to argue *first* that social theorizing comprises a diversity of context-bound exercises in argument making, each an exchange between context, theorist and audience, each a discrete mode of social theoretic engagement and *second* that social theorizing is disciplined by received tradition, in which case, the tradition which this author inhabits is the classical European tradition of social theorizing, concerned with the elucidation of the dynamics of complex change in the ongoing shift to the modern world.

The manuscript has been assembled over a lengthy period of time but as the intellectual issues addressed are both entertaining and enduring there has never seemed to be much of a rush to finish. The work has been pursued in the company of friends, students and colleagues in various locations in Singapore, Scotland, Germany, Japan, England and Hong Kong and I am happy to record my thanks to them all.

1
The Practical Nature of Social Theorizing

If one stands back from the day-to-day demands of professional routine, it becomes clear that an intellectual trajectory is not organised in advance, we do not begin by surveying the intellectual ground before deciding upon a line of enquiry; rather, as Hans-Georg Gadamer[1] might put it, we fall into conversation; our starting points are accidental, our early moves untutored, they are not informed by a systematic professional knowledge of the available territory, rather they flow from curiosity; we read what strikes us as interesting, we discard what seems dull. All this means that our early moves are quite idiosyncratic, shaped by our experiences of particular texts, teachers and debates with friends/ colleagues. Thereafter matters might become more systematic, we might decide to follow a discipline, discover an absorbing area of work or find ourselves slowly unpacking hitherto deep-seated concerns. It also means that we can bestow coherence only retrospectively. This idiosyncratic personal aspect to scholarly enquiry is part and parcel of the trade, not something to be regretted, denied or avoided; nonetheless systematic reflection offers a way of taking stock, of presenting critical reflexive statements in regard to the formal commitments made in substantive work. This text turns to one familiar source of such reflection, the philosophy of social science, where claims about the nature, intellectual value and utility of social theorizing are routinely disputed, and offers a particular restatement of the classical European tradition of social theorizing, with its central concern for elucidating the dynamics of complex change, arguing that social theorizing comprises a wide diversity of situation-bound attempts to make practical sense of shifting circumstances; each a discrete instance of argument and action; each oriented towards particular audiences and objectives.

Characterizing social theorizing: science, language and politics

Social theorizing is both bounded and creative; it is not a narrowly professional discipline; it can assume many forms. It is routinely engaged, practical and robust. And as the practice of social science is diverse, so too is reflection upon its nature and three significant strands may be identified: first, arguments from the natural sciences; second, arguments from language and understanding; and third, arguments from political community. A critical survey of these debates reveals how social theorizing can be grounded in language, located within received traditions and deployed in multiple forms of practice.

****

Norman Foster,[2] in the context of a television series dealing with great buildings, where each slot was limited to a few minutes, devoted his time to celebrating the Boeing 747; a design icon of the late twentieth century, the vehicle whereby the era of mass long haul travel was inaugurated, and clearly, in line with Foster's architectural predilections, the product of both high-tech imagination and natural scientific achievement. Foster was right about the Boeing 747; the modernist project has made science central to contemporary forms of life; our social world is dependent upon natural science; it is one of the brightest jewels in humankind's cultural crown; and today it is the world we take for granted. Natural science has a familiar image; it is neutral, reliable and safe. The status of natural science is easily acknowledged and replicating its success in the sphere of the social if it were possible might have many benefits. Nonetheless, natural science is not a natural given, it is an elaborate cultural achievement, and it is susceptible to all the analytical machineries of a social science; or more substantively, natural science has its economics, sociology and politics. Anthony Giddens[3] characterizes the familiar image of natural science in the sphere of the social sciences as the 'received model'; a mixture of naive realism coupled to naive induction. It offers a particular intellectual self-understanding and social role, inviting an aspiration to the provision of value-neutral, technically precise causal knowledge so as to inform authoritative intervention. But this systematically misleads in respect of the nature of social science, making policy science central, and whilst it can be granted that the orthodox preference for policy scientific work can be expressed in diverse and subtle ways, their central claims to a detached technical role are not sustainable because they are making arguments on behalf of a particular audience. Against their self-understandings, the work they pursue does not capture the essence of social theorizing. As Alasdair MacIntyre argues, it is enough to note the unpredictability of human life in order to dismiss expectations derived from the natural science, and familiar managerialist claims to such knowledge are fiction.[4] There are better starting points, better ways to grasp the diverse subtle exchanges between context, theorist and audience which shape social theorizing.

The argument of critical philosophers concerned with language, that reflection on the nature of human life should turn away from concern with how the world works, the realm of facts, and should begin with an examination of the conceptual apparatus people inhabit, is at first meeting almost wholly incomprehensible; it seems wilfully perverse; the world is out there, given, a realm of hard facts, and human language, talk, seems evanescent and inconsequent. Nonetheless, the analysis of language has been crucial in twentieth century reflection upon the nature of human social life and the character of the intellectual traditions we inhabit; and it can be argued that systematic reflection upon the nature of human language is the key to a plausible social science. A key figure was Ludwig Wittgenstein, whose work is located in the cultural milieu of *fin-de-siecle* Vienna, the fading years of the Hapsburg Empire and the period of the rise of modernism, with its concerns for intellectual and ethical clarity. Wittgenstein acknowledges the general interest in language, and presents two approaches. The *Tractatus* offers the picture theory of meaning; language and the world relate to each other in that the former models the latter, thereby securing clarity. The *Investigations* make a series of new claims: the idea that language has one job to do (stating facts) is rejected, now language does many jobs (the metaphor of the tool box is introduced); the way in which language obtains meaning is changed, it is bound up in the use of language (the ideas of language games and forms of life); and where language rode on top of the facts in the *Tractatus*, in the *Investigations* there are no facts outside the language games we play; our language is not grounded on an external reality rather it is sanctioned in established social custom. The second philosophy caught the attention of English-speaking theorists.[5] Yet scholarly interest in language was well established in the German-speaking world: the philosophical hermeneutics of Gadamer centred on the language-carried, tradition-bound nature of human understanding. Gadamer argues that language is the ontology of human kind. In respect of social sciences, it is futile to try to accumulate objective external descriptions after the style of the natural sciences, because all social knowledge is suffused with ideas passed down through language-carried tradition. In the natural sciences it might make sense to suppress inherited ideas, so as to see the natural world clearly, but such a manoeuvre in the social sciences would cut away the very traditions which inform human life and formal reflection upon human life. Gadamer argues that historicity (being-in-history) is a clue to interpretive social science. We inhabit tradition, it is sedimented in our minds and comprises those ideas we inherit, inhabit and continually rework.

The territory of human language has been extensively investigated. It offers the basis of an interpretive social science, concerned with the elucidation of the patterns of language-carried social meaning within which individuals and groups make their lives. A further step is available in the acknowledgement of the political nature of human community. Arguments that affirm particular models of political life are familiar, as philosophies and ideologies. In the Anglo-American intellectual world the assumptions of liberalism pervade social science; the rectitude of serving the policy scientific interests of liberal state and corporate sector is affirmed in routine practice. But there are alternative positions, critical of liberalism and its associated social science, looking instead to a rational democratic society, which go on to offer novel ways of thinking about the given-ness of political activity within all human social life. Cast in terms of a simple distinction between liberalism and democracy, C.B. Macpherson[6] criticizes liberalism and its variant liberal-democracy; the former read as the political theory of the English bourgeoisie, radical in its day, and now unhelpful, with the latter judged untenable, and argues for a return to the idea of democracy. In a similar vein, Alasdair MacIntyre[7] claims that in contemporary society a self-deluding individualism and an equally foolish bureaucratic managerialism dance to the tunes of state and corporate power holders; and a return to an Aristotelian ethic of virtue is advocated, the social achievement of a decent selfhood, anticipated in republic democracy. These themes are repeated in the work of Jurgen Habermas who pursues the project of constructing a politics adequate to the present: reliably grounded and practical.[8]

****

These three strands reveal an extensive debate. Natural science has been widely celebrated. Interpretive and critical social sciences can be found in reflection on human language/meaning and the political life of communities. These ideas are not new; they are part of the classical European tradition. The tradition is practical; it has informed the unfolding shift to the modern world in Europe; it has produced elaborate conceptual machineries, available to be deployed in various idioms in pursuit of the objectives of diverse social groups.

Tradition, diversity and complex change

The business of making sense of the social world is generic to humankind; it is intrinsic to forms of life, a mundane, practical and routine social accomplishment. There are many available attempts to order such understandings; to make them self-conscious, organised and ideally more effective; these range from the materials of little traditions (common sense, folk wisdom and the words of witch doctors, shamans, politicians and so on) through to the work comprising great traditions (the efforts of priests, artists, philosophers and the like). The sphere of formal social science is one more attempt. Social theorizing is a family of loosely related attempts to make practical sense of the social world. Any instance of argument and action will be a circumstance-sensitive and problem-specific deployment of the intellectual machineries of received tradition ordered around specific conceptions of enquiry oriented to particular goals. The expectation of a particular sort of action is built into the analytical machineries that carry the argument. Such arguments are routinely made on behalf of a wide variety of anticipated agents, thus there are a diversity of discrete modes of social theoretic engagement. Matters could be left there, and reflection upon the nature of the social sciences would amount to accumulating examples, but a measure of convenient order, the better to locate and clarify different stands of argument, can be secured. A series of inter-related ways can be specified: first, the preparation of exemplars drawn from the social theoretic tradition; second, the preparation of an ideal-typical framework; and third, the accumulation of a personal stock of examples.

The specification of exemplars is an obvious strategy, deriving typical modes of theoretical engagement from the history of social science, the practice. The core mode of engagement is provided by the way agents read and react to enfolding circumstances in the process of the ongoing shift to the modern world. The key concern is with processes of complex change: thus (reflecting this author's trajectory), Karl Marx, offering arguments for a revolutionary proletariat, Emile Durkheim, presenting arguments for the progressive French bourgeoisie and Max Weber offering arguments for the German middle classes. Other figures could be cited; the list is long. The identification of the core mode of engagement allows other modes to be identified, analysed (in terms of their internal make up and practical concerns) and positioned (evaluated) relative to the core of the tradition. However, a simpler strategy is available; an ideal typical trio of modes of engagement can be presented as summarizing the historical experience of social theorists in the classical European tradition: politics, policy and scholarship. The arguments of political agents are shaped by structural patterns, balances of forces and immediate problems. The arguments of policy analysts are shaped by institutional locations, organisational contexts and contemporary problems. The arguments of scholars are shaped by cultural traditions, intellectual disciplines and current concerns. Arguments are always specific to place and audience and their multiplicity easily grasped via the accumulation of further ideal-types. And then, finally, the accumulation of a stock of working examples; this strategy points up the diverse environments within which social theorists operate, their multiple concerns and particular audiences. Thus: the mode of engagement of the colonial administrator/scholar arguing on behalf of the enlightened colonial authority; the political writer urging action upon a public audience; the administrator-planner, found in commercial corporations, quasi-government bodies and in the state bureaucracy offering narrowly focused argument in favour of distinct policy positions; the print media journalist offering commentary to a reading public; or the work of the scholar presenting arguments on behalf of humankind.

The received European social theoretic tradition encompasses the work of differently located theorists making arguments designed for particular agents/audiences. There is no one model of social theorizing; after Wittgenstein, it is a loose family of activities. Yet the diversity of modes of engagement is not unrestricted; after Gadamer, theorists inhabit traditions which offer both resources and constraints. A received tradition can be identified. In general terms the tradition centres upon concern for the detail of social processes, (the ineluctable core of social life), which finds (schematic) practical expression in the analysis of the dynamics of structures, agents and projects in the ongoing shift to the modern world. In turn this produces a characteristic set of concerns: for historical-structural analysis, tracing out the development trajectories of particular territories, typically, countries; for conjunctures, the ways in which a given territory is located within wider patterns of power; for phases in development trajectories, the periods of relative stability in structural patterns and agent response; for disjunctures, breaks in development trajectories; for the political-projects of elites, the institutional vehicles of such projects and the business of popular mobilization; and, thereafter, for the nature and extent of critical debate in the public sphere. The European tradition offers, in contrast to the orthodox consensus, a more sophisticated intellectual machinery, a more complex substantive analysis and a more ambiguous practical import: change as comprising matters to be deciphered and ordered (to the extent that they can be).

The culture that contemporary Europeans inhabit has been shaped in part by these resources: in its popular form, the story of the evolutionary achievement of progress, a Eurocentric official truth. However in recent years there has been a wealth of critical material displaying the multiple errors of this stance; its unreflexive intellectual apparatus; unexamined ethical commitments and disposition to the export of unexamined models of practice. All this opens up a series of problems for scholarship: first, to acknowledge that the contemporary world, for all its increasing inter-connectedness, is home to diverse voices and different ways of reading the intermingled common history of humanity; and secondly, to acknowledge problems in reconstructing a plausible narrative of the ongoing development of the modern world. Here the historical experience of Europe (or given its recent pre-eminence, the USA) cannot be taken to offer a universal model and suggestions for the substitution of a global-centrism for outmoded Euro-centrism do not help as received culture cannot be evaded; one cannot step outside one's own culture. A reflexive appropriation of received tradition offers a more plausible route forwards. The classical European tradition of social theorizing represents the materials that theorists and commentators in Europe deployed in formulating, ordering and responding to the shift to the modern world. A contemporary approach to analysing complex change (one that is intellectually plausible according to the tenets of this tradition and grants recent criticism), must be sceptical, dialogic and routinely open to debate and revision; that is, interpretive-critical.[9]

Putting it all to work

In respect of these ideas, putting it all to work, the upshot of these reflections is a particular view of the nature of social theorizing: the business of making sense of the social world is generic to humankind;

social scientific theorizing is one way of making sense; social theorizing is interpretive-critical, a matter of making arguments for a variety of possible audiences; social theoretic enquiries are shaped by contexts and audiences; they are partial, finite pieces of interpretive-critical analysis; the spread of familiarly social scientific arguments is intellectually diverse and admits of a variety of engagements; and the familiar materials of social scientific work constitute a tradition, the intellectual/ practical environment which sustains contemporary practice. The classical European tradition is concerned with the elucidation of the dynamics of complex change, those intermingled unfolding routes towards an ever-receding modern world; it is a vigorous tradition; it is rich in resources; thus, it can be asserted that the sceptical reflexive modernist project is alive and well and its relevance/role in the contemporary multi-polar world evident.[10]

2
Arguments from Natural Science

The successes of the natural sciences are not in doubt; our pattern of life is structured by the pursuit of science; our ordinary lives are suffused with its achievements, the cities and suburbs in which we live could not be sustained without routines and machineries built on the knowledge of natural science. The sciences are central to our form of life, they do not exist off to one side, feeding in novelties; their products underpin our form of life, their habits of thought suffuse our thinking and they provide the common paradigm of knowledge. Yet it remains a contingent historical cultural achievement. Norman Davies[1] has reminded us of the nature of the world before the rise of science: the key intellectual, moral and institutional mechanism was the Church; the world was constituted in theistic terms, and the shift to our world, centrally materialist in the philosophical sense, was long drawn out, not simply a debate about ideas but a conflict about power and livelihood, the business of implanting mercantile agrarian capitalism from the sixteenth century onwards. The sciences have a place within our society and the depth of their reach within our form of life is an important issue; but it is not enough to say that science is central, the benefits obvious; because, in particular, for us, there is the question of the nature of a social science.

The rise of a science of humankind

The natural sciences developed from the sixteenth century onwards,[2] with Isaac Newton's work dominating scientific thinking for two hundred years, up to the turn of the twentieth century. Inevitably, and perfectly sensibly, theorists in other fields looked to the example of the new science and accommodated themselves accordingly; the model was widely embraced, and it came to inform the work of social scientists. The trajectory of that enthusiasm, the disputes it has provoked and its relative decline can be tracked as empiricist celebrants of science contended with a variety of critics.

The orthodox empiricist/positivists[3] argue from a particular view of the nature of natural science to a characterization of social science and thence its proper social role: they argue either that the epistemology of the natural sciences can and ought to be shifted to the sphere of the social (the unity of method) or make an ontological commitment that the human world is an integral part of the natural world and can therefore be studied in the same way (unity of subject). These two are different routes to the same end point; that is, a naturalistic science of the social. But the goal is contentious; and there are strategies of formal reply. The *weak hermeneutic objection* suggests that approaches appropriate to the natural world are not appropriate to the social. Wilhelm Dilthey distinguished natural and social science by their content; social sciences entailed the pursuit of interpretive understanding. Heinrich Rickert[4] stressed a difference in method between individualizing and generalizing. Max Weber[5] attempted to integrate interpretive and causal understanding. Later, Peter Winch drew on Wittgenstein to argue that natural and social sciences are conceptually distinct. And the Frankfurt School rejected arguments from natural science to social science because they involved technical manipulative reason invading the broader cultural sphere. The *strong hermeneutic objection* is bolder: Hans-Georg Gadamer's philosophical hermeneutics insists that all human activity is lodged within language-carried received tradition; consequently natural science is an historical cultural achievement; so too interpretive social science; both are specific, restricted human creations, neither accesses an extra-linguistic realm. A final response is the *strategy of dual reworking*; the unity of science is achieved in the simultaneous reworking of conceptions of both natural and social science as disciplined, theory-driven and public enquiries.[6]

Our contemporary debates rehearse established lines of argument and enquiry; we do not, as the orthodox empiricist/positivists would have it, move smoothly into the future, ours is a reiterative and not a cumulative pursuit and work is lodged within a long-fashioned, contested intellectual/practical tradition. The European tradition embraces empiricist/positivist, interpretive and critical contributions, but at the outset, here, it is the optimistic line of the Enlightenment[7] that is considered; later we turn to other strands of work that cast doubt on these formulations and thereafter to the hermeneutic and critical theoretic alternatives.

Mapping the field I: the Enlightenment, a trajectory of social scientific work

Many have written on the Enlightenment, and as the tradition is diverse any report claiming to identify its core elements could be challenged; here a simple rehearsal of ideas, culled from the available literature,[8] in order to make the point that contemporary social theorists inherit and inhabit a long, contested tradition of argument and practical activity. The theorists whose work now constitutes that tradition were engaged thinkers not passive observers and their ideas – tested against experience – provide the materials for today's social theorists in the areas of epistemology and social/political theory. It is important to acknowledge these resources; contemporary social theorists deploy a repertoire of concepts whose accumulation began in the seventeenth century.

The pre-modern world was agrarian, feudal and theistic; the church was a central institution; and the shift to the modern world involved a series of changes in the economic, social, political and cultural spheres. The intellectual changes were profound; in brief, a move from medieval Aristotelian reasoning *apriori* about humankind, the natural world and the realm of the divine to a recognisably modern stress on the importance of the mundane detail of the natural world. The rise of natural science was crucial. Isaac Newton worked on physics, astronomy and mathematics, and these materials were circulated in popular form,[9] and, with others, he engineered the shift from Aristotelian metaphysics to modern physics. It was a complex intellectual shift and a series of key ideas can be associated with seventeenth century natural science: (i) *ontological*, the nature of the world changes, and in the movement from theistic to materialistic schemes there is an affirmation of a mechanical philosophy which presents an ontology of matter and causes; (ii) *epistemological*, the getting of knowledge changes, and in the movement from medieval rationalism to empiricism the natural world becomes a sphere for the deployment of human reason (iii) *methodological*, the organisation of enquiry changes, and in the movement from *apriori* reasoning to the use of experiment[10] a central role is made for the accumulation of mundane detail coupled to the use of experimental method; (iv) *ethical*, the expectation of the ends of human action changes, and in the movement from the pursuit of perfection to an accumulative perfectibility hope for the future is embedded in the quotidian realm;[11] and (v) *pragmatic*, the nature of praxis alters, and the use of reason comes to inform human life and progress. And as the seventeenth century turned into the eighteenth, these ideas flourished, were enthusiastically translated into the territory of social/political thought and are recalled now as the Enlightenment; it was an exchange of ideas/practices which transcended national boundaries.[12]

In social/political theory and epistemology, Thomas Hobbes and John Locke, responding to the crisis of the seventeenth century English Civil War, put the new ideas to work.[13] In political analysis Hobbes drew on the new sciences for his method, the identification of logically primitive ideas followed by a reconstruction of complex reality: in the pre-social state of nature there was war of all against all; the social was constructed because it was prudent; and the contractual constitution of a sovereign power mitigated the effects of individualism. Natural and social laws constrained the individual; the former governed the competitive pursuit of individual satisfactions, whilst the latter backed by the power of the sovereign secured order.[14] Locke offered a variant; the state of nature was not unrestrictedly competitive because humankind lived in families; natural law now encompassed property; the contracted social law safeguarded property; and the sovereign was empowered by the consent of the governed. Locke went on to unpack the epistemology: the empirical world impressed itself upon receptive humankind, the mind was a *tabula rasa* upon which experience wrote; science advanced; and philosophy embraced the role of under-labourer. And these matters – social/political theory and epistemology – were pursued during the early eighteenth century in the particular circumstances of the Scottish Enlightenment.[15] In social/political theory Adam Smith affirmed the method of proceeding from first principles in order to reconstruct the complexity of the observed world; the wealth of nations was to be found in the complex division of labour and the invisible hand of the marketplace; and the system was buttressed by the established moral sentiments of the community. And in epistemology, David Hume advanced experience as the basis for knowledge, asserted the distinction between facts and values, argued that reason was the slave of the passions and stressed the role of custom or habit in buttressing knowledge claims. Hume's philosophical ideas run through to the present as the taken for granted underpinning of empiricism.

In France the *philosophes* sought radical change through an educative role in clubs, societies, pamphlets and the creation of the Encyclopaedia. There were a number of major figures: Voltaire, Condillac, Helvetius and Rousseau.[16] In a slightly different way Charles de Montesquieu[17] in *The Spirit of the Laws* sought to make history intelligible by reducing observable diversity in socio-political life to the operation of a few underlying factors, thus enabling effective political practice. Aristotelian political philosophy provides three models of government, (Republican,

Monarchy and Despotism); the material and social causes of all three are indicated (and here, size, climate, land holdings, and trade patterns, for example, are invoked); and on the basis of these analyses the example of England and the pursuit of material progress via the establishment of liberal democracy was presented as the route to the future for France. Montesquieu's legacy is his affirmation of determinism (thus chance does not rule the world, rather it is structured by underlying laws), rationalism in the general sense (thus the human intellect can discover these laws) and social structural analysis (thus characterizing and explaining the causal structuring of distinct polities).

In the early nineteenth century social theorizing was shaped by the democratic and industrial revolutions. The French Revolution was not the first bourgeoisie revolution, that claim could be made for the English Civil War or the American War of Independence, but it was the first to be explicitly democratic;[18] it was self-consciously pursued and analysed in newspapers and pamphlets. A wealth of philosophical work emerged, so too positive social science. Henri de Saint-Simon[19] published a series of texts in which he affirmed the power of human reason, stressed positive applied science and eventually generated a scheme of social engineering centred on the role of an intellectual scientific elite. Saint-Simon affirmed progress; history was moving forward, and with the use of science, including social science, this movement could become self-conscious and faster. Saint-Simon saw progress involving phases: organic periods of stable development (classical Hellenic, medieval Catholic and a third organic period, scientific, was emerging); and critical periods, the destructive and confused transitions from one organic period to another. The present phase was a critical period that had started about the time of the Renaissance and saw the slow rise of scientific industrial society. In all this Saint-Simon offered the first recognizably modern discussion of a range of social scientific concerns: the role of intellectuals, the nature of socialist reforms to unfettered markets, the nature of social class and the character of industrialism; plus the growth of bureaucracy, professionals, finance and the spread of the European industrial system. Theory was translated into practice via clubs and he had adherents spread around the world. August Comte,[20] his secretary and co-worker, took these ideas and produced an influential systematic general theory detailing the evolution of humankind and the development of the social sciences.

In the late nineteenth century Charles Darwin's theory of evolution via natural selection offered an explanation for the proliferation of living organisms and identified the mechanism whereby some survive;

thus chance variation and adaptation to the environment underpin the evolution of species. The arguments illuminated the development and character of the natural world and their extension to the human realm was an obvious albeit contentious corollary. Ideas of evolution were widespread and there was a two-way exchange between ideas of biological evolution and social evolution.[21] It took multiple forms. Herbert Spencer advanced a complex scheme of philosophical evolution; quickly simplified by his followers into social Darwinism, a celebration of late nineteenth century market capitalism. There were replies to Spencer:[22] the defensive reaction of biologists who did not like the extension of evolution into ethics; the favourable reaction of eugenicists like Francis Galton who saw a route to the improvement of humankind; and the reformist response which turned evolution back against its proponents and argued that if we could comprehend evolution then we could act to assist its longer run tendencies, thus social reform rather than *laissez-faire* could usher in the future. In Britain, the preference for reform produces the Fabians Socialists, L.T. Hobhouse and the British sociology of the first half of the twentieth century.[23] In the USA, Darwin's work was picked up by John Dewey and feeds into the reformism of the New Deal.[24] In France, Emile Durkheim, engaging with familiar debates, cast his work in terms of the organic solidarity of modern life.[25] In Germany, in the First Empire, the ideas of social Darwinism found widespread acceptance; and later they were recycled by the proponents of National Socialism.[26] Overall, the aggressive ideas of social Darwinism continue down to the present in residual/resurgent eugenics ideas, lately in the form of sociobiology, however, more familiarly, evolutionism has become submerged within functionalism and, thereafter, a general, vague expectation of progressive change has become something of an intellectual habit of mind.

The Enlightenment project unfolded over the course of the nineteenth century; it found expression in the public realm, as states and nations were made;[27] in the natural sciences; in the social sciences; and in the arts and humanities. Yet the changes were not universally welcomed: conservatives criticized the apparent costs, and harked back to community, hierarchy and imagined stability;[28] others recoiled from the forms of early industrialization.[29] It is also clear that there was a broader response to the Enlightenment; a counter stress to instrumental reason on imagination, culture and the creativity of human ideas; offering an assertion of the value and needs of people as against the rationalizing demands of the system.[30] Such work was inaugurated around the turn of the century, in particular in mainland Europe, and developed quickly; and whilst its proponents were scattered in the 1914–45 catastrophe, the work resumed after the war and, notwithstanding the difficulties attending cold war, proved surprisingly resilient. It is in this line of work that we can find the roots of an alternate conceptualization of the nature and possibilities of modern life and of the prospective contribution of the social sciences; it is here that we find the interpretive and critical work; the efforts of those not disposed to legislation, rather interpretation,[31] and whose materials will be considered later: F.W. Hegel, Karl Marx, Emile Durkheim, Wilhelm Dilthey, Max Weber, Hans Georg Gadamer and latterly Jurgen Habermas.

Mapping the field II: the process of disciplinization/scientization

The trajectory of social science in Europe over the period of the short twentieth century includes *expansion* (as the formal institutionalized pursuit of social science burgeons), *fragmentation* (as separate disciplines form and define themselves one against the other), *consolidation* (as disciplines develop their technical expertise and build up their stocks of knowledge) and *scientization* (as originally engaged scholarship subsides into professional technical expertise).[32] As the disciplines develop each lays claim to a particular object sphere, a relevant method, a body of accumulated wisdom and the status of a professional discipline whose expertise can be deployed in the knowledge marketplace.

In the English-speaking world, the key bridges across the great divide,[33] the self-understood movement from speculative philosophical thinking to the acquisition of scientific knowledge, were the marginalist revolution and the creation of academic disciplines within the American university system. In Britain, the study of political economy declined in the 1870s and was eclipsed by the time of the Great War[34] and there were methodological and political conflicts between proponents of economics and sociology. In the first, debate turned on the scope of sociology and its relation to economics and where Comte urged the priority of sociology a sharp reaction assisted the formation of neo-classicism. In the second, debate in respect of the claims of individualism and collectivism had both intellectual and political implications, and sociology was taken to be unreliably collectivistic in contrast to economics. These debates were paralleled in the USA where great wealth and deep conservatism co-existed and with no perceived need for structural change American social theorists pursued piecemeal reforms. One aspect of these matters was the process whereby economics and sociology were institutionalized; economics was established within the university world first and oversaw the later establishment of sociology. In consequence, in the

English-speaking world, economics became the hard social science and sociology became the study of social life more generally.[35]

In mainland Europe a similar process ran its course.[36] In France, history and philosophy remained prominent. After the 1870 Prussian invasion Emile Durkheim became influential and as the university system developed the position of sociology was assured as a practical reforming discipline oriented to the political project of the Third Republic. However, the Great War weakened the confidence of French intellectuals and in the inter-war period dispersed enquiries were pursued. In Germany, there was rapid economic advance and reform from above in the period from 1848 to 1914. A parallel intellectual debate revolved around the nature of social knowledge and the way in which it might inform action. The traditional view looked to the humanities and the arts as vehicles of personal cultivation and arguments in favour of a more practical social science were regarded as positivistic. However, as Germany shifted decisively into the modern world in the later years of the century the practical demands of the period became pressing. Max Weber made his ambiguous contribution to the illumination of the interests of the bourgeoisie and the German power-state, historical school economics were pursued and extensive work undertaken in economic sociology.[37] However, the debacle of the Great War, a failed revolution and the emergence of the fragile Weimar Republic had the effect of reducing the influence of the social sciences as the majority of intellectuals withdrew to the old traditions of the humanities.[38] Finally, it might be noted that as classical nineteenth century European social theory modulated into the discipline bound social sciences there were new intellectual departures[39] but the Second World War and the resultant destruction, division and occupation re-ordered debate; in the West, the American social science package of industrialism, convergence, modernization and the end of ideology was influential, and in the East, the doctrines of Marxism-Leninism supplanted indigenous debates; and, in both, commitments to rather different ideals of natural science were made.

Social science is always a drawing down on available stocks of ideas in received tradition, and an empiricist/positivist line is identifiable in theorists who have thus understood themselves. The history can be read in other ways, nonetheless, however one characterizes the history of the rise of the social sciences, familiar empiricist/positivist conceptions flow from long established reflection upon these matters. Yet to leave things at this point would be misleading. The model of the natural sciences thus far sketched was refined at the hands of early twentieth century philosophers and fed back into social science. In sum, the broad backdrop of discussions of the nature of natural science and the extension of these procedures into the sphere of the social comes to be reworked in a fashion stressing empirical natural science and logic; its apotheosis was logical positivism.

There had been extensive discussion amongst philosophers about the nature of natural science ever since the advances of the seventeenth centuries, in the late nineteenth century ideas of positivism were influential and round the turn of the twentieth century a new period of intellectual effort issued in the logical atomism of Bertrand Russell and Ludwig Wittgenstein: here was an equation of human knowledge with the natural sciences, and a characterization of natural science which saw it as systematic, disciplined and bound by cannons of logic. The Vienna Circle independently reached similar conclusions articulated in logical positivism. Discussions of the nature of social science within the ambit of the naturalistic orthodoxy have been pursued in the shadow of these recent variants of the broad cultural celebration of natural science.

Vienna Circle logical positivism

The later years of the nineteenth century saw a scientific revolution; there were fundamental discoveries in chemistry, physics, medicine and the biological sciences.[40] The celebration of science was widespread, finding expression across a range of undertakings, state, commercial and scholarly, and natural scientists, social scientists and the wider societies[41] were enamoured of these successes; in the domestic sphere progress was taken to be evident, and internationally the success of science was understood to exemplify occidental reason,[42] providing thereby one cultural element of the justification of empire.[43] In time diverse strands[44] of reflection crystallized into a particular and influential body of philosophical work, logical positivism, the doctrine of the Vienna Circle. The historical period was awkward. The later years of the Hapsburg Empire had been uneasy; nationalist sentiment had grown amongst the constituent peoples of the empire; there had been flows of rural migrants to the cities; critiques of cultural decadence were made; and significant early statements of modernism.[45] Following the Great War 1914–18[46] the collapse of the empire generated political uncertainty; there were programmes of progressive reform and strands of conservative reaction; and Vienna became the capital of a remnant of empire, Austria. The Circle's philosophical clarification of the language of empirical science was a contribution to wider scientifically ordered progressive social change.[47] Moritz Schlick, Rudolf Carnap and Otto Neurath were central figures.[48] Ludwig Wittgenstein's *Tractatus* was a key text.[49] Karl Popper was tangentially involved.[50] A number of major symposia were organised between 1929 and 1939, mostly in Europe, one in America.[51] The rise of European fascism dispersed the members of the Circle, and a number moved to the USA where the ideas proved influential.

The Vienna Circle drew on a series of influences: the work of Gottlob Frege on symbolic logic; the work of Ernst Mach[52] on the philosophy of science; the work of Bertrand Russell and the broad tradition of empiricism derived from Locke and Hume; and the general interest in the nature of language. Russell's work was taken to exemplify the requisite clarity in both the doctrines of logical atomism and the programme of analytical philosophy.[53] In contrast to earlier empiricists, who analysed knowledge as sensory experience ordered psychologically by human minds, the logical positivists, influenced by post-Kantian critical philosophy, concerned with the limits of language and thought, ran together two matters; meaning and knowledge, thus to comprehend a proposition entailed understanding both its linguistic meaning and its empirical ground. Philosophical analysis could clarify human thinking, distinguishing meaningful claims that had an empirical ground from empty talk which did not.

In 1929 the circle published a manifesto to announce their programme;[54] an unusual move amongst philosophers of science, though quite familiar in the communities of artists and intellectuals in Vienna, it was entitled *The Scientific Conception of the World: The Vienna Circle.*[55] The manifesto characterizes the environment of the Circle: its inheritance of anti-metaphysical scientific thinking; its place in Vienna, a site for much philosophical and scientific work; and its coalescence around the key figure of Moritz Schlick. The manifesto characterizes the broad prospectus of 'the scientific world conception': the pursuit of science and social reform informed by science;[56] the scientific world conception is empiricist/positivist, its key method is logical analysis and its task is the clarification of the tasks of science (and a number of key areas are noted). The philosophical work of the Circle revolved around the status of science and they pursued their search for logico-scientific clarity in the company of three main problems; the principle of verification, the elimination of metaphysics and the unity of science.[57]

The principle of verification stated that the meaning of a proposition is its method of verification; sentences were to be analysed out to their basic statements where these basic statements lodged empirical claims (or observation statements). These statements made claims about the real world, they could be checked. Complex sentences were built up of these basic statements. The verification principle offers a criterion of meaningfulness. Any sentence could now be analysed down into its observation-statements. The logical positivists also distinguished between analytic and synthetic statements; claims to formal truth (thus mathematics) or to empirical substantive reports. Statements could thus be analytical (true *apriori*) or substantive (true or false depending on how observation ran). They drew an important corollary; any sentence that could not be shown to be either analytical or empirical was meaningless. The verification principle acts as both a criterion of the meaningfulness of propositions (and thus their status as knowledge claims) and as a criterion of demarcation, distinguishing meaningful propositions from those that are meaningless; the latter included any abstract general intellectual strategies that claimed access to ultimate realities outside the empirical or analytic sciences. The commitment to the unity of science flowed automatically; either discourse was analytical or empirically redeemable or it was nonsense; thus there was only one fundamental form of meaningful discourse.

The argument advanced by the logical positivists is a radical expression of the empiricist tradition. The verification principle allows that natural science produces meaningful statements but denies meaning to metaphysics, ethics, politics or any other exercise that involves values; human discourse is split into two – natural scientific and meaningful and the non-meaningful rest. The verification principle was subject to close inspection, in particular the status of the principle itself? On the argument of its proponents it has to be either analytic or empirical; but it seems to be neither. If it is taken as empirical, a report on how meaning actually is assigned to sentences, then the necessary link between meaning and verification is broken as meaning could conceivably have been assigned to sentences some other way and still in future could be assigned some other way. The necessary link between meaning and verification must be sustained else verification cannot be used as a criterion of meaning and thus the whole project collapses. Alternatively it can be regarded as analytic; but clearly it is not analytic as maths and logic are. The logical positivists are forced back into unclear claims. Thus the verification principle can be read as a definition – but definitions are either stipulative, lexical, real, or persuasive and the last three are no good and the first, unsupported, looks like arbitrary *fiat,* so this strategy fails. At other times the verification principle was read as a methodological principle, but there are lots of these so there is nothing special here. The verification principle ruled itself out. It was neither analytic nor empirical, and attempts to label it a definition or methodological principle could only persuade those who already believed. Indeed, there were further problems with the programme. The elimination of metaphysics seemed to rule out things that people did want to talk about; Wittgenstein distinguished saying/showing; and Popper allowed that non-science could be relevant (aesthetics and emotion, for example) and provide a possible source of genuine scientific propositions. These were partial solutions, yet the final problem is more difficult: it addresses the idea of a unified science based on a particular idea of the relationship of language and reality. Wittgenstein in the *Tractatus* offers a scheme of how language works, analysable down to elementary propositions picturing reality and built up from these into complex sentences of ordinary language. As language at base works in this one way so the sciences must be unified. However many came to see this version of how language worked as unpersuasive. Wittgenstein rejects it completely in favour of the scheme presented in the *Investigations*,[58] there are many forms of life each carried in a language game; natural science is a diverse set of language games. There is no one model of enquiry. This is a major problem for logical positivism, and like the confusion with the verification principle strikes at the heart of their project.

However, notwithstanding these fatal problems the logical positivist celebration of natural science and the denial of the amenability to reason of matters of valuation had a profound cultural impact. In the USA, W.V.O. Quine helped to introduce the ideas, later the emigres.[59] In Britain A.J. Ayer's *Language, Truth and Logic* came to be regarded as something of a textbook of logical positivism.[60] The social reformist aspects are lost; the core arguments about natural science remain and Ayer argues that all genuine propositions can be allocated to one of two categories of meaningful propositions: empirical or analytic. Any proposition that could not be so allocated was judged to be senseless; a condition afflicting much philosophical work whose proper role is analysis, the clarification of the propositions of science. Overall, Ayer declares himself in close agreement with the Vienna Circle.[61] Ayer then confronts the realm of ethics, where people routinely argue about what ought to be done and take these arguments to be about ethical judgements (not facts or analytics). Ayer argues that these are simply expressions of emotion, thus neither true nor false. The work of moral philosophers is characterized as comprising four sorts of propositions; definitions of ethical terms, descriptions of moral experience, exhortations to moral virtue and actual ethical judgements. Ayer takes the view that only the first propositions are appropriate to ethical philosophy. The second belong to sociology and psychology, the third are ejaculations or commands and the last sort remain to be clarified (but clearly do not belong to ethical philosophy). Ayer rejects both utilitarianism (which reduces ethical statements to matters of pleasure and pain – thereby translating them into matters of fact) and subjectivism (which reduces ethical statements to feelings of approval – again, a sort of facts) on the grounds that these schemes are not '… consistent with the conventions of our actual language.'[62] Ayer's view is that ethical judgements add nothing to factual statements or the explication of analytic relations, they are 'pseudo-concepts'[63] designed to provoke certain feelings and encourage action;[64] the apparent discussions of ethics which people undertake turn out to be arguments about matters of fact conducted within habitual, taken for granted ethical frames, which are provided by common patterns of life; in this context agreement about matters of fact will in practice occasion agreement about ethical judgements.[65]

The lasting impact of logical positivism

The logical positivists shaped empiricist thought in the 1930s: offering a strong celebration of the work of the natural sciences, their views exerted influence within the social sciences where there were extensive debates about state planning. But as cracks began to appear within logical positivism, the status of social science was queried; there were problems of values, the nature of the role of the investigator, difficulties of prediction, the scarcity of laws and the paucity of hard facts. In the event, debates surrounding the optimistic celebration of science were overshadowed by a descent into barbarism, with disruption, scattered personnel and issues reworked in new contexts.[66] The Second World War saw the division and occupation of Europe; there were novel intellectual/cultural influences, in the East the Soviet Union and the materials of official Marxism-Leninism, in the West the profound impact of the USA. These were extended and subtle exchanges; indigenous scholars confronted novel perspectives as denizens of the European intellectual heartland attended perforce to voices from the peripheries, east and west, offering in each case their own traditions, both in empiricist/positivistic guise.[67] There were lines of resistance; in Britain, Keynes and ameliorist welfarism, in Germany the reconstituted Frankfurt School and in France[68] major thinkers in existentialism, Marxism and structuralism. Nonetheless the influence of the USA fostered the naturalistic analysis of industrial society. Alongside these developments debates continued in respect of natural science and its precise relationship with the social sciences; it is here that we find the social scientific orthodoxy of the years following the Second World War. Over the 1950s and 1960s one might speak of the presentation of a softened celebration of natural science, a mitigated positivism; but after the confusions of the sixties it rapidly fades.

Achievement/dissolution: Karl Popper, W.V.O. Quine and Ernest Nagel

The unfolding trajectory of engaged practical social theorizing was accompanied by formal reflection. The work of logical positivism was revisited. The new work offered tangled insights: as enquiry into the nature of natural science deepened the understandings of the logical positivists seemed less and less reliable; the inappropriateness of shifting the understandings of natural science of the logical positivists into the sphere of the social seemed less and less tenable; and, more radically, the further enquiry into natural science was pushed the more it seemed to be a thoroughly social activity. The opening moves in this slow dissolve of formal confidence can be associated with the work of Karl Popper W.V.O. Quine and Ernest Nagel; all three were influential within the Anglo-American world in the years following the Second World War.

Karl Popper's package deal: science and social reform

Karl Popper's work was presented in the distinctive milieus of pre-war Vienna and post-war London. It forms a coherent package, critical rationalism, but the contexts within which it was deployed significantly coloured its expression. In the former, the successes of natural science offered a clue to a progressive politics of reform during a period of great confusion and violence. However, the environment of London was quite different and here modest domestic social reform – the creation of a welfare state – was joined by a virulent politics of cold war anti-communism which left little space for respectable dissent; Popper accommodated himself to the environment; and in time became an isolated, somewhat reactionary figure.[69]

However, the bulk of Popper's work was accomplished in his early years in Vienna. The environment of city in the late years of the Hapsburg Empire was multicultural and tolerant, a place where assimilated Jewish liberal progressives could operate. Popper's work celebrated science and the open society. The years after the Great War were more difficult with tensions between left and right radicals that culminated in the rise of National Socialism; the tolerant milieu dissolved, and work begun in Vienna was continued in London, yet the environment was quite different and the political analyses were assimilated to cold war anti-communism. However, the material on natural science proved influential; in outline, the body of work combines a putative non-empiricist/positivist philosophy of science, a means of distinguishing science and non-science and a defence of liberal-democratic pluralism plus piecemeal social reform as appropriate to our knowledge-getting abilities.[70]

The first issue is the nature of science. The empiricist/positivist position affirms a notion of scientific procedure which entails observation and induction to generate laws and/or theories which are then elaborated by the method of deriving claims which must be true if the law/theory is true and testing them experimentally. The body of natural scientific knowledge thus grows accumulatively as a hierarchical set of claims (covering laws, general theories, specific hypotheses) based, finally, on the observation of facts. Popper proposes an alternative scheme of conjecture and refutation: natural scientific procedure involves making bold conjectures from which specific testable claims are derived. If the theory survives the test it is corroborated (not verified); so theory in natural science is the present collection of conjectures that have withstood attempts to prove them wrong. The body of natural scientific knowledge grows haphazardly: it is a collection of conjectures (guesses, theories, hypotheses) oriented to problems and proffered on the basis of experience (tradition) and imagination that have thus far escaped refutation. The image of science changes from the modest disciplined accumulation of verified knowledge to the bold imaginative use of collections of as yet un-refuted conjectures.

On the second issue, the logic of enquiry offers a clue to the demarcation of science and non-science. Popper's[71] philosophy of science revises traditional empiricism. Orthodox empiricism took the logic of science to be inductive where this involved the observation of many particular instances as the basis for generalized statements or laws. Popper argues there is a logical asymmetry between the weakness of confirming instances (which can never secure a general claim) and the strengths of a disconfirming instance (where one instance is enough to refute any general statement). So in place of a logic of enquiry which claims that science proceeds by collecting many observations of particular instances as the basis for inductive generalization and subsequent confirmation by further observation, a trio of steps taken as respectively, implausible, untenable and not credible, Popper proposes a logic of conjecture, a guess more or less well educated, followed by the derivation of specific empirical claims which are then tested leading either to refutation of the conjecture or provisional support. This conjecture is kept so long as it is not refuted in tests. Natural scientific knowledge is thus never final, but if a hypothesis escapes attempted refutation it is thereby corroborated (rather than confirmed). Natural science proceeds in this falsificationist fashion. It may be objected that scientists in practice are not readily disposed to abandon ideas or experiments that do not work. On this Popper declares that logically he is naive falsificationist, but methodologically he is more tolerant as constructing and interpreting empirical tests of a theory is in practice a laborious business. Thus the second issue is addressed: the notion of falsification serves as a key to the solution of the problem of induction (and the reconstitution of the logic of science) and as a criterion of demarcation between science and non-science. A scientific theorem can be falsified because it will make restricted empirically testable claims; non-scientific theorems do not have this quality, noticeably Marxism and psychoanalysis.[72]

The third element of the package is the political stance. *The Open Society and Its Enemies* examines the relationship between intellectual enquiry and socio-political organisation. Plato and Marx are analysed and in both an early optimistic epistemology conjoined with a libertarian politics of emancipation gives way with the rise of inevitable disenchantment to a later conjunction of pessimistic epistemologies with authoritarian politics of elite direction of society; Plato shifts from the early Socratic dialogues to the later schemes of *The Republic*, Marx from the libertarian optimism of the *Paris Manuscripts* to the authoritarianism of the scientific socialism of *Capital*. Popper notes that scientific knowledge is tentative and the social world is hugely complex, rejects the historicism, arguing in *The Poverty of Historicism* that it suggests the social sciences aim for large-scale historical prophecy, and advocates piecemeal social engineering; modest alterations to our social world can be proposed, thereby enabling precision and allowing control of the unintended consequences. Popper argues that critical rationalism enjoins piecemeal social engineering, the rational policy science of a liberal pluralist society.

In regard to this package, and its various elements, there have been criticisms: the status of critical rationalism has been queried; the utility of the notion of falsification has been challenged; and the persuasiveness of the model of politics has also been called into question.

It has been argued that Popper's critical rationalism is ungrounded in the sense that there is no rational basis for our adoption of this stance; we simply decide to use this procedure. Thomas McCarthy[73] suggests that Popper refuses to follow through the implications of a transcendental grounding of knowledge produced by his own stress on critical reason. Popper is committed to a correspondence theory of truth, a classic empiricist position; he inverts induction and affirms correspondence, now natural science gets closer to the truth by accumulating definitely wrongs. Popper's commitment to critical rationalism turns out to be a version of seventeenth century philosophical celebration of scientific method. The costs of this position are that whilst claiming to be progressive it fails to secure a coherent notion of progress,[74] abolishes learning for the random accumulation of novelties[75] and in place of the progressive display of the truth we have merely a collection of theorems that have thus far survived attempts at refutation.

One of the original intentions of Popper was to provide a means whereby science could be clearly demarcated from non-science. The solution to this problem was found in the notion of falsification. Science tests its theories, that is, attempts to falsify theorems via empirical examination of deduced hypotheses. The notion of falsification drew much support from its apparent simplicity. But on closer examination it becomes evident that there is a conceptual difficulty in deploying the notion because what is to count as a disconfirming instance is open to debate. Putting natural scientific theorems to the test involves interpreting experimental results, so falsification is not the simple criterion it is presented as being. The notion of falsification was also taken by Popper to be the key to reformulating the logic of scientific discovery so as to evade the problem of induction. Hume had argued that inductive reasoning, from observed particulars to general statements, was logically broken backed. Thus, in Popper's example, no matter how many observations we make of white swans we cannot logically argue that all swans are white. However, we can decisively refute the general claim by making one observation of a black swan. This insight is built into the heart of Popper's scheme of critical rationalism. All our scientific theorems are provisional: we can corroborate (rather than confirm) our theorems by testing empirical hypotheses deduced from them, and we test by attempting to falsify. If a theorem survives attempts to falsify it then it is corroborated. However, we have already seen that what is to count as a falsification is inherently ambiguous and thus corroboration by testing is also undermined. Popper's scheme of corroboration rests on induction in that we are enjoined to move from particulars (exercises in empirical testing) to the general (the provisional acceptance of the theory as corroborated).[76] Or, again, Marjorie Greene suggests that Popper uses both inductive reasoning and its familiar prop of the assumption of regularity in nature, when he assumes that what is refuted today (particular) will be refuted tomorrow and permanently (general).

Popper's political views pervaded his work; the rejection of the claims to scientificity of Marxism and psychoanalysis informed his work on natural science. The politics were presented directly in two influential texts: *The Open Society and Its Enemies* and *The Poverty of Historicism*.[77] The first was written at a time of crisis in European politics. It is often noted as opposing totalitarianism of the left and the right. It is true that the text figures routinely in the self-understanding of the Western bloc political system – that liberal trading system which was constructed primarily by the USA in the cold war years following the end of the Second World War – but the text has its occasion in the political life of pre-war Vienna, when social democrats confronted communists and both had to deal with reactionary conservatives; thus, it belongs to a vanished era. The second text offers an extended critique of Marxism; the material is foolish, but the text is significant in the self-understandings of the post-war cold war Western world as it was appropriated as a species of conservative liberalism. Perry Anderson[78] comments that the reception of Popper – and other émigrés – was not surprising as they offered a strong celebration of British pragmatic conservatism in the context of a host community which was in large part intellectually moribund.

Overall, Popper's work reveals how epistemology, ethic and practice run together.[79] It is latent in all social philosophical/social theoretic work, and one must be sensitive to the package being sold in otherwise seemingly innocent claims. Popper's work revolves around an idealized de-socialized model of science; it recalls the splendid enthusiasm for science of *fin de siecle* Vienna, but it carries its own limitations. Popper's logic of scientific enquiry centres upon the creative anticipation of nature; it recalls the seventeenth century philosophical stress on scientific method; and as an elucidation of the nature of science it has been criticised; and in the territory of the social sciences, looking to their agendas, in particular, it is not enough; the stress on scientific method is misleading as it offers no guarantees of social progress.

W.V.O. Quine: empiricism questioned in favour of pragmatism

W.V.O. Quine studied in Vienna and worked with some of the key figures in the fields of empiricist/positivist philosophy of natural science; he helped some of the émigrés fleeing from European fascism;[80] and was instrumental in introducing these materials to an American audience. However, later he rather changed his position, writing an influential paper that undermined empiricism/positivism before going on to represent the very different American tradition of pragmatism.[81]

In an essay entitled *Two Dogmas of Empiricism*,[82] Quine made two challenges to orthodox empiricist/positivist thinking: the distinction between analytical/synthetic truths; and reductionism, the idea that meaningful statements are finally grounded in direct experience. These two ideas are rejected. There is no defensible distinction to be made between analytical and synthetic truths. Quine comments:[83]

> It is obvious that truth in general depends on both language and extra-linguistic fact ... Thus one is tempted to suppose in general that the truth of a statement is somehow analyzable into a linguistic component and a factual component. Given this supposition, it next seems reasonable that in some statements the factual component should be null; and these are the analytic statements. But, for all its apriori reasonableness, a boundary between analytical and synthetic statements simply has not been drawn.

And nor do meaningful statements reduce to direct experience, rather they are part of a complex web of beliefs; Quine comments that: 'The unit of empirical significance is the whole of science.'[84]

Quine[85] offers a scheme of conceptual pragmatism; natural science is central to our culture, offering theories we accept as useful; these schemes are always liable to revision, but this has costs as our ontology also changes; thus our thinking constitutes a web of belief and we are at liberty to discard any element of the web, but inevitably there will be a resultant reordering of the web and the costs will be the greater the more important the concept we discard. In all this, natural science is the paradigm of knowledge getting; science counts because it has proved efficient at ordering the flux of experience; and the role of philosophy is codifying the ontologies of science, thus language analysis can show what entities we have to have and which can go, thereby eliminating notions that are surplus and consequently changing our thinking.[86] Such pragmatist ideas have become more influential; debate turns to human social practice, social institutions and social learning. Claims and truths are contextual and contingent; extra-social guarantors disappear and a new agenda opens up for reflection upon our various claims to knowledge. And this includes the social sciences, where pragmatist thinking, it has been claimed, has been central to American progressive social reform politics throughout much of the twentieth century.[87]

Nagel: blurring the distinction between natural and social science

Ernest Nagel, born in Prague, in the Hapsburg Empire, resident in the USA from the age of ten,[88] sympathetic to logical positivism, and with Quine a key figure in its acceptance within the American scene, was the author of a key text in the philosophy of science, *The Structure of Science*,[89] which offered an elaborate set of ideas about explanation in the sciences and extended them to the social sciences. Nagel affirms the unity of scientific method, redefines natural science away from controlled (laboratory) experimentation towards systematic enquiry and eliminates the apparent differences between social and natural scientific enquiry by characterizing a series of problems as merely technical. A social science is possible. The first move contrasts scientific thinking with common sense. Science is systematic whereas common sense is not, it rests content with the received stock of knowledge plus occasional additions; it is folk knowledge. Science makes limited claims, common sense does not; its claims are never precisely formulated. Science is consistent, but common sense is not. Scientific explanation is quickly overthrown by better explanations, whereas common sense knowledge is enduringly flexible. Science tests its claims, whilst common sense does not. Science has a short life, common sense a long life. Most importantly, science aims for abstract general claims, whereas common sense aims at specific practical claims. The differences are clear. And this is a familiar stratagem within the empiricist tradition; theorists committed to the priority of natural scientific reasoning offer a plausible comparative sketch of what it is to pursue science. However these are not even handed investigations of different modes of cognition, they are illustrative distinctions drawn from a position of strong partiality; natural science is the standard against which other modes are to be judged. Moreover, the distinctions offered can be challenged; maybe common sense is tested but over a long period of time, folk medicine has been discovered by orthodox medicine and it turns out that some folk medicine is efficacious; or again, peasant farmers have knowledge of local conditions generated over years. Nagel adopts a position that is suffused with evaluative judgements about knowledge of a most complex kind; this is by no means an innocently obvious starting point. However Nagel takes the idea of science as systematic enquiry and turns to social science; running a two-pronged argument: first, blurring the familiarly accepted differences between social and natural science, and second claiming that if it is not impossible to conceive of a naturalistic social enquiry then any present problems are only technical. The argument runs through a review of a series of objections brought to the idea of a naturalistic social science: experiments, laws and subjectivity.

Nagel begins with the matter of controlled experiment; it is crucial in natural science, impossible in the social. Nagel distinguishes controlled experiment and controlled investigation; the latter is what counts and is available to social science, and in any case it is the way natural science really works; controlled experiment is not so important. The gap is bridged and the criticism deflected. But this is not a plausible position: controlled experiment is the way the physio-chemical heartlands of natural science operate, and controlled investigations in social science are feeble in comparison. Next Nagel discusses laws; history-bound in social science, but absolute in natural science. Again Nagel attempts to blur the differences, arguing that laws in natural science often have only restricted generality and that limited attempts at laws have been made in social science (and here he instances, in particular, neo-classical economics), adding that there is no logical reason why there should not be social scientific absolute laws at some stage when procedural problems are resolved. However, the *formal* restrictedness of natural science laws is not the same as the *cultural* restrictedness of general statements made in social science, and the laws of neo-classical economics are culture bound.[90] The idea of social scientific absolute laws is absurd, however what is interesting is the appeal to the possibility in logic; it is a fine thread upon which to hang an argument.

It can be argued that the natural scientific approach cannot be transferred to the social because this is centred on inter-subjective experience. Nagel argues that subjectivity can be tackled naturalistically; hermeneutics can produce hypotheses, which could be investigated in an objective way. In a similar way, it can be argued that social science is inevitably caught up in valuation because researchers are also social actors. Here Nagel makes three points: that valuation can enter in choosing questions, but enquiry should proceed naturalistically; that ethical valuation can enter social science work, but extirpating such biases is perfectly possible; and finally, that we should distinguish between characterizing and appraising judgements where the former judge types of phenomena whereas the latter express approval/disapproval because if these can be distinguished then a value free social science survives as a possibility. However, human beings study society with purposes in mind; these are embedded in schedules of values. Finally, Nagel notes that social scientific knowledge is available to other actors; research output can change the original phenomena. Again, he moves to defuse the issue; observing that there is experimenter effect in natural sciences, he argues that controlling experimenter effect in social science is essentially the same procedural problem. However, the position of the social scientist in relation to that which he studies is radically different to the position of the natural scientist; the objects of social scientific enquiry have their own understandings of the social world, there is a double hermeneutic in social scientific research, experimenter effect does not simply disturb the object sphere it changes it.

In sum, Nagel downgrades the role of controlled experiment in natural science in favour of systematic enquiry and upgrades this characteristic in social science, thus blurring the differences; thereafter arguing that if a naturalistic social science is not logically impossible then it is only a matter of sorting out the technical and procedural inhibitions to a fully expressed naturalistic social science. Both these elements are set against the unsystematic nature of common sense. Neither element of his argument is persuasive. However, by way of an appreciation of Nagel's efforts in respect of elucidating the detailed procedural nature of natural science, it might be noted that if his position is cut loose from its anchorage in a prior commitment to the cognitive superiority of natural science conceived empiricist fashion then natural science appears as one more internally diverse sphere of human thinking/acting, and these turned out to be themes pursued by scholars more sceptical about the status of the natural sciences.

The materials of post-empiricism

As debate in respect of science unfolded, one group of theorists moved away from the received model of natural science by adopting social scientific perspectives on natural scientists: Thomas Kuhn presents the idea of paradigms, Paul Feyerabend argues that science is a form of life and Bruno Latour dissolves science back into human society.

The idea of paradigms: Thomas Kuhn

Thomas Kuhn[91] offers a revision to the orthodox empiricist/positivist model of natural science: in place of the careful accumulation of the facts of experience or the creative anticipation of nature, science is presented as a thoroughly *social activity*. The historical social practice of natural science is seen to be the sustained elaboration/exploration of an agreed paradigm. This paradigm offers both an area of enquiry and a method of enquiry. It will be constituted as a discipline. Natural scientific practice proceeds normally as members of the community fill in the details of the paradigm. Over time it may be that anomalous observations will occur and accumulate. Kuhn sees a period of disciplinary crisis ensuing during which time some members of the discipline will advance a new paradigm: abstract and general debate plus disciplinary politics will be necessary before the new paradigm is accepted and normality re-established. Progress is evidenced in better problem solving; the ideal of movement towards given nature is not affirmed. Kuhn did not discuss social science but many saw direct relevance: one response was to argue that social science had no agreed paradigm, but that once it had then a reliable empirical science would be established; another was more relativistic, a paradigm can look like perspective or ideology, and debate was seen as fissured by adherents affirming different paradigms, and the implication was that much debate was wholly useless as advocates of one paradigm simply spoke past those affirming another; and a further response was to simply celebrate theoretical diversity.[92] Kuhn's work provoked widespread debate; he was a major figure in sowing doubt about the empiricist/positivist position; his work made science a social undertaking.

Kuhn's historicized picture of natural science, the elaboration over time by a community of enquirers of truths taken consensually to be correct until such times as the weight of accumulated and routinely ignored counter-evidence necessitated a change of consensus, was both widely admired and condemned. The broader admiration flowed from a positive response to Kuhn's picture of natural science as a socially and historically located practice: natural science was now seen to develop over time and to have its internal frailties as flesh and blood scientists struggled against nature and each other. The condemnation flowed from philosophical anxieties occasioned by precisely the fully rounded, so far as it was, picture of the otherwise admired natural sciences. It seemed to the orthodox that epistemological matters were being superseded by sociology of knowledge considerations; symbolically, from the correspondence theory of truth to some sort of sociological consensus theory. Kuhn retreated when attacked, affirming available distinctions between context of discovery and justification which allows the history and sociology of natural science to be separated from issues of truth. Nonetheless, Kuhn's revisions to received ideas of natural science have contributed to moves beyond received models of both natural and social science.[93]

Science as a form of life: Paul Feyerabend

Where Kuhn sociologized natural science, seeing it as the professional practice of adherents to a discipline of learning (which can be characterized with reference to the internal practices of the group), Paul Feyerabend goes one step further and reads it as a socio-cultural practice, or form of life. Natural scientists are now seen internally as a social grouping displaying all the usual sociological and psychological styles and habits of human beings in their pursuit of knowledge; externally they are seen to be acting just like any other group in society, arguing their corner. Feyerabend argues that natural science has no special method; there is no key. Natural scientists try anything in discovery and internal dissemination; if it works and you can persuade colleagues to accept it then it is knowledge. The external realm is a realm of suppliers of resources or political support, and so on, plus customers.

Feyerabend[94] argues that none of the usual methodologies of natural science actually deliver the goods: inductivism, falsificationism and research programmes are all plausible schemes, but the history of natural science shows that these methodologies are not followed and if they had been we would not have had Galileo, Newton or Einstein. Thus the theories, procedures and data (interpretations/observations) of Galileo were not evidently superior to Ptolemy; Galileo won out via persuasion. Feyerabend concludes that methodologically anything goes; there are no fixed rules. This does not however mean that there is no difference between the natural scientist and the crank because the former group know and are bounded by their discipline, the intellectual frame that offers the possibility of doing natural science.

Feyerabend argues for the key role of theorizing. Theories rest on assumptions, these generate the possibility of observations, and actual observing will depend on expectations. Thus Galileo had to interpret observations made by telescope and did so in the light of prior expectations. Natural scientific practice is a package: theory plus assumption plus observation. And theories are incommensurable; there is no one common measure of performance. On Feyerabend's view two theories can be confronted with the world to see how they perform – for example classical mechanics and Einsteinian relativity – but evaluation will be across a range of criteria, including factual adequacy, elegance and coherence. Any choice between theories is not just narrowly rational it is also subjective.

Natural science is a form-of-life; it is a particular cultural practice. Feyerabend looks at the realm of natural science not merely through the eyes of historians but also sociologists and anthropologists. The procedures of natural science are rational inside that cultural sphere but not necessarily outside it. The superiority of natural science over other modes of cognition is, thinks Feyerabend, blithely assumed without ever being argued for by both practising scientists and their social theorist spokesmen. These unselfconscious adherents of the cultural form – natural science – never actually compare it with other forms. Further, Feyerabend argues that the familiar assumption that there is a universal scientific method, to which all other patterns of activity lodging knowledge claims should conform, is simply wrong. This is scientism. The rationality of natural science is culture specific. Feyerabend offers a relativistic scheme; there are varieties of knowledge; different ways of construing the world; and natural science is one such internally diverse strategy. Feyerabend's final step links his thoughts on natural science with his political position; the appropriateness to humankind of a libertarian anarchist politics.

In discussions of natural science the crucial novelty of Kuhn was the introduction of the history of the enterprise into reflection about its nature. Ordinarily natural science obliterates its own history as it goes along; textbooks are continually updated, the enterprise inhabits a timeless present. Upon this basis theorists of science produced their statements in respect of its character. Kuhn put the history back into natural science and discovered the social world of natural science: the disciplinary matrix embodied in an exemplar and the whole sustained by social discipline as well as intellectual conviction. Feyerabend goes further: history, society and culture are all back into the story. The upshot is that natural science can now be seen to be a particular form-of-life, with its own internal rules, and engaging the outside world as customers/suppliers. Familiar ideas of natural and social science need revising so that both come to be seen as discipline based groups arguing their corner, peddling their wares in the market place of society, culture and history.[95] Yet the modern world is unimaginable without natural science; it is not just one more form-of-life, it is the basis of the world we inhabit. Feyerabend's attack goes too far. However, Feyerabend and Kuhn accomplish much: first, they have shown that natural science must be tackled in its social, cultural, historical and political-economic contexts; second, that the standard tale of the timeless asocial world of natural science is not believable; and third they have shown that natural science like other cultural practices has at its heart an interrogative theorizing process, and finally, the familiar empiricist/positivist ideal of neutral reportage is simply unbelievable.

The re-socialization of science-science and technology studies

The work of Kuhn proved influential and the social scientific study of the natural sciences developed; the sociology of knowledge provided a broad resource, but over time other diverse strands of reflection were pursued, including feminism, cultural studies and postmodernist social critique. The earlier work looked at the detail of natural scientific practice – work in the laboratory – and contrasted the slow haphazard production of natural scientific knowledge with the tales of clarity and precision told by rationalist philosophers;[96] thus the social production of knowledge was seen to run into the heartlands of natural scientific practice. The later work was ambitious; science was read as a male, power-oriented Western meta-discourse. The overall field was energetically elaborated; in time a reaction emerged, criticising the social scientific study of science, objecting that it falsely reduced science to just one more form of social knowledge and series of emblematic quarrels emerged: realism versus relativism; science versus ideology; knowledge versus opinion.[97]

The work of science and technology studies made natural science not less but more interesting, however the material was read as a cognitive/ social status challenge. The debate was confused. The status of natural scientific knowledge was not in question; claims to its asocial nature were, because it is a social product. The practice of natural science was not in question; claims to its asocial purity were, because science has its economics, sociology and politics. And the results of natural scientific enquiry were not in question; claims to their definitive (cognitive/ social) status were, because science is not an asocial mode of knowing, it is as Gellner remarked 'the mode of cognition of industrial society'.[98] Yet as these debates unfolded, the received model of natural science, a mix of naïve realism plus naïve induction, the standard empiricist/ positivist image, continued to inform the development of the social sciences.

Discipline bound positive social science in the years after the Second World War

After the Second World War the logical positivists who had migrated ahead of the European catastrophe exerted a significant influence on the development of social science in the USA and thereafter the Western world. The familiar spread of disciplines, established around the turn of the twentieth century, revisited their self-understandings and the empiricist/positivist model of science was affirmed in economics, sociology and politics. The affirmation of this distinctive model of natural science took different forms in the various disciplines; these disciplines had their own histories, intellectual characteristics and questions at issue; their intellectual status and form was but one concern; but the impacts of positivism can be tracked in broad terms, and the process of its more recent partial dissolution indicated.

(a) The notion of positive economics[99]

The discipline of economics took shape around the turn of the twentieth century as the hitherto influential political economy approach[100] to the social production of wealth gave way to the neo-classical analysis of the competitive market place. Proponents of neo-classical marginalist analysis eschewed politics in favour of putatively scientific analysis; the reaction against political economy gave economics its pervasive naturalism and the split between macro and microeconomics; with the former being inductive, statistical, aggregative and leading into econometrics, and the latter being deductive, mathematical and leading into formal modelling. All this produced an economics of liberal markets. Yet economic thought in the years before the Second World War was dominated by the eclipse of hitherto seemingly reliable liberal economics as the Great Depression, the construction of empire trade blocs and the rise and apparent success of the state-planning system of the USSR all combined to sow doubts and confusion in respect of both analysis and policy. The situation was rescued, so to say, by the demands of wartime mobilization as production became the overriding preoccupation of those governments involved in war fighting and economic thinking was thus reoriented. Amongst economists the story was of the rise of the influence of J.M. Keynes who showed how the state could intervene in the marketplace in order to remedy the depression equilibriums which were the central problems of inter-war capitalist economies. These ideas, plus the demands of war production coupled also to the political imperative of welfare reform, placed the idea of planning firmly at the centre of policy making and thus on the agenda of professional economists. However, there was always a dissenting line and conservative figures, such as Friedrich von Hayek, made early objections: first, political,[101] the increased role of the state was equated with socialist un-freedom; and second, analytical,[102] the nature of the available economic knowledge was put in question (and here the curious position advanced might be summarized as being that whilst economics was a positive science and thus produced reliable knowledge, its reach was limited, more particularly, it was not good enough to inform a state planning machine, and moreover nor should it aspire to do so, precisely because it was, or ought to be, value free). As these debates unfolded down the post-war years, the proponents of liberal economic systems gained ground. An influential statement of the claims of positive economics was made by Milton Friedman[103] who argued that the task of positive economics was to provide generalizations in order to make predictions and he insisted that '... positive economics is, or can be, an "objective" science, in precisely the same sense as any of the physical sciences'.[104] In time, the influence of Keynesian work was purged from economics and the neoclassical work was reinstated and has remained the dominant force in the economics profession.

The proponents of the liberal competitive markets theorized in neoclassical work make four maximization claims (it is a package): *first*, in the economy, as competitive markets are optimally efficient, to the maximization of material welfare; *second*, in society, as responsibility for action resides with individuals, to the maximization of moral welfare; *third*, in politics, as human welfare is best decided by freely choosing individuals, to the maximization of political freedom; and, *finally*, in respect of knowledge, as science is the yardstick, to the maximization of economic knowledge. The opening trio of claims can be challenged on various grounds;[105] in respect of the last noted it is clear that the status of knowledge claims within economics had long been at issue; doubts as to the nature of the business flowed from the inability of economics to produce the sort of hard knowledge its scientistic self-understandings anticipate;[106] it has been argued that if the profession could attain consensus in regard to methodology then perhaps matters would come right, however, other critics suggest that the crucial problem for mainstream economics at the present juncture is its pervasive naturalism.[107]

Overall, the self-understanding of positive economics affirms a claim to the value-free technical analysis of given economic systems; but it is an implausible claim; and positive economics seems only a variant of familiar liberal political ideology.[108] It has proved to be influential. Yet all these debates are known to economists and material exists which points to more sophisticated ways of grasping the business of livelihood: thus there are other traditions within economics (institutionalism and political economy[109]); there are other disciplines attending to these matters (economic anthropology, economic sociology or cultural studies[110]); there is a wealth of experience from the developing world and East Asia;[111] there are the new/old enquiries of the burgeoning field of international political economy;[112] and there are further critiques which draw on these materials in order to radically re-theorize the territory of orthodox economics.[113] It can be argued that there is no continuity in economic theory, rather there are discrete epochs, as economic theorizing is shaped by the questions asked and these in turn are shaped by real world circumstances; economic theories do different jobs; thus it could be that these debates might, once again, be revisited following the practical impetus provided by the neo-liberal American financial crisis of 2008.[114]

(b) Sociological theories of the middle range

Sociology developed around the late nineteenth century; it took different forms within various national communities;[115] thus, in mainland Europe its development had been bound up with state and nation making; in Britain, it had been disregarded as the polity had expanded overseas within the frame of empire; and as the USA expanded its grip on its newly acquired continent, and welcomed inward migration, scholars pursued studies of urban and rural communities, later reading nineteenth century European theory.[116] These distinct lines of development continued into the twentieth century. However, after the Second World War, the influence of the USA and USSR flowed into the European scene; the former offering the orthodox consensus of the naturalistic study of industrial society (especially, structural-functionalism);[117] and the latter, the official Marxism of late period state-socialism. But in the sixties events provoked change: in the American sphere political change provoked reflection whereas in the Soviet sphere blocked change slowly led state socialist thinking into a dead end from which it recovered only after the events of 1989/91.

In the West, in the sixties, the status of sociology was called into question. The intellectual claims of sociology – to the status of positive science – were examined and anxieties addressed. Thus Robert Merton[118] offered a familiar diagnosis of the failings of sociology: an immaturity in enquiry, evidenced by failure to agree goals and procedures, occasioned by a hangover from the past (founding fathers not put in their place) coupled to status anxiety (trying too hard to be scientific and thus rushing to generalize). The solution was the strategy of theories of the middle range ordered by an overarching paradigm. Merton advanced the notion of theories of the middle range, where these are intermediate in scope between all inclusive general theory and small-scale empirical research.[119] A middle range theory comprised a clearly specified and inter-linked set of statements having empirical referents. A middle range theory could guide empirical research. The middle range theory should be assembled with precision, because theory was a precise set of statements about relations between variables and not just an orientation to data. Such middle range theories were to be modest but demonstrably secure. Merton's notion of theories of the middle range was presented as a realistically modest programme in the light of the extant state of social science. Over time social science could reasonably expect to accumulate such middle range work and eventually begin to aggregate them in the light of an overarching paradigm, and here Merton specified functional analysis.[120] At the heart of this scheme was a commitment to the idea that social science ought to become like the natural sciences, that is, an empirical accumulative enterprise. Merton argued that it would take time, because social science, as evidenced by its extant internal confusion, was an immature discipline. The immaturity of the discipline, the lack of clarity about goals and procedures, continued, argued Merton, because of a series of misapprehensions about both classical sociology and natural science.

Merton distinguished the history and systematics of theory and noted that in the natural sciences the history of theory was wholly neglected except insofar as that history was represented by formulations within the currently accepted systematic statements of the disciplines' theory. Merton argued that history suffered obliteration by incorporation: the natural sciences were interested in the elaboration of the systematics of theory (that is, naively, adding to the stock of knowledge of the real world). The history of natural scientific theorizing was of antiquarian interest only. In contrast, observed Merton, the social sciences continually made reference to the history of theory – new formulations were quickly absorbed in formulations and anticipations of earlier theorists: social science made no routine attempt to distinguish between the history and systematics of theory. Merton urged this as a prerequisite to attaining a measure of agreement on goals and procedures. An appreciation of the importance of the systematics of theory would enable the adoption of the middle range theory proposal. It was of the essence of the idea that theory was not some sort of vague, quasi-philosophical orientation but was rather, like the natural sciences, a precisely formulated set of statements built upon a good stock of real data. Theory in social science should be regarded as like that of natural science – summary statements of observed regularities, produced by inductive reasoning.

Merton wanted to set sociology on the path to a coherent realisation of its inherent scientificity. It was implicit in his work, though never reflexively examined, that sociological knowledge, once properly constituted, would be informative and useful. Merton looked to a sociological stock of knowledge akin to that of other professional groups. Merton presented sociology as a naturalistic enquiry which although presently immature could by following his procedural advice both con-stitute itself as a coherent scientific enquiry and catch up with the natural sciences. Merton argued from the natural sciences to the sphere of the social sciences, addressing problems in terms of the notion of intellectual disciplinary immaturity, diagnosing present confusions, detailing their occasion and offering means to their successful and productive allevia-tion: social science was naturalistically conceived; there were no insuper-able problems to this project; and a resolution of present confusions would enable progress to be made. The whole effort was elegant, subtle and plausible, but reflective debate continued.

(c) Scientism in political analysis

Contemporary political analysis comprises three intermingled streams of argument: political philosophy, political science and international relations; the first noted centres on European work, the latter have been predominantly American. In the first matter, a recent survey[121] of political philosophy identifies a number of enduring preoccupations – the nature of political life, the role of institutions and the possibilities of empirical analysis – which move into and out of fashion, and which in turn are influenced by debates about the foundations of the dis-cipline; in the immediate post-war period, logical positivism directed political philosophers towards the model of the natural sciences and a preoccupation with clarity in political philosophical formulations; later, theorists of liberalism sought foundations in basic human values; others found reliability in ideas carried in tradition; whilst some, invoking the work of postmodernists, denied that there were any foundations, political philosophy was the wholly contingent product of debates amongst theo-rists. Some recent work has looked to the resources of hermeneutics and critical theory; the former points to the role of understanding, the latter to dialogue; it has been suggested that it is here that a plausible contem-porary variant of political philosophy might be located, reading the logics of the multiple polities now extant within the global system and resisting any attempts at theoretical closure. Then, second, in more substantive vein, a recent judicious survey of the post-war period reveals three major approaches to the analysis of domestic political activity:[122] thus, in the 1950s an older institutionalism gave way to behaviourism, which then in turn accommodated the 1970s rise of rational choice theory; behav-iourism and rational choice theory have understood themselves in terms taken from the received model of the natural sciences, that is, concerned with explanation and prediction; but most recently the 1990s have seen a representation of older, hitherto somewhat disregarded, traditions of institutional analysis. And, third, turning to analyses of international relations, there are three main strands of work: neo-realism, liberalism and recently social constructivism.[123] Of these, neo-realism has long been the core of a discipline dominated by scholars from America. The work of neo-realists was in aspiration scientific, associated particularly with Kenneth Waltz.[124] Much the same could be said about liberalism, with its links to the sphere of economics. However, in the newer, marginal, territory of constructivism alternate interpretive ways of conceiving enquiry have been considered. The debates around the empiricist/positivist ideal of science have been sharp and in this context an interesting contrast can be drawn between the neo-realist affirmation of positive science and the earlier realist work of E.H. Carr.[125]

Carr's 1939 text *The Twenty Year Crisis* advocated a pragmatic accommodation with the other great European powers, Germany and Soviet Union. Hans Morgenthau reportedly liked his book, but Carr was out of fashion in positivist cold war years.[126] Carr argued that social theorizing was bound by context and shaped by purpose (audience); it was not disinterested; it ran after events, interpreting. Carr advocated scepticism and looked for a limited clarity of understanding; in social theorizing there was always a mix of utopian and realist thinking, the former is *apriori*, voluntaristic and disposed to timeless truth, the latter empirical, deterministic and disposed to relativism. Carr argued that the utopianism of the nineteenth century liberals carried over into the Wilsonian League of Nations; aprioristic and voluntaristic theorizing, an idealist recipe and bound to fail; realists explain why, arguing that grand ideas serve no general purpose, they only disguise particular purposes; thus the Wilsonian system was illusory; it is better to focus on how the world actually is and be sensitive to context and the social dynamics of the time as they set the lines of possible advance and the limits of what is feasible; at the same time realist cynicism is no good as it blocks all forms of looking, thinking and acting; hence a mix of utopian and realist thinking is needed. It can be argued that the orthodox international relations view of Carr as a proto neo-realist is mistaken;[127] Carr was working in the 1930s and 1940s – realism meant adjustment to reality (for UK, alliance with USA, no cold war and domestic welfare planning). Jones[128] calls him a 'political romantic' and the core of his work was a 'pragmatic realism'.

The development of neo-realism marked the emergence of the discipline of international relations in its contemporary form – predominantly an American discipline, largely committed to the ideal of positive knowledge and concerned to inform policy. It is a distinctive position. It also generates very sharp debates. Crawford[129] suggests that there are three main reasons for this aggressive debate: (i) *disciplinization* – international relations has tried to become a 'closed discipline' – it was previously a mix of diplomatic history, law and current events; (ii) *scientization* – international relations tries to become like the natural sciences, positivist and looking for 'theories of the middle range' so that the accumulation of empirical studies can generate a better and better picture of reality; and (iii) *parochialism* – assumptions build around the model of the USA and the methods of its social scientists are unselfconsciously affirmed. In this context, a return to the critical work of Carr with its thoughtful balance of idealism and realism and its attempt to work pragmatically through problems would be helpful.

Finally, looking to the analysis of matters political in general, Charles Taylor[130] has argued against the positive scientific pretensions of mainstream political science and international relations; in this vein a series of typical arguments are made: *first*, the political scientists of the orthodox consensus argue that an affirmation of the distinction between facts and values coupled to stringent techniques of empirical enquiry can shift the study of politics out of the realm of ideologically suffused debate and into the sphere of positive social scientificity (exemplified for many by the work of orthodox neo-classical economics); and *second*, such enquiry is taken to be the route to a professionally vehicled role in policy scientific work (ways of advising clients in general and governments in particular). Against this position critics such as Taylor point out that: *firstly*, all social scientific work is suffused with valuation and that a professionally expressed resolution to try very hard to be 'objective' is both procedurally self-deluding (it does not work); epistemologically naive (it could never work); and as it turns out politically biased (as the political scientists argue in an unreflective way for a position taken as objective which on examination turns out to be value based they merely lend unselfconscious support to one ideological stance); and *secondly*, the role of policy science not only does not exhaust the range of possible ways of putting social science to work but also promotes a marginal activity in place of core traditional concerns (with elucidating complex change so as to inform action in the public sphere).

(d) Rorty's critique of analytical philosophy

The image of natural science has influenced not merely the familiar realms of the social sciences but has also rolled through the most abstract areas of intellectual reflection. It has had a clear impact upon the self-understandings of philosophers. Richard Rorty[131] offers a critique of contemporary analytic philosophy, the Anglo-American mainstream, in terms of its inheritance of a futile tradition (the post-Cartesian attempt to find in 'knowledge-in-general' a role for philosophy in the wake of the collapse of religion and the rise of natural science) and its recent more specific preoccupation with 'scientific rigour' (the mostly post-war exchange with imported Vienna Circle logical positivism). The upshot, suggests Rorty, is that analytical philosophy has disappeared into a professionally delimited, technical, scientistic, intellectual dead end, cut off not merely from the surrounding arts, humanities and social sciences but also separate from the one native school of American philosophy, pragmatism, and the very much richer mainland European or Continental tradition.[132] The resources of these two streams of reflection allow us to take the idea of contingency seriously; our claims to knowledge have no ground (and don't need one, what is important is solving practical problems); our claims to ethics have no ground (they are lodged within the culture – itself contingent – which we inhabit); and our culture itself can claim no particular priority (it is merely the one with which we are familiar and whose benefits we can advertise). The practical import is a celebration of intellectual conversation; there is always the chance for a persuasive re-description of our circumstances, a better way of going about our lives; and that is all that is available to the liberal ironist.[133]

An unfolding line, new directions

The rise of natural science was followed by the rise of social science; thinkers concerned with the practical issues of ordinary life looked to the procedures of the natural sciences, if it works in the realm of objects might it not also work with persons? There is nothing to regret in the social scientific appeal to the model of the natural sciences, it would have been odd if no such appeal had been made. What is at issue is the nature of the appeal to the model of natural sciences, whether it has been helpful, and if so, how? A familiar complaint points to the original promise of better practical social understanding becoming lost in the creation of state/corporate claims to authoritative technical knowledge.

The deployment of the received model of science in the sphere of the social involves a double commitment; first to the idea of theory as an elaborate passive report on how the world actually is, and secondly to the idea that the role of the social theorist is that of a compiler of value neutral reports on the world. The orthodox self-understanding looks to the provision of value neutral, technical reports on how the social system, conceived on the analogy of natural systems, actually works. The empiricist/positivist package feeds an orthodox politics: talk of social laws and causes implies authoritative manipulation of the system. The knowledge sought is the social analogue of the output of natural science; detailed technically precise causal knowledge; what Bauman called legislation.[134] The agent is the social scientific analogue of the natural scientist, the technically competent knowledgeable authoritatively placed state/corporate policy scientist. The ways in which this policy scientific commitment can be cashed are diverse and subtle; and any reworking of familiar conceptions of social theorizing will present considerable problems.

The issue might be put this way: the social sciences embrace a diversity of discrete modes of social theoretic engagement and the appeal to the model of the natural sciences can form a part of a number of modes of engagement (most obviously, the state/corporate sector bureaucrat-planner – thus, there is nothing wrong with having the trains running on time), but the appeal to natural science cannot inform a definitive mode of social theoretic engagement; it cannot justify an exercise of theoretical closure; *there is no single definitive way of doing social science*. The appeal to the model of natural sciences so as to inform the social sciences does not produce a secure starting point; rather, it mistakenly privileges a subordinate form of technical social theorizing; one subordinate to the demands of the state and corporate bureaucratic spheres. It is an old theme:[135] Kant identified the creativity of the structures of the mind, delimiting the sphere of science, leaving space for ethics; and later theorists have distinguished the sphere of the natural sciences, criticized any social scientific appeal to the sciences and proposed that the social sciences are centred upon the lives of ordinary people.

3
Arguments from Language/Understanding

The social world is one that is familiar; it embraces the spheres of routine action, it embraces the spheres of routine understanding and it is a world that requires no explanation to its inhabitants, those whose practices constitute that world. Social theorists in Europe have addressed in numerous ways the 'given-ness' or 'taken-for-granted-ness' of the ordinary social world: in terms taken from ancient Greek philosophy, in terms of the sacred texts of the Christian church, in the empiricist inflected theories of the liberal philosophers of early capitalism and – recently – in terms of the idea of language. The interest has found various expressions and all have it in common that the realm of human 'being-in-the-world' is understood as both constituted, and amenable to reflexive grasp, in language.

At this point discussion turns to the work of a series of streams of thought which have it in common that they reject the notion that talk about social science must begin with natural science and assert that the social world is a realm of lived human experience and that this is where discussion should begin. All centre their work on reflections on human language: first, directly, in the philosophy of language; then, second, with reference to the tradition of hermeneutics; and, third, more formally, with structuralism (together with post-structuralism). The first group, the philosophers of language, looked at patterns of ordinary use in order to address long-standing philosophical puzzles, and this encouraged the social theorists to attend to the patterns of meaning inhabited by actors in the social world, linguistic meaning (rule) and social meaning (rule) were taken to coincide in ordinary practice. The second group, hermeneutic philosophers, originally concerned with clarifying the meaning of biblical texts, insisted that meaning was central to human life; thus if the social world is conceived as a text-analogue then it can be approached in terms of inter-pretation and understanding. And, finally, structuralists looked at the cognitive/social underpinnings of the familiar world of ordinary exper-ience and whilst early work located structures in social practices, later discussions centred on power and language.[1]

Putting the matter generally, the thinkers to be considered here centre their enquiries on the claim that the social sciences do not con-front an extensive realm of objects having physical causes, rather they are interpretive practices which are themselves lodged within particular communities comprising persons having understandings, reasons and intentions. Together these offer an idea of social theorizing which does not rest upon the natural sciences; yet the rejection of their para-digmatic status does not entail abandoning enquiry, rather the reverse, when the social world is grasped directly much can be said.

Wittgenstein: language games, forms of life

Ludwig Wittgenstein belongs to the second wave of critical philosophy;[2] downstream from Kant's Copernican revolution and reflexively con-cerned with the creative nature of human thought, the focus is on human language. Wittgenstein[3] advanced two philosophical positions concerned with the nature of human language; the first combined direct statements about language coupled to an under-stated subjective ethic of personal responsibility; thus language could state facts, ethics could be directly experienced/felt, and the clarification of language was a central contribution to the advance of ethical life;[4] the second identified lan-guage as the vehicle of conventional, finite and contingent human social practices, with philosophical reflection turned to the therapeutic dis-solution of deep-seated general confusions.[5] The work generated extensive philosophical commentary[6] and attracted the attention of social theorists; in this context, for present purposes, two issues are crucial, first the deep-ened appreciation of the extent to which human-beings are not merely users but are inhabitants of language,[7] and second the realization that these claims about language opened the way to a different social science.

Wittgenstein and language

Wittgenstein's scholarship has a double context: Vienna and Cambridge. It also has a clear trajectory as conception and intent are successively amended. The work embraces a spread of issues within philosophy which defy simple summary, however contextualization indicates something of the occasion of his work, whilst also advertising the exegetical complexities faced by Wittgenstein scholars. But, to reiterate, the concern in this text is only with two aspects of his notions of human language: first, its unavoidable centrality in human practice/understanding; and second, the implications of these ideas for our notions of the possibilities of social science.

Wittgenstein was a member of cultured bourgeoisie Vienna;[8] the capital city of empire, home to government, commerce and the arts; and his concerns reflected this distinctive milieu. In *fin-de-siecle* Vienna intellectuals rebelled against perceived aesthetic, ethical and political decadence; and the clarity evidenced in natural science[9] was sought in music, the visual arts and philosophy. Clarity in language itself was sought. Wittgenstein wrote the *Tractatus* in the years of the collapse of the Hapsburg Empire. The text has a double aspect, logical and ethical: the former translates the clarity of natural scientific argument into the sphere of language, we are shown how language works, what can be said and what cannot; the later aspect is characterized indirectly, ethics are not science, they cannot be spelled out, action is crucial and understanding is achieved indirectly, evident, for example, in art. The text contributes to Viennese debates and in turn these are one root of European modernism. Viennese contemporaries regarded the text as a whole as an ethical statement.[10] However, where Wittgenstein began his work in *fin-de-siecle* Vienna with its political tensions, social reform movements and modernism, he pursued it in Cambridge where Bertrand Russell,[11] G.E. Moore and J.M. Keynes attended to science, philosophy and ethical/aesthetic experiment.[12] The *Tractatus* was read as a contribution to the elucidation of the logic of scientific discourse; a progressive text advancing philosophy, science and humankind through clarification and the excision of nonsense in all three areas. It might be added that the later work of the *Investigations* fits rather uneasily into this context, Russell reportedly was unsympathetic, but it was read into the technical concerns of the analytical philosophy school.[13]

The theorists of the Vienna Circle linked the intellectual concerns of Vienna and Cambridge; they too assimilated the *Tractatus* to their own programme, logical positivism. All these philosophers were enthusiastic about the achievements of natural science and novel work in formal logic.[14] These commitments/resources gave their work a distinctive intellectual style: natural science revealed definitively what was and was not the case, logical analysis exemplified clarity, allowed the formal delineation of the sphere of science, (what could and could not be said) and offered a method of logico-analytic or linguistic analysis.[15]

The Vienna Circle logical positivists were celebrants of natural science, the key to wider programmes of practical social reform.[16] They had three technical philosophical concerns: establishing the principle of verification (criterion of meaningfulness of propositions and criterion of demarcation of sense/nonsense); eliminating metaphysics by checking to see if propositions could be analysed down to statements of facts, if so fine, otherwise they were dismissed as empty metaphysics; and affirming the unity of science.[17] The idea of analysis was important; it was understood to be the intellectual means whereby the language of common sense could be broken down into its component parts. Philosophical problems were to be analysed out so as to dissolve them away. Wittgenstein never joined the Vienna Circle; but his influence was strong in the late 1920s and early 1930s.[18] The *Tractatus* itself was much admired by the members of the Circle. In the *Tractatus* Wittgenstein offers a picture theory of meaning, which is very close to the idea of the verification principle, asserts that if propositions are to have meaning they must analyse down to stating facts, otherwise all we have is noise, and agrees that as propositions were meaningful *qua* fact stating (when analysed down) then science was the paradigm of meaningful discourse and inevitably unitary. The crucial difference lies in the attitude to ethics/metaphysics; the logical positivists dismissed these, Wittgenstein did not.[19]

There has been much discussion of the trajectory of the work; style and orientation shift from the earlier to the later work. There is scope for confusion. Janik and Toulmin argue[20] that Russell and his contemporaries misread Wittgenstein, assimilating the *Tractatus* with its neo-Kantian concerns for the structure of language to neo-Humean British empiricism. The Vienna Circle also misunderstood, assimilating it to their programme of logical positivism. Janik and Toulmin,[21] looking at the context of the work, identify a Viennese thinker concerned with moral engagement in the modern world. Wittgenstein used the technical language of Gottlob Frege but turned it to distinctive concerns, the pursuit of clarity in language; the *Tractatus* is an austere expression of a wider Viennese concern for modernist simplicity, not a narrowly technical contribution to the philosophical elucidation of the formal language of science. The work of the *Investigations* is a further expression of interests in social practice and human language, pursued in a different idiom oriented to a broader agenda.[22] It might be said that the enduring concerns are with language, practice and ethics, but the early austere science-invoking vocabulary gives way to the more anthropological style of the later material. Yet the key for present purposes is the pervasive concern with human language: its centrality for human being/thinking, its radically social nature and evanescence/solidity.

The idea of language in the *Tractatus* is distinctive; language models reality. The text is dominated by the terms logic, language, thought and reality.[23] The central problem is the apprehension of the limits of thought – as with Kant – this time via the analysis of language rather than any discussion of the inherent structures of the mind. At the centre of the *Tractatus* is the picture theory of meaning. It addresses the issue of the relationship of reality and language. The world is modelled in language. To atomic facts are attached names. Names in combination give us elementary propositions. Elementary propositions can be combined until eventually we get the propositions of our ordinary language. At this point two other notions can help us grasp the vision on offer: truth function and truth condition. For the former we have the story of the subjection of elementary propositions, arrangements of names of atomic facts, to the repeated operation of the logical operator N (which is taken to encompass all formal logical machineries). The idea is thus of elementary propositions which model states of affairs, reality, which are then worked on by the machineries of logic to generate the familiar linguistic realm we inhabit. Then for the latter, truth conditions, we have the rather more readily intelligible idea that for any proposition to be meaningful it has to coincide with a possible state of affairs, that is, be empirical, and for it to be a true proposition it has to correspond to an actual state of affairs, a particular distribution of elementary propositions and collections of names of atomic facts. What we find here can be expressed thus: reality is modelled in language; reality is grasped by language via modelling (names plus logic machinery); the relationship of reality and language is thus precise and specifiable (because it is a model); and language is thus guaranteed because it is underpinned by reality.[24]

Wittgenstein came to reject this view of language.[25] The *Investigations* is dominated by the metaphor of language games; language is not asocial, it is inseparable from human social practice, language games are the vehicles of forms of life.[26] Wittgenstein's continuing preoccupation is with the nature of language, however, where language was underpinned by reality, it is now the language that we have which gives us the reality we inhabit. In the *Tractatus* the picture theory aimed to characterize language; the nature of language was determined by how the world was and any sentence could be analyzed into its the basic atomic propositions. The task of philosophy thus reconstituted would be to sort out meaningful from non-meaningful statements (beginning with the statements of philosophy). But now the idea of language games points to the routinely social nature of language, to its role in ordinary practice. And the idea that language has one job to do, stating facts, is rejected; the opposite is now seen to be the case, language does many jobs in the social world. The metaphor of the toolbox is introduced. The nature of language as presented in the *Investigations* is conventionalist; patterns of language use are embedded in the ordinary routines of social life. Wittgenstein denies that language has a firm base; there are no facts outside the language games we play. Language is not grounded in an external reality rather it is sanctioned in established social custom. Wittgenstein now sees language in a completely different way: the early logico-formal models of language/reality give way to the fluidity, flexibility and diversity of patterns of use sanctioned by social custom. Wittgenstein speaks of families of concepts clustering together, each cluster being a language game, in turn constituting a form of life. A vertical model of language is replaced by an horizontal survey; the task of philosophy is the therapeutic dissolution of superstitions of the intellect, it has no systematic method, nor does it have any quasi-scientific task of formal clarification. The *Tractatus* characterized the essence of language as picturing facts, showed how to distinguished sense from nonsense, underpinned a programme for the resolution of all hitherto existing philosophical problems and contributed to the ethical critique of late-Hapsburg society. In the *Investigations* philosophy cures diseases of thinking; it is unsystematic, offering no programme. The philosophical critique of language now plots its ordinary social use rather than attempting to specify its essence; human language games are expressed in a variety of forms of life and it makes little sense to try to order them into a two-category hierarchy of sense and nonsense as each has a particular use. Philosophy can plot the limits of language from the inside in a piecemeal unsystematic fashion, reporting on patterns of use. The world does not structure language, it is the other way round; language constitutes the facts, the world, it does not ride on top of them. In Wittgenstein's discussions human beings are thoroughly social and language carries this social nature; we are inhabitants of language.

Wittgenstein and a new route to a social science

At the outset two points can be made: first, the centrality of the idea of language games whereby human action and talk 'slices up the world'[27] makes Wittgenstein's second philosophy anti-positivist, dethroning empiricist accommodation to the given facts and socializing natural science; and second, the preoccupation with the detailed description of language games brings him close to the concerns of the social sciences, in particular, anthropology[28] and sociology.

The reflections on language are crucial. In the earlier *Tractatus* language works because it models material reality; it is reality that underpins language and guarantees the truth/falsity of propositions. The study of reality is typically the business of natural science: natural scientific discourse deals with facts and it alone is genuinely meaningful. The sphere of ethics cannot be similarly characterized; it is accessed subjectively and directly. In the *Investigations* Wittgenstein rejects this scheme and places humankind at the centre; language informs all social practice, stating facts is merely one task, and ethics is not radically distinct as human practice is full of social/language rules. It is a conventionalist account of language; forms of language use are the vehicles of patterns of life and the coherence of forms of life is a coherence-in-use. The radically social characterization of language presented denies any role to extra-linguistic guarantors, language games carry forms of life and stability in meaning/understanding is sustained via socially carried rules.[29] It is a position with wide implications. Peter Winch introduced the material to English-speaking social theorists in an influential text;[30] arguing, first, that philosophical and social scientific concerns overlapped, and second that the conceptual framework of social science was distinct from that of natural science.

In regard to the roles of epistemology and sociology, Winch finds a coincidence of interest in rule-governed behaviour. John Locke identified the philosophical role of under-labourer to natural science, the role of clearing conceptual confusions in aid of natural science, a position popular with empiricist/positivist thinkers but not the only way of conceiving the task of philosophical enquiry. Winch points out that clearing conceptual confusions is not simply resolving terminological problems: 'Our idea of what belongs to the realm of reality is given for us in the language that we use.'[31] Conceptual reflection does access the world we inhabit; there is a great deal we can say about the world; we understand readily enough and we do not have to wait until we have gathered all the facts. Winch argues that it is the proper role of epistemology to concern itself with this matter; that the world is *apriori* intelligible. The nature of social life is readily comprehensible. Winch notes that we inhabit worlds we understand, worlds that we find intelligible and this intelligibility is constituted in sets of ideas; thus if one wished to understand the pattern of life of a monastery one would have to have some idea of the sets of ideas that the inhabitants routinely drew upon to order their lives. The notion of intelligibility is explicated further using Wittgenstein's notion of rule-governed behaviour; language use is social because like any rule governed behaviour there has to be a common set of rules (one cannot set one's own rules and check one's own compliance). The epistemological project of elucidating the nature of intelligibility *per se* involves analysing instances of rule following, and these are embedded in language games, the vehicles of forms of life. Turning to the relationship of philosophy and sociology, Winch notes that whilst there has been doubt as to the position of sociology in relation to other social sciences, it can be clarified by noting that however that question is answered a major role for sociology must be elucidating the nature of the social in general. Sociology is concerned with the elucidation of strategies of understanding in social life, specimens of rule following. Sociology and epistemology coincide in a concern for the rule-governed basis of intelligibility.[32] Winch secures the first of his two main points.[33]

Winch turns to his second broad question, the nature of meaningful behaviour, and argues that it has to be understood in terms of following rules; human behaviour is intelligible if it exemplifies rule following, the mad man follows no rules.[34] The rules need not be immediately available to the actor; it is not necessary that the actor self-consciously know what rules are being followed. Winch observes that habit-governed behaviour certainly counts as rule-governed as this is exemplified in intelligibility, or meaningfulness. The familiar naturalist view of social theorizing (in particular, J.S. Mill and Vilfredo Pareto) begins with the view that social science is the same as natural science in its basic logic and differs only in the complexity of the material it handles. Winch disagrees; the issue is not empirical but conceptual as '... the notion of a human society involves a scheme of concepts which is logically incompatible with the kinds of explanations offered in the natural sciences'.[35] The key natural science term *cause* is unusable within the sphere of the social sciences. Explanations of human behaviour rest first on motives. One can only understand a person's motives in terms of the reasons for action. These reasons are context-dependent. The context encompasses the actor's social world. It is clear that motives, reasons and contexts are not causes; once again, social scientific enquiry is drawn into the web of rule-governed meanings that social actors inhabit. There is a further complication; the language game of social science has its own rules, there is a double hermeneutic.[36] Winch secures his second point;[37] the social and natural sciences inhabit different conceptual realms, different language games.

The general lesson is that social actions embody concepts; that is, the relationship of concepts and actions is internal. Winch invites us to imagine a biochemist discovers a new disease-causing germ: clearly, the existing stock of knowledge has been augmented. Now compare this discovery with the first formulation of the germ theory of disease; this required entirely new ways of understanding and acting. A doctor familiar with germ theory, concerned with reducing the incidence of disease and ignoring rules of hygiene would be '... behaving in a self-contradictory and unintelligible manner'.[38] A new idea thus implies a new set of ways of conceiving the world and acting within it. Winch ends by suggesting that relations between social actors are better compared to the exchanges within a conversation rather that the causal interactions of a physical system. It is a counter-position to orthodox social science; resting upon the work of Wittgenstein, Winch offers the intellectual core of a non-naturalistic social science whose task is interpretive. In the scientistic context of the late 1950s these ideas were controversial, raising questions about social theorizing: conception/intention (how and why were arguments made?); idealism/realism (was everything just a matter of ideas?); relativism/universalism (was everything bound by cultures?); and multiple rationalities/single rationality (was science not universal?). There were practical anxieties: if the pursuit of authoritative technical expertise was eschewed as unavailable in principle in favour of the interpretive elucidation of sets of distinct cultural ideas then what was the role of the social sciences?

Anthony Giddens[39] suggests that when social scientists came to consider Winch they were both attracted by and simultaneously unhappy with his notion of rule-governed behaviour. He argues that the notion of rule-governed does too much work. Generally, the objection seems to be that Winch fails to distinguish varieties of rule governed-ness. Giddens distinguishes language rule and social rule and adds that where Winch sees rule following as essentially unproblematic, social scientists typically ask whose rule? Giddens is getting at the difference between an abstract-general realm of application of the notion of rule, in Winch, philosophically considered linguistic rules, and the specific concrete realm of the social application of the notion of rule, which is the more familiarly social scientific sphere. It could be said that Winch (following Wittgenstein) recalls attention to the experiential depth of human social life, whereas Giddens looks to the matter of concrete historical social relations. However, it would be foolish to dismiss-by-misrepresentation the arguments advanced by Winch who was concerned: first, to characterize the core of social science; and second to specify its relation to philosophy (which is just what he says in the book's title). Winch did not claim to be offering an elaborated theory of social science. However, that said, it remains the case that there is much to be done to the Wittgenstein/Winch material if it is to be brought into close and fruitful contact with the familiar realm of the social sciences.

Alasdair MacIntyre offers insights into these debates; in particular three arguments: first, on causality,[40] where causes are rejected for interpretation thereby reinstating the notion of ideology; second, on ideology,[41] where it is argued that causes/reasons are not mutually exclusive; and finally, on putatively rational bureaucratic managerial expertise, where a-moral manipulative and/or justificatory claims to scientificity are criticized as untenable.[42]

On the issue of the relationship of belief and action, MacIntyre notes that social theorists have typically stressed one or other before retreating into speaking of a two-way interaction. The arguments presuppose that beliefs and actions are separate sorts of things and that they are contingently related by cause. MacIntyre argues that belief and action are not separate and their relation is not causal and contingent. Consider a head movement: is it a nervous tick, in which case it is caused physical behaviour; or is it a nod, in which case it is human social action and only intelligible within the context of social rules. Social rules inform understanding and action. MacIntyre considers the example of a man whose roses have greenfly, and shows that we understand his behaviour in spraying the roses with insecticide in terms of his belief that greenfly are bad for roses. We do not suppose that his belief caused his action rather we say that being a keen gardener and not spraying your greenfly infested roses is so odd as to be unintelligible. 'Actions, as much as utterances, belong to the realm of statements, concepts and beliefs; and the relation of belief to action is not external and contingent, but internal and conceptual'.[43] MacIntyre thinks that many sociologists have made this mistake; thus Max Weber argued that Calvinists who were committed to predestination gave way under psychological pressure (a species of cause) and began saying that doing good works gave a clue to God's intentions. MacIntyre argues the shift was required by the internal logic of Calvinism; it asserted contradictory claims about good works, psychological tension was irrelevant; thus the role of belief in social action is demonstrated, which is what Weber wanted anyway.[44]

MacIntyre now makes three points: first, that for an action to be such it must be recognised as such in terms of the socially available stock of meanings; second, that for the action to be my action it must be recognisable to me; and third, that whilst others might more aptly characterize my action my report has final authority. There is a crucial extension to the argument:

> ... an agent can do only what he can describe ... The limits of what I can do are set by the limits of the descriptions available to me, not those I posses at any given moment. And the descriptions available to me are those current in the social group to which I belong ... If the limits of action are the limits of description, then to analyse the ideas current in society is also to discern the limits within which action necessarily moves in that society.[45]

The business of the social scientist is no longer with causes and effects but with spelling out how sets of ideas shape social worlds. Human beings inhabit structured webs of meaning. Yet these change through time. MacIntyre argues that the key to social change is rational criticism that may be fostered or restricted: to elucidate individual, group or societal change is not to look for antecedent causes, but at available choices and ask why one was made rather than another.[46]

MacIntyre offers the example of Stalin: the Bolsheviks came to power in a rural country, however their notions of Marxism saw democracy as growing out of liberal industrial societies. They faced a dilemma; pursue industrialization or pursue democracy. A variety of answers were given, Stalin's was to pursue industrialization and call it democracy. The only problem was the Bolshevik old guard who knew that there were alternatives. Stalin publishes a book on Marxist theory that presented a mechanistic materialism in which ideas are just parts of causal chains, thus he could argue: 'If actions cause ideas, and Stalinist ideas reflect proletarian class interests, and non-Stalinist ideas reflect hostile class interests, the conclusion follows that to have had non-Stalinist ideas means you must have been performing non-Stalinist actions'.[47] Dissent entails that there has been disloyalty; hence Stalin's show trials where the accused confessed and were liquidated, thereby closing the circle of Stalinist ideology. Once inside the system it all makes perfect sense; the circle of ideas is maintained by circumscribing critical thinking. MacIntyre notes that the interpretation renders intelligible otherwise bizarre behaviour; it also saves social scientific effort as all the theories about Stalin's psychology, the need for figureheads, irrational cults of violence amongst Russians and so on, are not needed.

However, when thinking about ideology, matters are un-clear: MacIntyre returns to these awkward issues, suggesting that a focus on interpretation has the effect of blocking the social scientific analysis of the context-determination of actions; we can distinguish between the rules an agent professes to follow and those he actually does follow. MacIntyre now wants to show that causes/reasons are not exclusive strategies for analysing behaviour; the key argument is the example of the post-hypnotic suggestion. MacIntyre invites us to consider the example of a post-hypnotic suggestion; an agent/victim is hypnotized, given the suggestion that is later triggered. The agent/victim reports reasons for triggered action that we would disregard for a causal explanation. Thus there are professed reasons and actual causes. Thus the stress on rules blocks important questions in respect of both contexts of actions and patterns of change. Winch, thinks MacIntyre, gets us as far as seeing that we must begin by characterizing the form of life in question – the ideology – but then leaves us unable to proceed. However the example is ambiguous. An alternate reading of the example points to a different conclusion. The victim is loaded by talk: please do 'a' when I ask and also forget all about this conversation; this is verbal collusion. The victim is triggered, by talk, please do 'a' now, and the victim does so and when invited to explain this behaviour the victim does not refer to the collusion but offers reasons. The mystery here is the collusion; causes/reasons can stay exclusive. These are difficult debates. It might be speculated, after the intervening enthusiasm for structuralism and the attention paid to structure and agency, that MacIntyre is looking for a notion of structure; a way of characterizing the determining/enabling contexts within which individual and group action moves.[48] Thereafter, his criticisms of the underdeveloped nature of Winch's positive suggestions as to the nature of an interpretive social science are not unreasonable; the point could be granted by Winch.

Finally, in a later text, the nature of the claims and practice of nominally rational bureaucratic managers becomes the focus of concern. In *After Virtue*[49] MacIntyre argues that the rise of the modern world saw the established power of the church broken and attempts made by theorists of the Enlightenment to reground morality in asocial human nature failed; all they created were individuals.[50] Thus the rise of the modern world has bequeathed to us the pseudo-morality of liberal individualism. The consequences of this invention are manifold. In the political sphere, autonomous subjectivist agents cut loose from community confront bureaucratic managerialism. MacIntyre dismisses liberal individualism; an asocial ethical system misses the point, ethics are embedded in community. Nor can the claims of state/corporate bureaucrats to technical expertise be sustained; they seek a realm of morally neutral facts and law-like generalizations, but the social world is filled with knowing agents, it is radically fluid in organisation, it is not regular and it is not predictable. MacIntyre comments:[51]

> The concept of managerial effectiveness is after all one more contemporary moral fiction and perhaps the most important of them all. The dominance of the manipulative mode in our culture is not and cannot be accompanied by very much actual success in manipulation ... the realm of managerial expertise is one in which what purport to be objectively-grounded claims function in fact as expressions of arbitrary, but disguised, will and preference.

The ideas of autonomous facts, the disjunction of facts/values, notions of social laws and the autonomous individual are all products of the rise of the modern world, yet none are as self-evidently plausible as our common culture supposes. The analysis in *After Virtue* is moral critique, however the unhappy inter-linkages of liberal-individualism, subjectivist protest, state/corporate managerialism and empiricist/positivist social science are sketched in rich and plausible detail.[52]

Wittgenstein: responses, other work, crucial lessons

The anti-positivism in Wittgenstein's *Investigations* attracted attention. Human thought had no extra-linguistic guarantee in a putative realm of facts; language was social; forms of life were carried in language games; the relationship reciprocal; the ensemble of linguistic and social practices were secured in rules; and as rules could be changed, what finally 'gives the practices their stability is that we agree in our interpretations of the rules'.[53] Pears calls this an extreme anthropocentrism.

In the *Tractatus* language works because it models reality: it is reality which underpins language and guarantees the truth/falsity of propositions. Reality is thus the extra-linguistic guarantor of our activities. The study of reality is typically the business of natural science: natural scientific discourse deals with facts and it alone is genuinely meaningful, the rest is noise (although Wittgenstein was tolerant of this noise). This package, the ontology of things and the centrality in epistemological reflection of the natural scientific display of the facts, is objectivism.[54] In the *Investigations* Wittgenstein rejects objectivism and puts humankind at the centre – hence the anthropocentrism. The given is now language practices, or forms of life. The problem for Pears is how to give up objectivism. Wittgenstein is re-read: in place of the dictum – what has to be accepted, the given so to say, are forms of life (embedded in or expressed by language games) – an alternative is presented – what has to be accepted, the given so to say, are the *facts* of language use. Wittgenstein is presented as a linguistic naturalist, or a subtle kind of positivist; thus Wittgenstein is read as enjoining philosophers to attend to the detail of linguistic practice. But there are two problems here: first, Pears continues to use the word facts and this smuggles in through the backdoor what Wittgenstein has just thrown out of the front door, namely, the objectivist package, thus in place of deference to the facts of the real world we now have deference to the facts of the linguistic realm; and second the objectivism opens the way to radical re-readings of Wittgenstein's work, one such being the presentation of the *Investigations* as the base for a naturalistic sociology of knowledge.[55]

Pears grants that Wittgenstein's later philosophy has a naturalistic flavour in the detailed attention to the uses of language but adds that this is only one side of the story, the other is 'his resistance to the thrust of science, which, he felt, must not be allowed to encroach on other modes of thought'.[56] Later Pears returns to this theme and notes that throughout Wittgenstein's work there is the idea of the danger to thinking of the contemporary prestige of natural science. It is clear that Pears has a problem: he cannot let go of objectivism and so he cannot see that Wittgenstein did. In the *Investigations* the positivism of the *Tractatus* is rejected in favour of a conventionalist account of language: forms of language use are the vehicles of patterns of life. The coherence of forms of life is a coherence-in-use. The extra-linguistic guarantor of language in a separate reality is not needed. Pears tries to square the circle – what he perceives as anti-positivism and the positivism of his linguistic naturalism – by talking of divergent tendencies within the work of Wittgenstein.[57] But this is wrong. Wittgenstein dethroned natural science. This Wittgenstein was picked up by Winch.

Many philosophers had difficulty accepting Wittgenstein's anthropocentrism;[58] affirming the priority of language games entailed both abolishing the realm of real material guarantors of knowledge and dethroning natural science; yet many also recognized that Wittgenstein's work was to be seen as all of a piece: a species of positivism is affirmed in the *Tractatus* and decisively rejected in the *Investigations*. Wittgenstein is an anti-positivist and the philosophy of language is non-positivist. The naturalism is an aid to solving philosophical problems – to do this Wittgenstein tells us that what has to be accepted are forms of life, that is, the sphere of natural languages, wider than the technical discourses of traditional philosophy.

David Bloor,[59] alluded to above, has produced some thought-provoking discussions of Wittgenstein, in particular in respect of the development of the sociology of knowledge. Wittgenstein is read as an anticipator of a scientific sociology of knowledge.[60] Bloor achieves this result by first ignoring the *Tractatus* and then reading Wittgenstein as a naturalist reporting upon patterns of language use. Bloor suggests that Wittgenstein did not go far enough. Thus one can take the ideas of finite language games and by adding structuralist anthropology, generate a quadripartite formulation of the available forms of human life[61] – characterized in terms of rules governing ranks inside a group and rules governing the boundaries of one group and another – which scheme provides the basis of a comparative positive sociology of knowledge. Dismissing those who have taken Wittgenstein as an anti-positivist, in particular Winch, who is taken to have misled everybody by reporting Wittgenstein as focusing on meanings rather than behaviour, Bloor reclaims Wittgenstein for the scientistic style of thinking which he was at pains to leave.

Overall, Wittgenstein's work entails that social science must centre upon the business of language; Winch offers a preliminary indication of how this might be done; MacIntyre offers an extension of this line, sketching out a non-natural science referring social science where the key idea becomes ideology, both micro (the sets of rules inhabited by actors can be contextualized to group and society) and macro (the ideologies promulgated in societies can be unpacked so show how they work to shape society). These themes find echoes elsewhere: hermeneutics and semiotics. K.O. Apel[62] argues that the material of the *Investigations* offers much to hermeneutic reflection, notwithstanding its allusive style, static image of language and disregard of society and history. And in semiotics, Saussure[63] read language as a formal system; where Wittgenstein plots language games to dissolve philosophical puzzles, Saussure constructs a model of structure of language. The coincidence of interest lies in the affirmation of the centrality of language.

Wittgenstein offers crucial lessons for the idea of a social science: first, the lesson of the centrality of language for humankind and the ineluctably social nature of human beings, expressed elsewhere as the decentring of the individual; second, the lesson of diversity, multiple language-games, multiple modes of practical social theoretic engagement; third, the lesson of family resemblance, concepts have no core meaning, rather family resemblances, so too the loosely related activities of social theorizing; fourth, the lesson of the priority of interpretive attention to the particular case, where such explications can be accumulated and ordered but not systematized; fifth, the lesson of the importance of the therapeutic treatment of philosophical problems, which arise from the mis-working of language, and which are amenable to dissolution via therapeutically intended attention to detail of actual linguistic usage, thus in social science there is no one method or procedure and aspiration thereto misleads because the process of social theorizing in all its diverse guises is primary; and finally, generally, the lesson of anti-positivism, attention must be turned to language-carried social practice.

Hermeneutics: tradition, culture

The success of the natural sciences in the eighteenth and nineteenth centuries encouraged empiricist/positivist thinkers; the product of disciplined enquiry, understanding, came to be equated with the restricted idea of causal explanation, itself centred upon laboratory-controlled experiment. The final resting point of this intellectual contraction was equation of explanation and prediction. Hermeneutics rejected this collapse; it stands in opposition to the empiricist/positivist tradition, whose claims it regards as not merely in error but culturally pathological.[64] Hermeneutic analysis is concerned with the recovery of meaning. It originally designated procedures in biblical exegesis; techniques whereby obscure material could be clarified and its meaning recovered. This tradition reached an apogee in nineteenth century German Romanticism; the focus shifts from texts to culture;[65] a little later Wilhelm Dilthey moved hermeneutics into the centre of social scientific enquiry, insisting that all knowledge was context bound and history was the key discipline; thus what Bauman[66] calls the 'hermeneutic challenge' was clear, to grasp human meanings with the discipline evident in the sphere of the natural sciences.

The main claims of hermeneutics are these:[67] firstly, empiricist/positivist social science contrives to miss what is characteristic about human life, its experiential meaningfulness; secondly, hermeneutic understanding is different from empiricist/positivist notions of explanation; and thirdly an hermeneutic interpretive science of the social is needed. Hermeneutics centres on interpretation, the elucidation of the nature of a form of life and the techniques of interpretation have been various:[68] the recovery of meaning via close textual exegesis, the psychological empathetic recovery of the intentions of social actors and a more recent focus on patterns of language use which reads culture as a text-analogue. Charles Taylor argues that an empiricist/positivist epistemology in which the culturally specific is eschewed for general formulations ends up offering empty abstract characterizations of society: a refusal to close with the culturally specific produces ahistorical ethnocentric work; truth is not displayed, it is obscured. The contrast with empiricist/positivist social science is sharp; hermeneutics is a moral science.[69]

Hermeneutics and method: Wilhelm Dilthey

Stuart Hughes[70] argues that around the turn of the twentieth century in Europe there was a reaction against the intellectual, cultural and political package that celebrated the modern industrial/democratic world. There was a revolt against positivism. Hughes identifies four preoccupations: the idea of the unconscious, the nature of time, a concern for a new critical politics and the epistemology of the cultural sciences. There are specifically German strands of reflection; neo-Kantianism, the reflexive concern with the grounds of enquiry; and Romanticism, a deeper reaction against the demystification of the world that finds expression in phenomenology, existentialism and hermeneutics.[71] And Dilthey was concerned to critically delimit the sphere of historical analysis, to display its categorial frame. The early material is psychologistic,[72] understanding involves the empathetic recovery of meaning; the later work sees an Hegelian[73] influence reappearing as understanding becomes the part/whole hermeneutic diagnosis of cultural forms.

Dilthey is concerned with the intellectual grounding of the human sciences, in particular as they relate to history.[74] Intellectual strategies informed by the natural sciences are rejected; they 'truncate historical reality'.[75] Dilthey argues that whilst it is true that the natural and human sciences are implicated in the study of humankind, they are different;[76] the human sciences begin with reflection upon practical experience of humanity.[77] Dilthey states:

> So man becomes the subject matter of the human studies only when we relate experience, expression and understanding to each other … A discipline only belongs to the human studies when we can approach its subject matter through the connection between life, expression and understanding.[78]

In the human sciences we learn; we learn about human life and our participation in human life is the basis of our learning:

> The lives of individuals are infinitely enriched through their relationships to their environment, to other people and to things. But every individual is also a point where webs of relationships inter-

sect; these relationships go through individuals, exist within them, but also reach beyond their life and posses an independent existence and development of their own through the content, value and purpose which they realize. Thus they are subjects of an ideal kind ... At this point society and history unfolds before us.[79]

Thus individuals learn about the cultural sphere in which they live; the basis of learning is routine participation; and the culture flows through people, it transcends the being of the individual persons who carry it: 'Life, knowledge of life and human studies are thus, internally related and constantly interact'.[80] Such learning is an interpretive deciphering of patterns of life, not the piecemeal accumulation of causes. It is constrained/secured by the common culture and the resources of the particular discipline of learning:

> The great outer reality of the mind always surrounds us ... Every single expression represents a common feature in the realm of this objective mind. Every word, every sentence, every gesture or polite formula, every work of art and every political deed is intelligible because the people who expressed themselves through them and those who understood them have something in common; the individual always experiences, thinks and acts in a common sphere and only there does he understand ... We live in this atmosphere, it surrounds us constantly. We are immersed in it. We are at home everywhere in this historical and understood world; we understand the sense and meaning of it all; we ourselves are woven into this common sphere.[81]

The sense of being-in-the-world suffusing everyday routine practical activity is the starting point for reflection. It displays the common cultural themes upon which individuals and groups necessarily and routinely draw. The human sciences comprise the reflective study of broad cultural forms – subjects of an ideal kind – enfolding individuals and groups; practical experience, reflection and scholarship are internally related as strategies of understanding and causal natural science need not be invoked. In all this, understanding is the key:

> Understanding is the rediscovery of the I in the Thou: the mind rediscovers itself at ever higher levels of complex involvement: the identity of the mind in the I and the Thou, in every subject of a community, in every system of a culture and finally, in the totality

of mind and universal history, makes successful cooperation between different processes in the human studies possible.[82]

The key to strategies of enquiry is the centrality of language in cultural forms:

> Because it is in language alone human inwardness finds its complete, exhaustive and objectively comprehensible expression that literature is immeasurably significant for our understanding of intellectual life and history. The art of understanding therefore centres on the interpretation of written records of human existence.[83]

The natural and social science are separated around the issue of the internality of relations of understanding; cultural learning involves the interpretive deciphering of received meanings, not the accumulation of causally related facts. The project of offering a critique of historical reason, the extension of Kant into the sphere of the historical and cultural sciences proved fruitful; the Copernican revolution that put humankind at the centre is taken one step further, human kind are now flesh and blood, not just intellects. All human life is founded in routine practical activity; such activity is lodged in received tradition; and the embedded knowledge can be accessed – brought to reflective consciousness – through the detailed exegesis of texts/text analogues.

Dilthey has been criticised for making hermeneutics a method, distinguishing natural and social science in terms of strategies appropriate to objects (thus both natural and social science are sciences as they both study their objects in an appropriate fashion so as to produce objective knowledge), but such claims, implying a narrowness of vision, are misleading; the remarks on understanding make it central to human life. Dilthey's work was both a part of a tradition – sometimes tagged the 'philosophers of life'[84] – and a forerunner of more explicitly anti-positivist work.

Hermeneutics as ontology: Hans-Georg Gadamer

As Hughes reported, a movement amongst late nineteenth century philosophers, the philosophers of life, opposed the dominant empiricist/positivist work and instead affirmed the centrality of human experience; and the work has been developed further and can now be read as a distinctive stream within European social philosophy. It encompasses the closely related fundamental ideas of phenomenology and hermeneutics; and in turn these materials have found recent further expression in schemes of liberal irony and deconstruction. It is a rich line of thought, and in respect of the early material three intermingled strands can be identified:[85] work informed by the inheritance of research in psychology which gives us the idea of 'lived experience'; work informed by the broad inheritance of European metaphysics, which gives us the idea of 'being-in-the-world'; and work informed by traditions of scholarly biblical exegesis, which gives us the idea of 'the experience of the world in language'. All these materials have fed directly into the social sciences; illustratively, phenomenological work has been produced in sociology and psychology; and hermeneutic work has informed a wide range of interpretive work (texts and text-analogues) in the social sciences, the arts and the humanities.

(a) Edmund Husserl and Martin Heidegger

The notion of phenomenology grows out of late nineteenth century discussions of empirical psychology, investigations into the nature of the mind; as these are developed by Edmund Husserl[86] the focus turns towards the task of characterizing the realm of ordinary experience, that is, subjective lived experience; and materials are produced relating to the procedures of phenomenological analysis and the presentation of the results thereby gained. In brief terms,[87] Husserl's phenomenology is constructed in opposition to the 'naturalistic attitude', the commonsensical apprehension of the world as a realm of things that developed alongside the rise of the natural sciences. It is symptomatic of the rationalization of the world consequent upon the inappropriate extension of ideas/attitudes drawn from the sphere of natural science to other areas of human practice. It displaces more appropriate conceptions of the nature of human social life; causes are substituted for the realm of meanings. Husserl's philosophical project is centred on the 'life-world'. A philosophical analysis of the nature of human knowing is undertaken. A reflexive, critical 'transcendental reduction' uncovers layers of assumptions that are progressively identified and set aside. Eventually the raw experience of pure subjectivity is uncovered and from this point of philosophically secured purity and surety the analysis works forwards to reconstruct the world of ordinary lived experience as a complex cultural construct.

The material is picked up by Martin Heidegger who reworks it extensively via a return to the broad tradition of European metaphysics. A deeper ground is identified and explored and the basis of enquiry is identified as human being itself, centrally, the notion of 'being'. Heidegger's background is late nineteenth century Germany; he was conservative, deeply religious and for a while had nursed plans for the priesthood. He lived through a chaotic period in German history, including the Great War, the Weimar Republic, National Socialism and finally the post-war Federal Republic; a disastrous political mis-step in the thirties damaged his reputation and he retired into seclusion in southern Germany.[88] As indicated, Heidegger's central concern is with the nature of 'being':[89] the material is metaphysical, theological and philosophical and it is remote from the work of social scientists.[90] Schematically, there are three moves: first, 'being-in-the-world' is made central from the outset (in Husserl it appears rather late and with some difficulty as the shift is made from solitary subjectivity to the familiar inter-subjective world); second, being-in-the-world is lodged in history (in Husserl the analysis of subjective experience moves in the sphere of pure subjectivity); and third, the ensemble of ideas and practices that constitute such human experience are carried in language[91] and so understanding is routinely evidenced in ordinary human experience (in Husserl understanding was made a consequence of an ascetic purification procedure, the business of the recovery of pure subjectivity).[92]

One aspect of work focusing on subjective experience was the role of language (a late nineteenth century preoccupation); experience was not a simple given of human life, rather experience was mediated in language; and this exchange had to be elucidated. The role of language had been identified by Heidegger, and his work was the point of departure for his student, Gadamer. The consequence of these concerns was that work cast in terms informed by psychology or philosophy of mind or metaphysics was supplemented (or replaced) by work informed by reflections upon language. Gadamer produces a philosophical hermeneutics; now the experience of the world is lodged firmly in language. Thus in the work of hermeneutics, attention turns to the sets of ideas inherited and inhabited by people. And with Gadamer, human beings are constituted in language, lodged in society and these in turn are located within unfolding time, history.

(b) Hans Georg Gadamer

Gadamer returns to the Romantics, in particular their criticism of the Enlightenment preference for technical rationality and affirmation of human understanding, and rejects the latent scientism of modern culture, evidenced in the routine celebration of method within the social sciences, in favour of the inherent worth and dignity of human experience. In Dilthey, hermeneutics was arguably a method, but in Gadamer it is presented as ontology; understanding is central to human life.[93] *Truth and Method*[94] is a key text in the tradition of philosophical hermeneutics.

Gadamer presents his position via a dense and complex dialogue with post-Kantian interpretive philosophy; the text has three elements: a critique of aesthetics; a critique of historicism; and a summary statement in regard to the language centred nature of hermeneutic scholarship.

In part one Gadamer asserts that the truth of art is immediate and autonomous. The truth-saying quality of art should be acknowledged says Gadamer. Post-Kantian aesthetics both makes the direct experience (merely) subjective and couples this to the view that the truth of art needs external demonstration via a 'scientific aesthetics'. This is all error argues Gadamer, but to refashion aesthetics demands reconstituting the centrality for human sciences, including aesthetics, of hermeneutics, the elucidation of tradition. Interpretation is the key: interpretations are located, they are lodged in society and history, they are thus bound by rules and these are transmitted by tradition. Interpretation is informed by rules carried in tradition; individuals participate and learn; it is not a quasi-private subjective experience at all, it is social and historical.[95]

Part two is a critique of historicism. Gadamer argues that Dilthey's was in error focusing on hermeneutics as a method. Historicism must be rescued from this deforming deference to method. Hermeneutics must shift from method to the core of living: tradition is present in our language and consciousness and reading the past is thus dialogue not neutral reportage. It is with reference to the work of Heidegger that a new movement forward can be made: it was understood that tradition was embedded in our thinking, a vehicle of thought. The concepts of prejudice, authority and tradition are reaffirmed. All interpretation is context-bound and there is no neutral point (neither external objective/scientific nor internal privileged subjective) from which to survey the world. The culture we inhabit flows through our heads: prejudices shape readings; tradition carries these prejudices; and the resources of tradition are not available in a voluntaristic way, they are demanding, in the form of effective history. Any particular exercise in interpretation thus takes the form of a dialogue or conversation, shaped by received ideas and an expectation of possible agreement, a regulative idea; but the process is reiterative and open ended.[96]

Then, in part three, *Truth and Method* concludes with a section on language and hermeneutics. The language-centred nature of hermeneutics is clarified; language is central to being/tradition, truth is disclosed in dialogue. Gadamer begins by noting:

> We say we conduct a conversation, but the more fundamental a conversation is, the less its conduct lies within the will of either

partner ... Rather ... we fall into conversation ... Understanding or its failure is like a process which happens to us.[97]

And he then reviews the linguistic character of the process that happens to us and expands its scope to cover the exchange of scholar and text (and text analogues). In the paradigm case of conversation there is equality of opening to the meanings of the other, 'each opens himself to the other person'.[98] The resemblances between ordinary conversation and hermeneutic enquiry are close:

> Thus it is quite correct to speak of a hermeneutical conversation. But from this it follows that hermeneutical conversation, like real conversation, finds a common language, and that this finding of a common language is not, any more than in real conversation, the preparation of a tool for the purpose of understanding, but, rather, coincides with the very act of understanding and reaching agreement.[99]

From this point of linking hermeneutic enquiry with ordinary conversation, and having noted that both have understanding built into their structure as conversation, Gadamer moves to point up the linguistic nature of this understanding, where we have a fusion of language, thought and practical experience. Gadamer comes to the position of noting that:

> We have, then, a confirmation of what we stated above, namely that in language the world presents itself ... The experience of the world in language is 'absolute'. It transcends all the relativities of the positing of being, because it embraces all being-in-itself, in whatever relationships (relativities) it appears. The linguistic quality of our experience of the world is prior, as contrasted with everything that is recognised and addressed as being. The fundamental relation of language and world does not, then, mean that world becomes the object of language. Rather the object of knowledge and of statements is already enclosed within the world horizon of language.[100]

And a little later on he remarks 'Being that can be understood is language'.[101]

Gadamer's position generates a rich stock of ideas for reflection on the nature of enquiry in the social sciences.[102] The natural scientific dictum of open-minded enquiry is misleading in social science as all knowing is suffused with foreknowing; the creative anticipation of results generated by the flow of tradition. The suppression of fore-knowing in natural science may allow enquiry to begin, but in the social sciences the procedure would involve suppressing the substance of the enterprise. Gadamer argues that historicity, being-in-history, is a clue to interpretive social science. History and culture are sedimented in our minds, carried in our ordinary language and reworked in the ordinary routines of life. The key idea is tradition, the set of ideas we inherit, inhabit and rework. But tradition is not a passive thing, a given stockpile of notions; it is rich, diverse and fluid, we can rework it as our personal horizons and concerns shift. Hermeneutic enquiry is thus a dialogue between the interpreter and what is being interpreted; pro-gress comes from successively refining formulations, broadening and deepening the context of understanding. Tradition is rich and inter-pretation is open ended and growing. Any text or text-analogue can be variously read. The enquirer learns in the dialogic discovery of tradi-tion. The scientistic pursuit of external description is futile; hermeneu-tics looks to the dialogic reading of received tradition; and an external realm of objects is not relevant, nor is the natural scientific notion of objectivity.[103] And underpinning this learning is our possession of lan-guage. It gives us the world we inhabit; tradition is expressed in lan-guage, interpretive dialogue is communal, internal to the language we inhabit.

(c) *Hermeneutics debated*

Like many early twentieth century theorists Gadamer reacts against pos-itivism. There has been extensive debate; here noted: first, the implic-ations of hermeneutics for the social sciences; second, the nature of the politics seemingly entailed by hermeneutic informed social science; and, finally, the broader question of the scholarly reliability of the material.

Taylor[104] argues that the hermeneutic dissolution of un-clarities in a field of meaning-for-subjects is central to any plausible social science, and radically distinct from orthodox empiricism. Taylor argues that inter-pretation is generic to humankind: human beings interpret their own lives, reflect upon it and social scientists reflect upon both. Hermeneutic interpretation is thus hierarchical; interpretations aim to decipher for a subject by situating or contextualizing their taken for granted world. Thus behavioural political science (and analogously social science) that focuses empiricist/positivist style on correlations/causes of observed social behaviours is radically misconceived; it produces nonsense-in-general (although it may throw up interesting particulars). Taylor does not note the technocratic-ideological role of this sort of material, but he is clear about the lack of veracity of the results, ethnocentric, biased and spuriously value neutral. Taylor[105] insists, contra those who argue in the wake of the presentation of post-empiricist philosophy of natural science that both natural and social sciences are theory-driven and thus, broadly, interpretive,[106] that the understanding sought in these two areas is different and any collapsing of the two areas is a mistake.

Richard Bernstein[107] also addresses the issue of hermeneutics and the attempt to re-read natural and social science as coinciding in theory-driven enquiry. Bernstein identifies unease within the contemporary humanities, social sciences and philosophy in respect of what he calls 'objectivism' and 'relativism'. The former is associated with the ortho-doxy and is in retreat, yet the alternative seems unattractive. Objectivism can be characterized in terms of a commitment to a realm of objects, accessible to enquiry if the method is correct. This is the empiricist/positivist package. Relativism can be characterized in terms of the insight that knowledge claims are culturally context dependent and enquiry and claims for enquiry should be appropriately restricted. The debate between objectivists and relativists brings a 'Cartesian anxiety' into play – the concern that our knowledge of the world (and thereafter ourselves) is either well founded and hence reliable, or it does not work at all. Bernstein claims he is not taking sides, preferring to read the terms as dialectical, thereby opening a possible way to moving beyond the exchange in order to reconstitute both areas of enquiry. The post-empiricist work of Thomas Kuhn is noted as having shown that natural science has an hermeneutic dimension. In the natural sciences the epistemic unit is now the community of scientists. This draws us into the realm hermeneutics. Bernstein thinks that the upshot of the attack on objectivism, and the simultaneous re-presentation of hermeneutics, generates the need for a dual reconsideration of natural and social science. At which point, it might be recalled that the hermeneutics set aside discussion of natural science and established independently and persuasively an interpretive social science. It now seems that hermeneu-tics can expand and embrace the area of natural science. But if the self-understanding of both social and natural science is now to be cast in hermeneutic terms why insist on a dual reconsideration? Why not simply recast the now failed objectivist work? It seems that this insistence upon rethinking both is an apologia, if not for natural science (recalling Feyerabend,[108] why would they need it?), then for all those social scien-tists who preferred an imported model of enquiry to the task of detailing their own.

On this it might be said, more broadly, that what is at issue is priority: should reflection on human beings and knowing begin with the humanities and social/cultural sciences or with the natural sciences? The intellectual tide in recent years has been for the former. The defensive manoeuvres of 'dual reconsideration' can be rejected. Thus, for the present: first, if we want to comprehend social theorizing then its a good idea to attend to the detail of what social theorists have been variously doing; second, similarly, if we want to comprehend what natural scientists are doing then its a good idea to attend to the detail of what they are variously doing.

Turning to the detail of the practice entailed by hermeneutic philosophy, it has been argued that the hermeneutics is in some sense conservative; thus, critical theorists object to the allegedly passive nature of hermeneutic work. Brian Fay[109] characterizes interpretive social science as focusing on the sets of meaning-structures inhabited by agents. Fay elucidates the practical aspirations of proponents of an interpretive social science by recording the expectations that such work will increase the possibilities of communication within society by proferring new explanatory schemas: new ideas about how the world is open up new possibilities for action. Fay identifies two objections to this: firstly, the theory of social science and secondly, the notion of the exchange of theory and practice. In social science the interpretive scheme leaves no room for the conditions that give rise to the actions, rules and beliefs that it seeks to understand: it does not involve crucial 'quasi-causal' explanations. It does not treat the latent functions of actions. It offers no way of analysing structural conflict and it neglects historical change. Moving on, in respect of theory and practice, there are two problems: the interpretive scheme does not treat social resistance to its free communication, thus social agents' self images are involved in their understandings of the world, so challenges to the latter may impact on the former – people might not want to know better how the world works; and secondly, it is rather conservative in that social tension is made to flow from breakdowns of communication and the possibility of real material inequalities is not addressed.[110]

However, there is a sustained attempt to advance in Jurgen Habermas, who points out that Gadamerian tradition/culture can encompass a systematically unequal material life. Habermas broadens the ontological characterization of human life, identifying technical, practical and critical understandings. Critical social science is a vehicle for a hermeneutic/critical enquiry into the structural conditions and present forms of distorted communication (ideology); thus critical or depth hermeneutics.

The prototype of critical social science is psychoanalysis; in dialogic exchange analyst and analysand bring to consciousness (and thus dissipate) psychoses that shape/deform patients life/behaviour. Critical hermeneutics has the theorist engaged in emancipatory dialogue with particular social groups. Habermas lodges such exchanges in a radically reconstructed historical materialism; human evolution is seen to take place in material, social and moral (power) spheres. The dissolution via critical social science of systematically distorted meaning patterns moves the process forwards. The veracity or otherwise of analyst/theorists' ideology-critiques are established, always provisionally, in dialogue governed by the language-inherent regulative and ethical standard of the ideal speech situation of open and reasoned debate. In sum, interpreted texts, or text-analogues, are contextualized, the real material history is put back in and their determining structures displayed by analyst/theorists who deploy reworked historical materialism, grounded in language, so as to proffer emancipatory ideology critique.

And, finally, returning to the hermeneutic challenge and the intellectual status of the material, Bauman[111] notes three important debates. First, interpretation can be understood as *technique or ontology*. Dilthey makes hermeneutic understanding a method of studying history, itself the key social science. All interpretive knowledge is context bound and thus relativistic but finally buttressed or secured by virtue of shared human life (of observer and observed). Gadamer represents the Romantic idea of human life as essentially subjective; Dilthey's historian as reporter is reworked into the historian as participant. Again it is the sharedness of human life that is the final ground for this work; in Gadamer the continually reworked tradition of our culture enfolds us in language carried structures of meaning. Then second, interpretation can be read as *passive re-description or as active engagement*. The work of the hermeneutic tradition displays two tendencies in the anticipated use of interpretive exercises; either essentially technical-scholarly (for scholars and dissemination through society via cultural-trickle down), or as potentially scholarly and popular (for scholars and wider co-inhabitants of the life-world). Finally, third, interpretation can read history as *progressive or reiterative*. The interpretation of cultural forms, meanings, has routinely been diagnosed as bound by history but the characterization of history made is not monolithic. The relativism of hermeneutics can issue in the view that social scientific enquiry is re-iterative and not cumulative and by extension (since our only access to history is through our interpretations of history) history itself is re-iterative rather than cumulative or progressive. But however these debates are resolved, hermeneutics is a rich tradition; a still unfolding body of scholarship, and those disposed to sympathy will judge the challenge well met.

Structuralism, post-structuralism and deconstruction

A final area of reflection centred on language is provided by structuralism: Ferdinand de Saussure takes the present of language and analyses it formally; meaning is a formal relationship evidenced in present usage. Meaning in social relations and meaning in system relations are two ways of coming at the same issue; language is conventional, it is a human construction.[112] Saussure offers a theory of language; a distinctive project. It has been argued that structuralism is simply a method,[113] but much more is on offer; centrally, language is grasped as a formal system and this has been read by some as opening a route to an objective, scientific, study of humankind as inhabitants of systems of signs. Structuralist analyses were utilized within the spheres of language, culture, literature and psychology, and in some cases grandiose claims were made to the supercession of modernity and whilst such confidence is now waning, the residues are of significance.

Saussure: language as system of signs

Saussure's *Course in General Linguistics*[114] is a highly technical discussion of the formal nature of language. The key idea is that language can be analysed as a system of signs, each sign having a form (signifier) and a substance, the idea (signified). The linguistic sign is arbitrary; form and content are established conventionally in the community of language users. Jonathan Culler remarks: 'Each language articulates or organises the world differently. Languages do not simply name existing categories they articulate their own'.[115]

A series of points in respect of Saussure's scheme can be made. First, signs are arbitrarily and relationally defined; language is a system of differences, thus brown cannot be ostensively defined only relationally as not red, not yellow, not green and so on. The sign works within a system of signs. Second, the formal system of signs, language, can be distinguished from speech, those acts that are possible within the system. Third, value and signification can be distinguished; language units have a value, meaning-within-the-language-system and when deployed in speech they have signification, or meaning-in-the-context-of-use. Fourth, synchronic and diachronic study of language can be distinguished; language slices up the world in an arbitrary way and is radically historical. The pattern is always in flux; it has no essences to anchor it, the sign is subject to history. The present is thus both the obvious start point for analysis and, oddly, a methodological fiction; the system is in flux, one state of affairs flows into another. Diachronic evolution is also a fiction (what is so special about presently tracing out an old track?). In sum, language is a human social convention; a speech community uses/affirms the conventions that reproduce language in their speech acts. Culler, notes that Saussure's wider influence flows from the thought that:

> Semiology is thus based on the assumption that insofar as human actions or productions convey meaning, insofar as they function as signs, there must be an underlying system of conventions and distinctions which makes this meaning possible.[116]

Language was one area of enquiry; but the field of meaning is vast, potentially embracing most of the humanities and social sciences.

The use of Saussure's insights into the formal structure of language within the broader cultural sphere involves a considerable shift; how is this understood and justified? In hermeneutics there is a key argument move; text to text-analogue as the justification of culture-critique centred on ideas of meaning/understanding. The proponents justify it with remarks about persons as bestowers and inhabitants of language carried understandings; a package centred on language/meanings. There is an analogous shift for structuralism; language as formal structure to culture as formal structure as the justification of cultural analysis based on ideas of structure. But the justification for this shift seems to be rather different. We could say this: it begins narrowly as a claim about methods; thus the method of structural analysis reveals ahistorical, trans-cultural, trans-subjective truths about the structures at back of cultural forms (this may be a narrow beginning but given that they are erecting a rationalist natural science of culture these are hardly modest beginnings) and thereafter it broadens into an implicit package (an ism) with its ideas of deconstructing and decentring the subject, here systems reproduce themselves and persons are merely elaborate points in the system; an anti-humanist view.[117] So, where hermeneutics justified its shift text to text-analogue by invoking commonly taken-for-granted ideas about human beings (meaning-bestowing and meaning-inhabiting), structuralism justifies its shift from formal language structures to formal cultural structures by invoking ideals of natural scientific explanation that entail abolishing commonly taken-for-granted ideas about human beings. So, whilst structural analysis might be seen as just one more strategy available to social scientists, the package of structuralism is much more ambiguous.

Language and power

Foucault draws on structuralist ideas, but softens the formalism; the work has been pursued in the form of historical analyses and both the method deployed and substantive claims advanced have attracted considerable attention.[118]

The method is a mixture of philosophy and history invoked, as author states, to make a history of the present.[119] It involves the quasi-structuralist presentation of the sets of conditions underlying patterns of more or less self-conscious thinking/acting. A number of key concepts order these analyses: discourse, episteme and genealogy. The notion of a discourse points to an institutionally ordered way of conceiving reality and thereafter acting within that sphere; reality is not simply given but it is constituted in the commitments we make, mostly unconscious or routine, in ordinary social action; we are fairly directly making-up the world as we go along. Such discourses are organised intellectually around a core set of ideas – these are claims to knowledge – they are the sets of assumptions drawn upon or invoked in discursive practice; they form historical blocs of meaning; ways of understanding and acting; and they are discontinuous – there is no process of smooth evolution – and incommensurable, once inside an episteme it works to make sense of the world, it is a self-contained sphere, like a paradigm. Finally, acknowledging that discursive practices carrying their embedded epistemes subsist within the flow of time, in history, the notion of genealogy allow us to grasp – in retrospect – the sequence of discontinuous transformations between discourses/epistemes. Thus, by way of an example, in respect of one intellectual/social phenomenon – 'the mad' – we can note that these persons have been successively understood to be inhabited by the gods (holy fools), bad (possessed of various ill-tempers), mad (having lives radically distorted and needing control/seclusion) and more recently mentally ill (having illnesses admitting of treatment): in each case an institutionally ordered strategy of reading and reacting to a particular group was in place; understanding and action were carried in social understandings. Such examples could be multiplied – in respect of any closed institution (prison, hospital or school) – in respect of many contemporary public collective activities (workplace, office or shopping mall) –and in respect of spheres of life usually taken in liberal individualist terms to be private, thus, sexuality.

Foucault's vision of the social world revolves around power – human beings are variously disciplined. The substantive claims focus on subject, knowledge and power. Modern civilization is diagnosed as centrally characterized by the subjection of the human subject to rationalized power. Foucault's response is a detailed case-by-case elucidation of power-in-action: in closed institutions such as prisons or clinics and later in regard to human sexuality.[120] The state is the central agency of these disciplinary enterprises. A key image is the panopticon but it should be noted that power, in these analyses, does not merely constrain some categories of human beings but reaches deep into the social being of all members of society. Overall, one might note that Foucault's role in these works seems to be that of an intellectual working in the public sphere – alerting subjects to their subjection. It would seem that the best that might be hoped for is a better grasp of the nature of the ties that bind.

Foucault's work shifted structuralist ideas into historical critique; successive ways of making sense of the world illuminate comparatively our present. The ideas of discourse/episteme recall speech/language. Successive states of the system (or residues thereof) would give us genealogy. All this recalls attention for social theorists to the value of the specific example. And the detail is persuasive; it can persuade when abstract schematic work leaves the audience unclear as to how material is to be understood/used. Foucault's focus is on the detail of contemporary cultural realm, characterized in terms of discipline (knowledge, power and subject). Foucault takes politics as omni-present and concerned with power but there is no expectation of progressive change; critics see him as both an irrationalist and conservative; but he might better be seen as a provocateur, challenging easy taken-for-granted ideas in theorizing (the formal aspects) and the easy acceptance of received social practices/prejudices (the substantive work);[121] of course, the risk is that such provocations might be mis-read.

Science and also deconstruction

The materials of structuralism can be used in radically divergent ways: sometimes to stress the goal of scientific status, at others to undermine received ideas of argument.[122] In anthropology Claude Levi-Strauss looked for common culture-forming principles of humankind; the structure behind surface reality was sought in terms of fundamental binary oppositions, us/them, male/female, insiders/outsiders and so on. These were taken to underpin otherwise diverse cultural forms. These building blocs could be combined variously; unity in diversity. Binary oppositions in concepts were characteristic of language, so the strategy opens the way to scientific analysis: 'There is more than a hint of Enlightenment rationalism that Levi-Strauss wishes to give to human universals'.[123] He rejected phenomenology and hermeneutics for their historical and subjective specificity, and for their scientific failure to distinguish appearance/reality. Science was affirmed; thus 'What Levi-Strauss seeks is the dissolution of the radical discontinuity of the human and natural sciences. Human life is placed back into nature by showing how culture is part of nature itself'.[124] And this theme was emphatically affirmed by Louis Althusser,[125] who offered a structuralist reading of Marx. Standing in opposition to the Hegelian Marx, the key idea was that of a symptomatic reading – a diagnostic analysis of underlying situations. Such a symptomatic reading disclosed the author's problematique – the complex set of problems, theories, methods, concepts and expectations. For Marx the problematique was an historical materialist science of history. The key text was *Capital* and the earlier work was pre-scientific and of no great moment. The key focus of historical materialism was on modes of production. These were abstract, timeless and formal concepts. They showed precisely the exchange of two classes in production. The mode of production was visible in the ordinary social scientific realm as a social formation. The mode of production was structured and reproduced itself. Formal models of modes of production could be made. Social formations, comprising articulated sets of modes of production, could thereafter be analysed. In all, in aspiration, a natural scientific Marxism. The early Marx was rejected as moralizing – so too was critical theory.

However, against the drive for scientificity, finally, another French theorist has pushed reflection on the nature of language and human being one step further. Language itself can be undermined. Jacques Derrida,[126] has returned to Heidegger and represented the notion of deconstructive reading. Derrida does not want to make systems; he offers deconstructive readings of texts by attacking their deep assumptions. A particular target is 'logocentrism' – the Western 'metaphysics of presence', the focus on states of affairs rather than the patterns of differences through which they are constituted. Derrida attacks language itself – he attempts to deconstruct language, producing an immanent critique of commitments made in language. Derridean deconstruction calls attention to the literary aspect of language; Derrida identifies subtle metaphors shaping thinking and self-conscious ratiocination. All of which is true; we dwell within language, we are all literary as well as literate people. Hence language is subtle, allusive, poetic and strong.

Language and social science

Twentieth century philosophy has seen a major preoccupation with the nature of language and its relationship to human thinking and culture; a key figure was Wittgenstein. The figure responsible for making this sort of material readily available to a wide audience of social scientists was Peter Winch, who argued, in brief, from the material of Wittgensteinian philosophy to the conclusion that social science was best seen as misbegotten epistemology concerned with elucidating instances of language-carried social rule following. At more or less the same time as the orthodox consensus began to crumble away, a large spread of material was introduced which derived in various ways from mainland European social philosophy. In addition to the language centred work of the philosophers of ordinary language there have been contributions from phenomenology and hermeneutics, Heidegger and Gadamer have proved to be of major importance. The implications of these changes in the focus of philosophy and social philosophy for social theory have been profound. Against the orthodox consensus view with its received model derived realism and inductivism feeding into essentially descriptive enquiry, social science is now taken to be ineluctably interpretive.

These ideas have been secured in dialogue with powerful and influential lines of argument. Wittgenstein offers a subtle analysis of language as the medium of human life and offers the key metaphors of language games and forms of life. Wittgenstein shows us that language is the medium of social life, and that language is a social construct. It is clear from Wittgenstein's work that social theorists must attend to specifics and diversity. Also from Wittgenstein powerful arguments can be taken which have the effect of radically blocking the naturalist project of a social science: reasons not causes. Gadamer proposes that hermeneutics be taken as ontology: we inhabit language carried tradition which is amenable to interpretive enquiry via dialogue. The hermeneutic line addresses directly the issue of how to conceive a social science. Empiricist/ positivist work is explicitly rejected at the outset. Hermeneutic enquiry is interpretive. It endeavours to unpack received historical cultural forms, to destroy the naturalness and given-ness of tradition and reveal its occasion and structure. Hermeneutic enquiry aims for plausible interpretation. It is dialogic. It is open-ended. It is a moral science.

Some have recoiled from the insights carried in language philosophy, phenomenology and hermeneutic work; a familiar prosaic complaint looks to relativism;[127] more directly the psychologist R.D. Laing, a noted figure in the 1960s anti-psychiatry movement, pointed to the intractability of the human condition; ending one text by remarking

'... then there is no end to it, words, words, words.'[128] Yet others rest content with the contingency of language, self and inherited practices.[129] However, neither anxiety nor complacency is required; that human beings inhabit language is a simple given, a starting point for reflection. For hermeneuticians language is the medium of human lived experience; human beings inhabit structured webs of meaning; carried in language, the vehicles of definite cultural traditions; the business of interpretation is central to human life; and language is the vehicle for reflection upon such experience.

The key to social sciences must be language. It is the medium of human lived experience and the vehicle for reflection upon such experience (lay and disciplinary). Philosophical hermeneutics is the starting point for enquiry in social science: we inhabit language and this is the vehicle of received cultural forms (tradition). This tradition we can critically recover in social science. In social scientific reflection theorists are able to draw down on received tradition in order to illuminate in a sceptical fashion extant sets of circumstances. Such episodes of scholarly reflection can be taken to represent a reworking of received tradition, and a contribution to its reproduction and transmission. At present the task of social science seems to be the reflexive discovery of tradition lodged in language. The critique of received cultural forms is seen as potentially liberating and progressive, although there is no immanent logic identified that would secure such advance. To advance matters beyond this point it would seem to be necessary to pay rather more attention to the intentions of theorizing than has thus far been the case.

4
Arguments from Political Community

Social scientists are not detached from the social world which they inhabit, nor are they separate from the political life of their communities; they are citizens; and this routine experience has prompted questions in respect of both the political logics of collective life and the possible roles of the social scientists. Any political community comprises many players with argument and action unfolding day by day; and social theorists are engaged in these matters, one more group of actors.[1] Unsurprisingly, the nature of political life and the character of apposite social theorizing have been extensively debated and they are still energetically disputed; schematically, in regard to the European tradition, there are conservative, liberal and democratic political lines;[2] invoking principles of tradition and authority, individualism and contract and dialogue and reason; and where each orientation embraces a distinctive view of the appropriate engagement of social scientific enquiry: hence piecemeal social engineering, instrumental-rational modelling and emancipatory political critique. Thus, in sum, the nature of the social sciences can be illuminated with reference to debates surrounding the business of ordering the political life of the community; and amongst these strands of debate, it is the later which will be the focus of this chapter; that is, the language-carried emancipatory critique.

Modernity, political debate and the critical analysis of society

The core of European received tradition is the modernist project, it embraces deep-seated assumptions about how the world might be understood and rationally ordered. It can be viewed as a cultural-project: the celebration of the cognitive mode of science, the deployment of reason and the demystification and rationalization of the world. It can be viewed as a social scientific project: the deployment of strategies of political-economic, social-institutional and culture-critical analysis oriented to the rational apprehension of patterns of complex change. It may be viewed as a (contested) political project: evidencing differing celebrations of the life of the community, most familiarly cast in terms of ideas of democracy.[3] Its best advocate has been the success of natural science;[4] yet natural science is a social activity, exhibiting a diversity of method/intention, it is not free of the features/problems found in other collective endeavours; and, therefore, to grasp the nature of modernity it is not enough to simply invoke 'science'.

The modernist project is bound up with the rise of capitalism; indeed, the notion offers one reading of that history; others reacted, offering different stories.[5] The project has unfolded unevenly; alliances of intellectuals and commercial groups brought together the ideas/interests necessary to initiate the sweeping changes involved; yet subsequently the bourgeoisie drew back from its radical implications[6] and sought a modest settlement around the ideal of the self-regulating liberal marketplace. The modernist project continues to be history-specific, appearing in various guises as agent groups read and react to changing circumstances; and so the core ideas admit of reinterpretation, misinterpretation and misrepresentation. However, overall, the modernist project can be taken to affirm the power of reason (we can grasp the dynamics of the system that enfolds us (celebration of science)), the efficacy of analysis (the system is read as inherently dynamic/progressive (future-optimism)) and the efficiency of human agency (collective endeavour secures progress). And within this unfolding form of life, where change reaches throughout the social world, political activity can be variously characterized, models of humankind invoked,[7] social relations characterized and an appropriate pattern of life for the community sketched out and thereafter the role (if any) of the intellectual commentator (amongst whose number will be social theorists) spelled out. Here three discrete strands of thought and action can be noted: conservative, invoking tradition/authority; liberal, invoking individualism/contract; and democratic, invoking dialogue/reason.

Conservative groupings have figured routinely in the modern history of Europe; they have frequently attained prominence; in the nineteenth century, in reaction to the rise of the modern world and its seeming displacement of old regimes;[8] in the crisis years of the twentieth century, in reaction to the burgeoning demands of socialism;[9] and in the years following the Second World War when the apparatus of the cold war was put in place in order to blunt reformist social change in Western Europe, resist state socialism in Eastern Europe and combat a variety of more or less reform minded nationalist elites in the new states of the former colonial empires.[10] It might be argued that the conservative line has fallen into the background at the present time; recent decades have seen an aggressive liberalism in the ascendancy with parallel streams of anxiety in respect of the fate of traditional authority and the dwindling status of representative democracy; but there is an enduring core. The conservative model of humankind is cautious: persons-lodged-in-communities provide the starting point, practical knowledge accumulates; it is enshrined in tradition, social and legal, and hierarchy is entirely to be expected/accepted. The collective wisdom of the community is thereby deployed and transmitted down the generations.[11] The vehicles for the use/transmission of accumulated wisdom/ideas are those of the established social/intellectual realm: churches, law and the senior professions where the claims of the practitioners are modest, piecemeal and protective of the status quo; it is a minimalist epistemic hope, an ethic of elite service/responsibility. Meddling with the established order is eschewed; neither the available dispersed collective knowledge nor the ethics of obedience and acquiescence offer encouragement; and thus, in principle, the role of any self-conscious social science is limited.

Turning to liberal strands, commercial/progressive groups have figured centrally in the making of the modern world.[12] The seventeenth century liberalism of Hobbes and Locke advanced a notion of possessive individualism;[13] and their arguments affirmed that the individual was sovereign over his own person and could enter contractual social exchanges to secure autonomously arising needs and wants (religious/feudal ideas lodged persons in a hierarchy of duty/deference). It was progressive as it offered a route forward from feudalism and civil war; it was the theory of the nascent bourgeois revolution.[14] In the later eighteenth century it was further developed; it intermixed with a wide affirmation of progress/science, in Scotland,[15] England[16] and France;[17] and in America the Lockean variant became a part of American nationalism.[18] In the nineteenth century, as the industrial and democratic revolutions unfolded, liberal ideas were further developed and the tradition unfolded into the twentieth century. Commentators suggest that it collapsed in the crisis years, and was only rescued by war economies. In the post-war period liberalism has given some ground to socialist ideas in the guise of welfare states, but towards the end of the twentieth century it has been resurgent in the economic policy field in the guise of 'globalization theory' in

America, Britain and parts of Europe. Again, a core set of ideas are identifiable. The liberal model of humankind is pragmatic: the autonomous individual-in-the-marketplace is central; relationships are practical, pragmatic and are entered into freely; and contract is central to the social world. Humankind has a basic set of needs; order and material well-being; and also has the individual wit and energy to secure these needs. The role of the state is restricted: it supports social order and the pursuit of well-being through a monopoly of legitimate violence and the apparatus of the law; and the key institutional vehicles of this form of life are the state and the market, where the required personnel include legislators, lawyers and merchants. The social world is ordered spontaneously. In principle, meddling with the system is not needed, although it may be needed in practice: states and markets can go awry, the practical knowledge/ethic embedded in them are not infallible but they are derived from basic needs/skills; there is a role for a social engineer, tracking the unintended consequences of collective actions, fixing problems, engaging in piecemeal social engineering.[19]

And, finally, picking up the democratic strands,[20] the idea of democracy threads its way through much of recent European history. The late eighteenth century put democracy onto the political agenda of the modern period; ideas from classical Greece via the Renaissance humanists are re-presented; and the French Revolution and the American War of Independence offer the possibility of republican democratic nation-statehood, celebrating liberty, equality, citizenship and law.[21] The ideal of democracy was contested, radical and quickly associated with violence;[22] the construction of modern states and nations unfolded across Europe; and whilst a series of democratic revolutions failed in 1848, with emergent social classes pressing for democracy, liberal-democratic systems were slowly installed.[23] The European general crisis 1914–45 saw a widespread albeit brief experiment with fascism, a longer period of state socialism and the establishment of welfare state systems.[24] Post-war political conflict was endemic and institutionalized in the machineries of cold war. The American sponsored Bretton Woods liberal trading regime system helped to generate recovery; as elite commitment to the welfare model softened, the 1980/90s Anglo-American liberal New Right became influential, subsequent celebratory globalization theory found many critics,[25] and arguments for democracy continue to be presented. The core ideas are familiar. The democratic model of humankind is optimistic: rational-individuals-dwelling-in-polities are central; individuals are rational, they reflect, they enquire and they can and do make sense of their social world. The polity both orders and shapes individual needs/wishes: the key institutional vehicle of the form of life is the public sphere; major elements include the machinery of the state, that is, formal parliaments, plus the dispersed apparatus of open debate present within the political community; and the central ethic of a democratic polity is the achievement of rational consensus. In this process there is a distinctive role for the social sciences – essentially, interpretive and critical – unpacking the claims of participant groups and arguing, in the terms of one noted figure, on behalf of humankind.

In this matter, the nature of political life and the possible role of scholarship, a number of political theorists have it in common that they reach back before the rise of liberalism, or to the very early phases of that era, when a form of democratic civil society had been sketched in practice, in order to recover and represent the idea of democracy. It is a strategy found amongst theorists working within the tradition of critical theory.

Early critical theory

The turn of the twentieth century saw changes in conceptions of social theorizing. Stuart Hughes[26] speaks of a revolt against positivism, taken as restrictedly rational at best and bureaucratic-irrational in its worst forms, and points to a spread of work in the humanities and social sciences. At this time in the 1920s[27] Marxist theorists attacked the Marxism-Leninism promulgated by the Second International, it too was read as positivistic and unsatisfactory; amongst these theorists a common strategy was reaching back to the original work of Marx in order to represent a philosophically sophisticated democratic critical theory.

The philosophical/scholarly background to the idea of critique can be traced to Immanuel Kant and G.W.F. Hegel; human kind is the starting point, human intellect and imagination the key; human beings collectively fashion their world;[28] and in this vein critical theory insists upon the active engagement of the theorist. It was exemplified in the early modern period by Karl Marx with his social scientific critique of political economy;[29] thus, theorizing unpacked in action, the unity of theory and practice. The concern for *praxis* informed the work of later theorists: Georg Lukacs, Karl Korsch and Antonio Gramsci; and the most influential group have been the Frankfurt School, Jurgen Habermas has inherited their mantle.[30]

Georg Lukacs, Karl Korsch and Antonio Gramsci

Lukacs offers the first humanist reading of Marx. The practical occasion is twofold: a reaction against the scientism of the German SPD, the Second and Third Internationals and the official theorists of the Soviet

Union; and the experience of the failures of the revolutions of 1918. The upshot was a concern for consciousness; how people read their circumstances was crucial for how they acted and claims to a science of revolution were dismissed. The available intellectual resources included Wilhelm Dilthey's hermeneutics, the neo-Kantianism of Max Weber and Werner Sombart, and the critical work of Hegel and Marx. Lukacs[31] presents reflections on method, class and reification.

On method, the key terms are dialectics and totality. The notion of dialectics points to the centrality in both the substantive material world and reflection upon that world of processes; dialectical reasoning uncovers the complex logic of processes. The critical nature of dialectics separates it from orthodox positivist social science (and Marxist positivisms) in both procedure and engagement: active reason rather than passive understanding and practical/political rather than spuriously technical/neutral. The notion of totality grants the context bound nature of social processes and insists that the social world – the ensemble of processes/reflection – can be critically apprehended as a coherent totality.[32] Lukacian historical materialism is a method; it allows the critical deciphering of the processual logics of given social totalities:

> Thus the objective forms of all social phenomena change constantly in the course of their ceaseless dialectical interactions with each other. The intelligibility of objects develops in proportion as we grasp their function in the totality to which they belong. This is why only the dialectical conception of totality can enable us to understand reality as a social process.[33]

Lukacs lodges his own work reflexively within these unfolding processes; the possibility of the method is occasioned by the shift to the modern capitalist world because it is only now that the social nature of human existence becomes clear. However in bourgeois society it is simultaneously disguised as discrete forms-of-life and reified as given and universal. The full realization of the social nature of human life and the possibility of rationally ordering it remains a task for the next phase of capitalist development which following the Marxist tradition (with its concern for linking theory and practice) was being generated by the practical activity of the proletariat. The elements – method, occasion and use – are run together:

> the essence of the method of historical materialism is inseparable from the 'practical and critical' activity of the proletariat: both are aspects of the same process of social evolution. So, too, the knowledge of reality

provided by the dialectical method is likewise inseparable from the class standpoint of the proletariat.[34]

On class, Lukacs rejects causal links between structure and thinking and writes of the historical materialist reconstruction in theory of the appropriate intellectual-political position of the proletariat; imputed class-consciousness; and thereafter, actual class-consciousness is situation-determined and must be social scientifically deciphered. The theorist distinguishes between class-consciousness indicated by the method of historical materialism and the empirical consciousness of class identified by familiar social scientific study. The systematic misreading of class situation, false consciousness, hinders the progress of the social system. The critical dissolution of false consciousness is required; it is the theorists' role. The sequence runs thus: first, class consciousness flows from structural position and may be radically misconceived; second, the imputed class consciousness of the proletariat provides a critical standpoint for the Marxian enterprise; third, the way the proletariat actually thought is crucial; and fourth, the vanguard can dissolve confusions thereby advancing social progress.

Finally, in regard to reification, Lukacs links it to Weber's rationalization: the social world takes on the form of an impersonal system governed by immutable laws and technical-rational thinking spreads. The dialectical analysis of the contradictions of contemporary society is the only route to the dissolution of such reified social relations and social thought. Critical analysis around the imputed class consciousness of the proletariat offers a chance to move the historical dynamic forwards, however, Lukacs concludes more optimistically (democratically) by noting that the transformation of society rests on the self transformation of the proletariat, that is, active and self conscious agency.[35]

The work of Lukacs proved to be influential and controversial.[36] The official reception was negative whereas the intellectual response was enthusiastic, not merely in respect of the recovery of the humanist Marx, but also in the related area of the critical analysis of the cultural forms of capitalism.[37] A number of themes were pursued: the rejection of positivistic social science; scepticism about the ideological power of natural science; the concern to fracture common sense thought and thus advance change; and the role of intellectuals in providing such analyses.

Karl Korsch,[38] writing after the failure of the 1918 revolutions and echoing Lukacian themes,[39] also addressed the relationship of theory and practice. Where the victorious bourgeoisie were concerned with social stability and positive social science, and Marxists with a trade union sponsored quietism that misrepresented Marx's remarks on the supercession of philosophy as enjoining a positivistic approach, Korsch argues that theorists must engage the sphere of ideas, not rest content with positivistic elucidations of inevitable proletarian victory.

Korsch notes the phases in Marx's work[40] and argues that a sophisticated critical analysis is maintained throughout the shifting substantive concerns. In contrast, followers of Marx 'despite all their theoretical and methodological avowals of historical materialism, in fact divided the theory of social revolution into fragments'.[41] In practical terms, later Marxists came to regard scientific socialism as a set of scientific statements, divorced from immediate political practice. In the political crisis of the early twentieth century available Marxism proved unhelpful: the orthodox clung to a dogmatic reading and the revisionists accommodated to the status quo. The historical materialist strategy had become merely a variant of positivistic social science; what was missing was the holistic and critical philosophical core. Korsch argued that materialist theory could not be divided into disciplines, nor divorced from practice.

And so orthodox and revisionist Marxist failings in regard to the political crises of 1918–20 revolved around a lack of appreciation of the importance of intellectual/ideological struggle. Korsch argues that patterns of understanding are threaded through patterns of social life and to secure change it is necessary to criticize ways of understanding at the same time as efforts are made to alter practical circumstances. The two tasks are linked:

> Just as political action is not rendered unnecessary by the economic action of a revolutionary class, so intellectual action is not rendered unnecessary by either political or economic action.[42]

Antonio Gramsci's[43] work pursued these matters. Gramsci was politically engaged from around the early years of the century, when he was sympathetic to the situation of the southern Italian peasantry (somewhat marginalized in Italy's move into the modern industrial world). Moving from Sardinia to the mainland in 1911 to attend university in Turin he quickly became involved in political activity; first in discussions of workers organizations, then the issue of Italian involvement in the Great War and after 1917 the whole business of revolutionary political change. The politics of left groups during the country's shift to the modern world – the late nineteenth century through until the end of the Second World War – were labyrinthine[44] and Gramsci was an active political figure until his 1926 arrest and imprisonment by Mussolini's regime; he died in 1937 shortly after his release.[45]

The theoretical work took shape 'in the context of an ideological debate with Bukharin's positivist Marxism and Croce's idealist liberalism with the intent of applying the Leninist political strategy to the Italian political conditions'.[46] Gramsci rejected the positivistic schemes of Nikolai Bukharin, characterizing the work as a deterministic and quietist; Benedetto Croce's idealism misdirected social scientific enquiry from the practical life of people; and the exchange with Leninism centred on a distinction between political and ideological hegemony, a focus on the machineries of the state versus a stress on the diffuse spread of ideas/practices throughout ordinary life. The key for Gramsci was practical activity; the routines of everyday life and the parallel demand that theorizing engage with this practical sphere.

Gramsci develops a political theory of change: there are sets of established material and ideological arrangements, historical blocs; established sets of widely disseminated ideas foster acceptance of the status quo (thus downplaying the role of violence), hegemony; and structural problems (contradictions) coupled to widespread challenge to received ideas and arrangements constitute an hegemonic crisis. As Gramsci came to realize the importance of the cultural sphere he considers the role of producers of ideas, intellectuals,[47] in particular noting the role of organic intellectuals, those embedded within the system. The role of the party, a 'collective intellectual', is to display the logic of the system, to foster its supercession. In sum, Gramsci argues that there is no automatic historical process to be revealed positivist fashion by scientific socialism; Marxism is a strategy of emancipatory critique/action.[48]

The concern for praxis and the role of the intellectual

The early years of the twentieth century saw a debate with positivistic social science both within established disciplinary traditions and the Marxian sphere; the arguments advanced by Lukacs, Korsch and Gramsci remain influential. The early humanist Marxist tradition rejected the positivistic Marxism of the early twentieth century; asserted an Hegelian Marxism, where historical materialism is read as dialectical, totalizing and critically engaged; diagnosed cultural resistance to the political left generated by the bourgeoisie (either reification and false consciousness, or the hegemonic power of the bourgeoisie liberal historical bloc); and suggested that the route forward was intellectual[49] critique to disturb the world taken for granted revealing the possibilities for the future.

The Frankfurt School

The Institute for Social Research was founded in 1923 at the instigation of a sympathizer, Felix Weil. It was a turbulent period of European history with intermingled economic advance, depression and social conflict.[50] In Germany there was dislocation following the Great War: first, political conflict in the form of the removal of the monarchy, the failed socialist revolutions of 1918–20 and the establishment of the fragile Weimar Republic; second, economic chaos in the form of hyper-inflation (on top of heavy war reparations paid to France); and third, social/intellectual confusion in the form of doubts about the reasons for the failure of the war, the viability of the new Republic and the shape of the future. The first Director was Karl Grunberg; succeeded by Max Horkheimer in 1931. The School was avowedly Marxist, although it was never associated with any particular party. Its early work involved political economy, archival work on the German labour movement, as well as the first stirrings of what was to become its most characteristic preoccupation, the critique of the cultural sphere of contemporary capitalism. The Institute left Germany in 1933 when the National Socialists came to power, continuing their work in Switzerland, the USA and subsequently the Federal Republic.

The programme of the Frankfurt School was characterized by Martin Jay[51] as a defence of reason on two fronts. One line of attack upon reason came from those who reacted against the growing rationalization of the world and celebrated in a romantic conservative fashion the non rational; the realms of subjectivity, moral striving, aesthetic experience and the like, an unlooked for legacy of the philosophers of life Friedrich Nietzsche, Henri Bergson, Georges Sorrel and Wilhelm Dilthey.[52] The other line was the celebration of positivism; human enquiry was restrictedly associated with a particular characterization of the natural sciences. Within this double defence of reason there is a Marxist aspect, a rejection of positivistic scientific socialism. The Marxian project in Europe was stymied when the Frankfurt School began its work; their approach to this situation is complex. The Marxian tradition is reconsidered and there is a double shift of conception and intent; a reaffirmation of the notion of reason as critical, coupled to a simultaneous shift in their attention to the cultural sphere. Some new work on political economy was accomplished but in the main extant analysis of the substructure is largely taken for granted and theorists moved to the project of the critical analysis of the cultural forms of capitalist society.

Before the Second World War Max Horkheimer, Theodore Adorno and Herbert Marcuse made efforts to assimilate Freudian psychoanalysis, researched the nature of authority and analysed mass society. Social control in industrial capitalism was discussed; and it was seen to be exerted not only in ever more intensive oversight by the state but also via mechanisms of cultural control in mass society. After the war Marcuse became involved in the 1960s New Left, Horkheimer and Adorno produced increasingly academic conservative work; nonetheless the crucial ideas of the Frankfurt School had been put in place.

At the centre lies the idea of critique: the Hegelian philosophical distinction between understanding and reason allows Max Horkheimer to offer a programme for the School. Horkheimer records that the familiar notion of theory entails the pursuit of a 'universal systematic science, not limited to any particular subject matter'.[53] This understanding of science is characterized as both product and servant of a particular stage in the development of the social world; the familiar conception of theory expresses the interest of the core groups of industrial capitalism in the manipulative mastery of their natural and social environment. Horkheimer remarks that this 'conception of theory was absolutized, as though it was grounded in the inner nature of knowledge as such ... and thus it became a reified ideological category'.[54] It produced essentially passive enquiry; uncovering what was given opened the route to universal theory. However, an alternative is available; a critical theory concerned to reflexively appropriate the grounds of knowledge claims thereby lodging them in history and revealing them as the products of rational agents. Horkheimer notes:

> Critical thinking is the function neither of the isolated individual nor of a sum-total of individuals. Its subject is rather a definite individual in his real relation to other individuals and groups, in his conflict with a particular class, and finally, in the resultant web of relationships with the social totality and with nature.[55]

In a postscript Horkheimer sums up:

> Theory in the traditional sense ... organises experience in the light of questions which arise out of life in present-day societies. The resultant network of disciplines contains information in a form which

makes it useful in any particular circumstances for the greatest possible number of purposes. The social genesis of problems, the real
situations in which science is put to use, and the purposes which it
is made to serve are all regarded by science as external to itself. The
critical theory of society ... has for its objects men as producers of
their own historical way of life in its totality. The real situations
which are the starting-point of science are not regarded simply as
data to be verified ... Objects, the kind of perception, the questions
asked, and the meaning of the answers all bear witness to human
activity and the degree of mans power.[56]

It might be added that critical theory 'very consciously makes its own
that concern for the rational organization of human activity which it is
its task to illuminate and legitimate'.[57]

Jurgen Habermas: theorist and critic in the public sphere

Habermas has constructed his critical theory in conversation with the
proponents of other positions in respect of the nature and possibilities
of social science; the resultant body of work is complex, here its trajectory, goal and grounding are sketched. The work may be divided
into two phases – early and late – with the former linked more closely
with the established work of the Frankfurt School whereas the latter
has more in common with contemporary Anglo-American philosophy
and social theory; here, the former is the main concern.

The phases of Habermas's work

An abiding concern for Habermas has been the construction of a politics adequate to the present;[58] a disciplined/scientific political discourse
that illuminated the circumstances of advanced capitalist societies. The
work produced since the 1960s falls into two phases.[59] The early work
sketches the notion of a critical theory of society;[60] it centres on a
quasi-Kantian notion of cognitive interests[61] that are taken to underpin definite areas of enquiry (scientific, interpretive and critical). However the intellectual status of this material was questioned and critical
theory re-centred on a general theory of language competence, the
universal pragmatics.[62] It is a 'reconstructive science', that is, the
empirical study of the structures that must underlie human activities.
The re-grounded critical theory is presented in *The Theory of Communicative Action*[63] whose themes are unpacked in a series of further
texts.

The overall project has been developed in critical dialogue with definite areas of social scientific and philosophical work: against positivism; against hermeneutics; against Marx and against systems theory.[64] Firstly, against positivism Habermas affirms a pragmatist notion of natural science as pursuing the useful (and so the positivists are wrong about natural science), and objects to the pervasive extension of positivism into the sphere of politics and culture, where the orthodox package generates a technocratic consciousness. Secondly, in his dialogue with hermeneutics Habermas takes this established counter-position to positivism to be correct in its stress on human experience as centrally one of understanding, with the consequent stress for social science on interpretive work, but wrong in its relativism and incipient idealism (which is evidenced in preference for persons as bearers of meanings given by tradition, rather than real historically located persons). Thirdly, in debate with Marxism, Habermas rejects the incipient scientism of Marx, fully expressed by Engels and subsequent scientific socialism, in favour of the recovery of the idea of critique and the focus on practical activity. Finally, against systems theory Habermas rejects its positivistic scientific pretensions and reworks the material to structure his discussions of the social context of hermeneutic tradition. The objective is a politics adequate to the present and critical social science contributes to the reconstruction of a public sphere of discourse that will replace technocratic regulation.

The first statement of the position is presented in a series of texts published through the 1960s and 1970s. A trio of knowledge constitutive interests underpinning scientific activity are presented with emancipatory interest the key to critical theory. The critique of ideologically occasioned distortions in communication fosters progressive evolutionary social change. The second statement is advertised in *Communication and the Evolution of Society* and pursued in the *Theory of Communicative Action*. The work is grounded in an idea of language, the universal pragmatics. The idea of critique is developed via a declaration that the obvious starting point of hermeneutic enquiry must be supplemented with: first, the critique of ideology so as to uncover systematic distortions in meaning patterns; second, an analysis of social systems in which meaning patterns are expressed or embedded; and third, a revision of historical materialism so as to allow the tendential evolutionary analysis of both distortions and system. The critical theory of society is dialogically oriented, substantively informed by a theory of society that speaks of social systems and committed to an evolutionist scheme of historical progress. The substantive analysis of contemporary industrial capitalism identifies system crises, presently one of legitimation; a solution can be found in the reconstructed public sphere, democratization in place of state/corporate managerialism.

The political project – towards a reconstructed public sphere

Habermas[65] distinguishes the original[66] ideal of political thinking as prudent understanding and the contemporary idea of rational decision-making; the Enlightenment links these otherwise remote eras, people are understood as rational beings able to understand and shape their world. In the nineteenth century this optimism saw expression (in the rise of natural science, in the development of social science, in the rise of the bourgeoisie and the promulgation of doctrines of republican democracy) and denial (in the beginnings of the subjection of natural scientific enquiry to state and commercial discipline, in the collapse of early nineteenth century social science into orthodox disciplines and in the denaturing of the democratic tendency as the bourgeoisie fixed themselves in place). By the end of the nineteenth century the Enlightenment notion of reason was lost; in its place were empiricist/positivist notions, and political thinking centred in all its ethically substantive forms upon means-ends rationality, a technocratic politics. The practical political sphere became absorbed by an essentially incoherent manipulative reason. A politics adequate to the present must recover political thought as prudent understanding of the social world and maintain the rigour of thought associated with the newly established natural sciences. The recovery of the Aristotelian notion of *phronesis* (prudent understanding) entails resisting technocratic forms of social decision taking in pursuit of the ideal of democracy (politics as discursive/public versus politics as the domain of the experts). The task is to reassert the autonomy of the political sphere: the objective, a reconstructed public sphere (anticipated in high tide of bourgeois liberal capitalism); the intellectual means, critical social theory (intellectually disciplined and democratic). The project can be elucidated with reference to early texts: *The Structural Transformation of the Public Sphere, Theory and Practice* and *Towards a Rational Society*.

In *The Structural Transformation of the Public Sphere* Habermas presents an historical sociological analysis of the development, nascent realization and subsequent decline of the public sphere. The text takes the form of a critical substantive narrative. This practical political institution is anticipated in Greece and Rome and subsequently extensively developed in modern Europe. Habermas characterizes the precursors in the epoch of feudalism and tracks the development of the public sphere (in Britain, France and Germany) in the period of the shift to the modern world, the emergence of mercantile capitalism. It is in Britain in the eighteenth century that Habermas finds the most compelling practical realization of the idea of the public sphere, a realm of social life separate from the state within which an independent bourgeoisie through a series of organizations (from newspapers, through learned societies to coffee houses) created an open public discussion of the requirements of their society. The exigencies of early mercantile capitalism restricted the extent of this public sphere; it was a liberal public sphere, the subaltern classes were not involved and the subsequent development of industrial capitalism with its extensive regulation – part functional part social reformist – meant that the state intruded on this public sphere and an arena of open public political debate is slowly circumscribed as the claims of one sort or another of bureaucrat/expert are advanced. Habermas takes the view that bureaucratic managerial capitalism has largely submerged the public sphere in a mix of parliamentary, corporate and media display; the key issue is whether – in a new guise – this public sphere can be reanimated in pursuit of democracy.

In *Theory and Practice* Habermas debates with Hobbes, Locke, Hegel and Marx, recalling the familiar story of the rise of liberalism and the counterstatement/loss of democracy. Habermas in the first essay 'The classical doctrine of politics in relation to social philosophy'[67] notes that the English revolution is theorized in the work of Hobbes and Locke. Aristotelian political theory centred on *phronesis*: it was a practical philosophy oriented to the community but in liberalism a technical manipulative politics is signalled. Ideas of natural and social science run together with liberal political philosophy; the natural world is material, causal and predictable, the social world is treated analogously and individuals regulated by the state calculate their interests and interact for profit. At this point classical political philosophy is replaced by familiar modern debate; Hobbes offers a social science instead of *phronesis*. If this is loss, Locke provides the gain; a concern for property secured by the state, a public sphere. Economists in the nineteenth century distinguish civil society/public sphere; the terms encompass the development of personal economic and political activity within the space guaranteed by the state. Thereafter, the usual problems of liberalism are mentioned, Hegel is cited as offering the next step forward and we may note: first, how close to familiar Marxian/democratic story all this is; second, the way these shifts are handled as involving losses and gains (there is no crude leftism); and third, the novel way Habermas identifies liberalism as furnishing the idea of civil society and public sphere – the creativity of the bourgeoisie is acknowledged and presented in a way that opens up the realm of politics as distinct from the realm of economics (and, this crops up also in the fourth essay, 'Labour and interaction: remarks on Hegel's Jena *Philosophy of Mind*,'[68] where Hegel and Marx are castigated for confusing the spheres of labour and interaction).

In the fifth essay 'On Hegel's political writings'[69] Habermas recalls that Hegel wrote journalism and edited a newspaper. The journalism should not be seen as peripheral to the philosophy: it was an initial point of contact with the world; the routine, diffuse, transient writings were an attempt to grasp events, a preliminary interpretation (rather than social scientific surveys). In the sixth essay 'Between philosophy and science: Marxism as critique'[70] Marx is criticized: the confusion of work and interaction skews enquiry in a scientistic direction; the focus on economics coupled to an expectation of crisis generated proletarian class action is redundant, in monopoly welfare capitalism the state is a key player and the proletariat demobilized. Marx must be read as critique. Again Habermas, like Max Weber, is drawing away from political economy to make room for politics. Habermas, in the seventh essay 'Dogmatism, reason and decision: on theory and praxis in our scientific civilization'[71] diagnoses technocratic rationalization. In economic production, in natural science and in the state dominated realm of politics the stress is on technical rationality, efficiency and order. This technocratic rationalization has developed through the seventeenth to nineteenth centuries along with the rise of the industrial capitalist system/ideology. The mode of thinking is now pervasive and inhibits progressive change. Habermas' political programme will have to re-establish the distinction made by Aristotle between technical and practical questions and the public sphere will have to be reanimated in order to foster democracy. Critical theory can contribute to the dissolution of false consciousness, reclaiming the practical sphere from the grasp of the technical expert. As technocratic rationality is pervasive in contemporary capitalism the task will have to be accomplished on a variety of fronts (routine political, policy, community, social theoretic and etcetera).

In *Towards a Rational Society* the direct programme is hinted at, the key term is democratization. The opening trio of essays deal with the democratization of the universities; that is, one major social institution, and the argument is applicable to other crucial institutions. The final trio of essays tackle the core issue of bringing natural scientific work back under public control: the democratization of natural scientific research (which is crucial to modern capitalism) is a fundamental task for securing progressive change and a major challenge to the extant system; locally there are many vested interests who would resist, and strategically the system would resist a shift from market oriented to publicly planned science.

The critique of technocratic rationality and the recovery of practical reason are central to a politics adequate to the present: one that is practical and intellectually rigorous. This sets the task of the critical theory of society. Habermas offers a familiar Frankfurt School line on the cultural achievement and failure of reason.[72] Perry Anderson[73] argues that the Frankfurt School have carried the flag of Marxist thinking in post-Second World War Germany and that in Habermas political circumstances and intellectual legacy issue in a brilliant social philosophy that has a distinctly pedagogic character. In the public sphere Habermas has been a doughty supporter of the post-war German polity, taking its firm embedding within the politico-cultural sphere of the West to be a major achievement.

Creating a critical social theory

The construction of critical social theory can be considered: the recovery of epistemology (the project's cognitive base); the process of carving out a space and shaping critical theory (the formal theoretical core); and how the work is deployed (theorizing in practice). Habermas proceeds through a process of debate with extant strands of thought.

(a) The recovery of epistemology

A crucial aspect of the Habermasian project of the reconstruction of the public sphere via the emancipatory efforts of critical social science is the rejection of pervasive habits of thought of technocratic rationality, the ideological counterpoint of industrial capitalism, and the recovery epistemology.[74] Alongside the rise of capitalism and its pervasive thought-style of technocratic rationalism we can plot the rise of positivism. It is the rise, character and supercession of positivism that concerns Habermas as he attends to the core task of creating a cognitive space for his enterprise in *Knowledge and Human Interests*. There are four steps: first, a review of nineteenth century positivism and its critics; second, a note on nineteenth century pragmatist and historicist replies; third, a discussion of the critique offered by Sigmund Freud; and finally fourth, the presentation of the knowledge constitutive interests.

Habermas argues that the philosophical discourse of epistemology collapsed through the nineteenth century into the philosophy of natural science, later contracting into the concern with methods pursued by logical positivism. Kant and Hegel failed to respond adequately to the rise of natural science: Kant splitting-off natural science and the realm of ethical judgements, and Hegel endeavouring to make philosophy the master science, left a clear space for positivism to develop; epistemology collapses, leaving the philosophy of science. Marx began to tackle this problem: in debate with Hegel – the materialist inversion via Feuerbach – Marx generates the core insight of historical materialism that human beings are centrally concerned with social labour (thus they make themselves and their societies in practical productive exchange with nature); however the materialist synthesis is too narrow, the essence of humankind is not labour but labour and interaction. The focus on a unitary *praxis* of labour and interaction (with labour as the key term) meant that Marx vacillated as to the status of his own work and by extension social theory. Habermas argues that Marx was never clear that his own work was social theory (critique) and thought it was (natural) science. The revised ontology proposed by Habermas – labour and interaction – gives us with interaction the clue and intellectual area of development of social theory (critique). Marx himself remains residually scientistic, a trait fully developed in orthodox Marxism-Leninism.

Habermas notes that if Marx does not escape the thrall of positivism, then neither does C.S. Pierce or Dilthey. They confronted the early positivist programme. Comte rewrites the history of the species in three stages and the present is the positive; natural science is celebrated as the study of given facts and the pinnacle of reason. The metaphysics of facts is pursued by Ernst Mach. A realm of facts constitutes the world which may be rationally accessed via technical science – objectivism. Pierce lodges pragmatist objections to objectivism: science is the effort of a community of enquirers and is practical in orientation; matters of usefulness and consensus are presented in place of accurate description of objects. Dilthey attends directly to the generic business of understanding within communities and could have shown how hermeneutics embraces all other sciences but remains haunted by positivism and narrows his efforts to providing a method for the cultural sciences as effective and appropriate as those used in the sphere of natural science. Dilthey also failed to show how systematic statements could be offered in cultural sciences, relativism remains. Pierce and Dilthey grasp that epistemology must attend to the social production of knowledge: they reject objectivism; but they do not grasp the more fundamental issue of knowledge constitutive interests.

Habermas finds the clue in Freud who offers a strategy of depth hermeneutic in the business of reading persons. The analytic procedure contextualizes patterns of behaviour using the structural model of psychoanalytic theory so as to emancipate the analysand from the thrall of confusions. The person grasps their behaviour through the structural model of psychoanalysis. The business of psychoanalytic critique and dialogue reveals the linkage between knowledge and interest. Psychoanalytic knowledge centres on the interest in emancipation: it is not a neutral mind-science, plus associated equally neutral mind-technology, which just happens to be useful in clearing up psychological problems. The interest in emancipatory therapy via dialogue suffuses the knowledge offered by psychoanalysis. The linkage of psychoanalysis (knowledge) and therapy (interest) is internal; a psychoanalytic theory that said it was not interested in therapy would be incoherent (recall Winch and MacIntyre). Freud thought psychoanalysis was a natural science and would in time be replaced by biochemistry (a better science). Habermas regards this as a self-misunderstanding; the style of critique presented by Freud is also that of Marx, it will be the key to critical social theory.

Habermas concludes *Knowledge and Human Interests* with a broad statement of his programme. Habermas argues that the Greek ideal of contemplative theory, which reveals the nature of the cosmos to humankind, comes to mean value free reports on facts; objectivism subsumes theory. Habermas offers a counter-position that recalls epistemology prior to the collapse into objectivism. A critical social theory will build on available social science and the cognitive-procedural model offered by Marx and Freud to offer an emancipatory critique of contemporary society. The rejection of objectivism opens the way to the recovery of the classical political tradition which offers the means to a criticism of the technological rationality of contemporary society. In brief, the recovery of epistemology clears the way for the Habermasian scheme of the knowledge constitutive interests; it makes the intellectual space for critical theory.

Habermas offers a philosophical anthropology of humankind. There are three fundamental aspects of human life, work, interaction and power, and they produce deep-seated human cognitive interests which inform areas of human knowledge: from work arises a technical interest and this informs the empirical analytic sciences; from interaction arises a practical interest and this informs the historico-hermeneutic sciences; and from power arises an emancipatory interest and this informs the critical sciences. Habermas' first technical cognitive interest underpins the spheres of empirical sciences; the notion of natural science is not that of the rejected positivist orthodoxy but draws strongly on the pragmatist line, natural science is the community-based pursuit of useful knowledge. The second practical interest flows from the need to maintain a coherent social world, one that works and is intelligible to its members. So this practical interest underpins efforts in the realm of communication: as formally constituted disciplines this is the realm of historical and hermeneutic sciences. On this account, as elsewhere in this text, the upshot is that the logic of enquiry of the human sciences is taken to be utterly divorced from that of natural science. The third cognitive interest associates with the concern for power. There is no extant discipline expressing this interest and Habermas has the task of constructing it: Habermas speaks of emancipation; as a project it cashes as the pursuit of democracy, thus we recover the passion for reason of the Enlightenment.

The scheme of knowledge constitutive interests allows Habermas to recover epistemology from the suffocating grasp of the philosophy of science and carve out an intellectual space for critical social theory. It is presented in phase one of his work. It has been much criticized; however for the present Habermas has secured the basis of a critical social theory (the intellectual space in the new epistemology and the interest in emancipation to give direction to such critical theoretic endeavours as may be accomplished); next we need a formal statement of the theory.

(b) Carving out a space and shaping critical theory

The formal outline of critical social theory can be sketched: the same ground is covered with a different question in mind; not carving out space, rather shaping theory. In respect of the theoretical core of critical social theory – tradition, system and evolution – Habermas proceeds via debate hermeneutics, functionalism/systems theory and Marx.

The debate with hermeneutics provides several ideas: the centrality of language based communication of meanings; the initial means for the dismissal of positivism in social science and natural science in favour of a version of pragmatism; the useful notion of tradition; and the hermeneutic recovery of tradition is transposed to the critique of ideology. As noted, Habermas tackles Dilthey in *Knowledge and Human Interests*. Gadamer is discussed in a series of comments over an extended period of time.[75] In brief, the hermeneutic counter-position to positivism is taken to be correct in its stress on the generic nature of understanding – and thereafter its stress on social science as interpretive – but wrong in its relativism and incipient idealism. Anderson *et al.*,[76] comparing the hermeneutics of Gadamer with the depth hermeneutics of Habermas make three points. First, Habermas objects that Gadamer does not consider the possibility that tradition is ideological, that it can encompass unequal material lives. Second, Habermas expands Gadamer's ontology/ epistemology. It is no longer unitary, with understanding expressed in history, culture and language, but tripartite, with the knowledge constitutive interests of work, understanding and power (the bases for natural science, hermeneutics and critical social theory). The interest in power is the base for a hermeneutic social scientific enquiry into the structural dynamics of presently existing forms of distorted communication (ideology): critical social theory, the result of this enquiry, is thus a depth hermeneutics. Third, the prototype of depth hermeneutics is found in psychoanalytic dialogue. Critical social theory is similarly dialogic in procedure. Psychoanlytic theory is generated to order or inform analytic dialogue. Then, continuing,[77] fourth, historical materialism is reconstructed to order or inform critical social theoretic dialogue and evolutionary change is characterized as possible (in principle) in material and communicative (social and moral) spheres of human life. The critical dissolution of distorted patterns of meaning moves the evolutionary process forwards. Fifth, the veracity of analysts (theorists) ideology critiques are established (always provisionally) in debate, and at base in the dialogue of the regulative ideal speech situation (critique is thus practically and morally grounded in language as truth transmitting). Thus, sixth, in sum, interpreted texts or text-analogues are contextualized, the real material history is put back in and their determining structures displayed by the theorist who deploys reworked historical materialism grounded in language so as to proffer emancipatory ideology critique.

The exchange with functionalism/systems theory is unexpected; such material fits uneasily with the humanist Marxian tradition. Habermas insists that systems theory can be taken into critical social theory; it provides a way of talking about the social frame (evolution) of meaning patterns. McCarthy[78] reviews these exchanges: the objectivist ideal of a self-regulating system amenable to natural scientific study is a chimera; functionalism can only be useful if taken as heuristic and pragmatic when oriented to stated goals. If we have specified our goal interests then we can order enquiries into social change by talking in terms of systems. Taken into critical social theory functionalism becomes a way of talking about the real world carriers of the meaning systems of tradition. All this overlaps with Habermas's borrowings from historical materialism: from Marx Habermas takes the ideas of critique and *praxis* (men make their own selves, societies and histories in their routine practical activity). Yet it is not immediately clear what is wrong with political economy. Nonetheless in *Legitimation Crisis* Habermas puts the system theory to work: the social system embraces and shapes the sphere of the life world. System crises impact upon the life world. Systems change around forces of production. Systems have a learning capacity and system flexibility depends on the level of learning capacity reached. Social systems evolve: primitive, traditional and capitalist and each social formation has a specific principle of organization. In capitalism problems are typically economic. Contemporary industrial capitalism is state-directed: there is an economic system, an administrative sphere and a legitimation system. The system faces problems – ecological, anthropological (motivation) and international (war) – and economic and administrative system failures generate the legitimation crises visible in political protest. Habermas argues that these legitimation problems must be resolved in open discourse. Thus we have critical diagnosis and prescription: it is cast in terms of systems.

In the debate with Marx two ideas are important: the idea of critique and the scheme of reconstructed historical materialism. First, Habermas[79] argues that Marx wrongly took his work to be (natural) science when he should have taken it as critique; the upshot is that Marx falls away into positivistic political economy and thereafter his followers make it ludicrous as scientific socialism. Further, Habermas[80] also argues that most of Marx is redundant and what has to be recovered is critique. Then, Habermas[81] argues that Marx's materialist synthesis is too narrow – humankind is not focused on labour but labour and interaction. In making his generalized history, the critical social theory analogue of Freud's psychoanalytic theory (the intellectual machineries invoked to order dialogue), Habermas begins with Marx's reflexively self-conscious philosophy of history, that is historical materialism – the notion that progressively we have become aware of how men make their own selves, lives, societies and history through their routine practice and how critique can move the process forwards. The creation of self and society is the key element taken by Habermas. But where Marx, given his ontology of labour, focused on change in the means of production, Habermas, with his dual ontology, can look at evolution in both the work and interaction spheres. The upshot seems to be an evolutionary, systems theory-informed version of historical materialism; it is discussed in *Communication and the Evolution of Society*.

In sum: Habermas takes from hermeneutics the idea of tradition; from systems theory a way to embed tradition in its real social carriers; and from historical materialism the idea of reflexively self conscious history-as-evolution. Linked to the idea of critique, it produces this schema: tradition is expressed in social systems that are evolving and critical social theoretic inquiry into distortions of communication can assist this evolution.

(c) Deploying/grounding critical theory

The recovery of epistemology allows Habermas to carve out an intellectual space for the core of a critical social science; it is then constructed using the notions of tradition, system and evolution. These machineries are then deployed in social theoretic practice: a trio of issues arise, specifically, procedures, methods and grounding. As before, what follows will be repetitive; Habermas's work is tightly integrated, any sequential rehearsal is rather simplistic. In the matter of deployment/grounding there are three aspects to consider: the procedure of dialogue (taken from psychoanalysis); the method of ideology-critique (therapeutic dissolution of distorted communication); and the grounding of critical social theoretic efforts in language.

Freud's[82] psychoanalysis provides a metaphor for the critical theoretic enterprise: the relationship of analyst and analysand mirrors the relationship of critical theorist and social audience. In the presentation of critical theoretic readings of the circumstances of the addressees the objective of the theorist is the dialogic transmission of this reading of the recipients circumstances. If the proffered interpretation is effective then the recipient will better grasp the nature of their circumstances and act accordingly. The exchange is dialogic, so proffered readings are amenable to debate (thus critical social theory does not offer recipes). Any proffered interpretation can be accepted or rejected. In the latter case the critical theorist begins again, the effort must be reworked. In the former case the question is how do we know if the theorist's interpretation has been grasped in the way intended. The answer centres on the transmission of the method of critique; if the proffered interpretation is good it will resonate with the experience/understanding of the recipients and generate a disposition to critical engagement with circumstances. Further, form and substance run together: critical theory is emancipatory; the correct grasp of proffered interpretations will be manifest in the recipient's use of substantive claims and techniques of critique. It is an open-ended procedure. In dialogue the partners are equal; dialogue is not a monologue of active expert theorist and passive non-expert recipient. All proffered interpretations are tested in dialogue. The only intellectually privileged element that can give a clue to the recipient's grasp is formal; the acceptance/use of the method of critique; the substance is up for dialogic grabs.[83]

The affirmation of the centrality of dialogue rests in the end on the view that reason and truth inhere in language/communication. Habermas distinguishes between action and discourse; communicative action rests on a background consensus and if this is disturbed then participants engage in discourse. The objective of discourse is to substitute for the now challenged taken-for-granted consensus a rational consensus achieved through argument. The proffered interpretations of the critical theorist are liable to challenge and thereafter the matter must be argued out; equally the theorist may challenge the claims of the audience. Again, one sees that critical theory is open-textured and open ended: carried and grounded in language.

The method involved in Habermasian ideology critique seems to be little different from the rest of the humanist Marxian tradition. The method of ideology critique is slotted into the evolutionary schema. Habermas has attacked the reduction to politics to technical rational expertise, the critique of the expert.[84] Habermas has attacked the reduction of natural science from free enquiry to the handmaiden of industrial capitalist production, the critique of narrow natural science.[85] More generally, Habermas has attacked scientism/objectivism, the critique of pervasive technical rationality in contemporary industrial capitalism. More substantively, Habermas attacks the dehumanizing impact of industrial capitalism upon citizenry, and the positive moment of ideology critique centres on the realization of democratic tendencies lodged within bourgeois capitalism.

Critical social theory has a dual grounding in language: its cognitive status (Habermas offers a consensus theory of truth to block any slide towards relativism); and a minimum ethic (critical theory is not just another ideology). In respect of the first, Habermas accuses Gadamer of being relativistic; the problem is avoided by lodging a disposition to truth within the structure of language itself. Any search for a rational consensus to replace challenged taken-for-granted consensus is guided by the ideal of free communication, that is, open dialogue in which the best argument is accepted, on the basis that language acts to transmit the truth. As Marx claimed every act of alienated labour carries within it the demand for free creative labour so Habermas claims that every act of communication that necessarily uses language entails affirming the notion of truth. It is a powerful point – a language that did not act to transmit the truth seems unimaginable (think of a computer: if it has an error in the software, a point where truth is not transmitted, then it is useless). It can be granted that the set of rules constituting language are complex, shifting and thoroughly non-obvious to casual scrutiny and that people lie, cheat, make mistakes and so on, but this does not touch the core idea that language must act to transmit the truth. Language also shapes ethics: every act of communication carries within it the demand for free communication and the circumstances allowing such free communication. Inherent within language use is a dual claim for truth (flowing from the intrinsic character of language as a formal system) and equality (flowing from immediate requirement of truth transmitting). This minimum ethic, the equality of participants in ideal dialogue, gives us the clue to a rich notion of democracy when full-blown ideology critiques are made and proffered to an audience.

The construction of a critical theory has involved carving out a space for critical theory, shaping the formal core and indicating how the exercises would be deployed/grounded. Carving out a space for critical theory is accomplished by rejecting positivism in favour of the scheme of knowledge constitutive interests: a represented epistemology freed from narrow restrictions of positivistic focus on methods of natural science that opens up technical, practical and critical knowledge spheres. As regards shaping the formal core of critical theory, so as to present the scheme of tradition expressed in social system which is evolving where such evolution can be aided via ideology critique, this is accomplished via a Freudianized historical materialism. In the case of delineating the deployment/grounding of critical social theoretic interventions, we have open-ended, dialogic, interpretation and action-contextualizing ideology critiques redeemed in discourse and grounded in language.

The substantive position: the critique of technocratic culture

The substantive position is embedded in the work; the concern with democracy was announced in *The Structural Transformation of the Public Sphere* and there are two other early sources, *Towards a Rational Society* and *Legitimation Crisis*. All this has produced a substantive analysis of a depoliticized society liable to social crises. Habermas attacks the prevalent technocratic ideology of the controlling organs of industrial capitalism and charges that the system is liable to crises of legitimation precisely because the state has now embroiled itself openly in securing economic success. The critique of the technocratic ideology is the prerequisite of the establishment of a broader democratic strategy of setting social goals and priorities.

Habermas has translated theory into practice in the form of numerous interventions within the public sphere, mostly focused on Germany, but also addressing issues related to developments in Europe and

America. A number of themes are present in these materials: first, a concern with the embedding of the German polity within the West, coupled to a concomitant rejection of any claims to a special national destiny for the country; second an insistence that reason is universal and that human rights and so on are similarly unrestricted in their nominal sphere of application; and third, an emphatic commitment to the possibility of consensus secured in dialogue. These ideas have run through numerous debates including the notorious 'historians conflict' in respect of the responsibility of the German polity towards the historical memory of the holocaust, the future of the European Union and more recently the errors of the government of George Bush in launching wars of choice in the Middle East.[86] It is possible to identify a change in tone in these materials as an arguably clear early Frankfurt School style slowly gives way to a more generalized progressivism, but this would be to cavil: Habermas has been justly celebrated as a 'critic in the public sphere'.[87]

Habermas phase two; universal pragmatics

There are continuities in the work: the concern for politics (scientifically adequate and practical; the concern to establish critical theory (as a distinctive intellectual sphere); and the concern for the democratization of bureaucratically ordered capitalism. A central concern has been with establishing critical theory as a distinctive intellectual sphere (otherwise, critical theory has no more claims on our attention than any other available ideology). There are three attempts to carve out and ground critical theory: first, the historical sociological identification of the late eighteenth century as the practical exemplification of the public sphere – a realm of open debate – restricted to the liberal elite, but a clue to the nature of a realizable democracy, and a clue to a critical analysis of contemporary society; second, the Kantian style philosophical identification of the trio of knowledge-constitutive interests – technical, practical and emancipatory – of which the last noted was the clue to an elaborated critical theory; and third, the analysis of the fundamentals of social interaction, initially, with reference to structuralist work (Noam Chomsky, Jean Piaget) and thereafter to Wittgenstein derived work on speech acts (J.L. Austin and John Searle), which offer a way of establishing a critical theory. There are two attempts to elaborate the logic of critical theory:[88] the first around the trio of knowledge constitutive interests and the second around the idea of communicative competence.

The work on communicative action has attracted considerable, often unsympathetic, attention. A comment on the relationship of the two formal phases is given by Perry Anderson[89] who speaks of three conceptual slippages: first, labour and interaction becomes labour and communication; second, communication becomes identified with language; and third, production (labour) is subsumed under communication by talking systems-style about learning processes and prioritizing communication and a subsequent extension gives communicative change the key role in general change; thus the revisions to Marx culminate in an abstract-general philosophy of communication/history. In a similar way, Thomas McCarthy takes the view that the material of communicative competence re-presents the earlier material in an abstract general fashion: it's all rather unhelpful.[90]

And Bernstein[91] takes a similar view; suggesting that the communicative competence material offers a systematic re-presentation of the early work in response to a set of problems: first, there is confusion between reflection and self-reflection, where the former Kantian idea denotes reflection on the grounds of knowledge whereas the later Hegelian idea denotes the dissolution of confusions inhibiting action; second, the status of cognitive interests is ambiguous, it is not clear whether they are transcendental philosophy or empirical anthropology; third, the early work stressed the knowing subject, thereby misrepresenting the social language-carried nature of knowing; and fourth, the early work had little by way of substantive social critique. And in *The Theory of Communicative Action* we have a systematic restatement of the programme. The Kantian transcendental strategy is retained yet reworked. Habermas turns to the analysis of language and speaks of reconstructive sciences of what logically must be universal species competences (two examples of such reconstructive sciences are Chomsky's linguistics and Piaget's scheme of cognitive development). Unlike Kant's procedures these reconstructive sciences are empirically testable. The language philosophy of Austin and Searle comes to the fore thereafter. The theory of communicative action and rationality is a more universal reconstructive science – it embraces the more restricted reconstructive sciences. Habermas calls this universal pragmatics – the bases of communicative action. Thus the first problem is tackled; the reconstructive science of communicative action provides the grounding (theoretical and ethical) for emancipatory critique. The second problem is tackled also: the trio of cognitive interests that were presented epistemologically/ anthropologically in *Knowledge and Human Interests* are represented in the reconstructive science of universal pragmatics as the spheres of purposive-rational and communicative action. The third problem is removed with the new reconstructive science of communication that focuses directly on dialogue embedded in language. The fourth problem is dealt with in terms of the unfolding logic and consequences of the demands of the system upon the life world.[92] Here the theory of communicative action and rationality can be seen to have both synchronic and diachronic aspects. Synchronically, the reconstructive science of communication and rationality begins with the analysis of speech acts that reveals the claims made in any speech act – to comprehensibility, truth, sincerity, and correctness. In speech these are all assumed but if challenged we shift to discourse where validity claims are tested/redeemed simply by open, free argument: this invokes the regulative ideal speech situation which simply inheres in language. Diachronically, picking-up the Weberian idea of rationalization Habermas distinguishes rationalization in the purposive rational sphere, better technique, and rationalization in the communicative sphere, better *praxis*, which involves removal of blocs to communication. This theory of communicative action lets us solve the fourth problem. Thus a critical social science will draw on insights from universal pragmatics to rework established social scientific themes. Universal pragmatics displays species competence in communicative action, and reveals drive for rationalization (progress) to be inherent in language.

The new general statement covers the ground set out in the phase one work. Established social science has typically studied either social systems (conceived as governed by purposive rationality and thus amenable to (natural) scientific analysis) or the life-world (conceived as the (subjective) sphere of creative actors) and did so non-critically. Habermas wants to treat these two dialogically and critically link them to the two spheres of rationality such that modernity is characterized by the invasion of the life-world by purposive rational systems. The technocratic style of present day society is the result of an overstress on one type of rationality to the detriment (neglect) of the other. All of which looks broadly like phase one Habermas but the changes in the theory are extensive and the doubt must remain that the latter position, as Anderson pointed out, has shifted significantly in overall conception and intent.

Criticisms of Habermas' work

It has been said that the overall project is an eclectic, over-general and implausible scheme with no very obvious agent in view; these criticisms relate to the first phase, grounded in knowledge constitutive interests; as regards the second phase, grounded in universal pragmatics, the overall criticism is reinforced and there are further technical philosophical debates. The phase one material is considered here, and, as with the exposition, so with the review of criticisms, the work represents a complex unity and exposition and criticism entail a measure of repetition.

In respect of characterizing the problem: the critique of technocratic rationality, the pervasive cultural style of industrial capitalism, and the recovery of the crucial distinction between technical and practical matters so as to foster the reconstruction of a public sphere of democratic discourse, are the essence of the political project. Jay details the rise of the Frankfurt School and displays the broad similarities of concern between Frankfurt School and Habermas: both are preoccupied with the pervasive irrationalism of the superstructure of industrial capitalism and both identify critique as some sort of response. Habermas inherits a tradition that moved away from the political economic analysis of material circumstances in the early 1930s and focused on culture. In a similar way, Anderson[93] lodges Habermas in his relevant context; the Germany of Konrad Adenauer, with Marxism marginalized and the left under pressure, and it produces a sober and pedagogic politics. Together we get one expression of a common criticism of Habermas – that it is idealist both in analytic strategy and in its programme. However, Albrecht Wellmer[94] offers a sympathetic report. Marx is characterized as utopian on two grounds: first, the neglect of analysis of social organization; and second the ill-considered ethic of free producers within a planned system. A crucial neglect flows from this utopianism, namely the neglect of the political dynamic of bourgeois society. Wellmer sees Weber as having said something about this – the idea of rationalization or disenchantment. Wellmer sees the Frankfurt School neo-Marxists as trying to integrate Marx and Weber – rationalization of the world could be made progressive with culture critique. However, early critical theory became pessimistic. Habermas is seen to be moving critical theory forward. Against Marx, Habermas is seen to argue that bourgeois law and morality are not just epiphenomenal but do represent genuine societal learning (rationalization in the sense of extension of reason). Against Weber, Habermas is taken to argue that this rationalization is more than mere bureaucratization. Against early critical theory Habermas is taken to be arguing that nascent democracy within capitalism is valuable and can be the basis of immanent critique. Habermas's critical theory then talks of rationalization in purposive and communicative spheres: the invasion of life-world can be remedied by critique thereby aiding evolutionary rationalization process in both spheres – the key is the extension of democracy, the sphere of communication. Anderson[95] calls this the priority of language before labour and the result of conceptual slippages that take Habermas from Marx to a pedagogic quietism.

In respect of carving out a space: the critique of positivism (objectivism) and the recovery of epistemology clears the way for a new statement in respect of the occasion, character and role of the three spheres of human knowledge. This is the key Habermasian scheme of the knowledge constitutive interests – it lets Habermas carve out an intellectual space in which to develop his ideas of critical theory (the vehicle for the political project): crucially the idea of critique. There are many criticisms of Habermas's procedure in carving out a space for critical theory.

Habermas has been criticized for his reading of Marx. First, Habermas argues Marx vacillated between seeing his own work as philosophy and as science and ended up misrecognizing it as positivistic political-economic based science. This seems to be a mistake. Marx's notion of science was both pre-positivist (in simple chronology) and catholic in scope and intention;[96] thus the Marx of *Paris Manuscripts* and *Grundrisse* uses the strategy of critique. Second, Habermas tackles Marx's philosophical anthropology of human creative labour, a key element in historical materialism. Habermas links this to the positivistic political economy. Habermas splits labour and interaction and thus opens up space for critique. But creative human labour involves interaction so Marx did not get it wrong (and nor was there any slide to positivistic political-economy). The effect of splitting work and interaction is problematic: Marx's human was a fully sensuous being whereas in Habermas the human is primarily a cognitive being (that is communicator via language). The idea of alienation drops away – instead we have embeddedness in patterns of distorted communication. And third, Habermas tackles historical materialism and in place of a substantive theorem of the self-creation of humanity via social labour, takes historical materialism as a strategy of reflexively appropriating history, thereafter expressed as evolutionary systems theory. The shift is related to Habermas's prioritizing communication/language over work. Habermas revises the agent of theory execution: the focus on proletariat is dropped in favour of an appeal to reason itself, that is, there is no very obvious agent at all. Marx is merely a resource for Habermas, and at the end of the borrowings there is very little of Marx left. One recalls Alice and the smile on the face of the Cheshire cat.[97]

Habermas makes a long and detailed discussion of Hegel, Pierce, Dilthey, Kant and Freud, as these thinkers offer responses to the rise of natural science. Thus Hegel (philosophy is the science) and Kant (who splits science and judgement) are seen to fail to adequately grasp the rise of natural science: the upshot of their work is, especially from Kant, subjectivism; that is, if it is not natural science then it is subjective opinion. Hegel's attempts to make philosophy the master science inevitably fail. Marx grasps the solution lies in focusing on creative human social labour, but with his positivistic self-misunderstanding (and other errors) fails to get to the idea of critique. Similarly, Pierce (stressing usefulness and community) and Dilthey (stressing understanding in communities) fail to break free of positivism. The new epistemology must grant the linkages of knowledge and interests and the variety of interests; thus technical, practical and emancipatory (the peak and base of the whole lot). All of which is, arguably, correct. However the treatment of Dilthey is unsatisfactory. What is interesting about Dilthey is his use of Hegelian themes of the historical embeddedness and recoverability of cultural themes, and his nearness to Gadamer. And then the clue to the linkage of knowledge and interest is found by Habermas in Freud: there has been doubt about Habermas's use of the metaphor analyst/analysand for theorist/social group addressed. It seems that Habermas wants the linkage, but only thereafter makes a sketch of how critical theory works. The problem with the later is the focus on communication, but what if communication is not possible or not wanted.

Habermas finds his space for a critical theory in the scheme of cognitive interests. This has been criticized and in phase two it falls away. The philosophical anthropology revises Marx: in place of human labour (*praxis*) we get work/interaction. This split has been criticized above. The knowledge constitutive interests identified as embedded in these aspects of the philosophical anthropology are characterized, after Kant, as quasi-transcendental: the general reaction seems to be one of deep scepticism in respect of this status. The subsequent reworking of all this in language is similarly complex. In brief: first, Habermas's critique of the collapse of epistemology into philosophy of science, and later simply the methodology of natural science, would be widely granted; second, Habermas's characterization of the positivist package, linking back to a political project, would also be widely granted; third, Habermas's view that a new space – allowing a range of human interests/ knowledges – is needed would (probably) be widely granted; and fourth Habermas's particular new space has been regarded with both interest and scepticism, probably more of the former.

In the matter of shaping the core: the formal core of critical theory, like all the other elements is constructed via dialogue with established areas of social philosophy. First, from hermeneutics, Habermas takes the idea of tradition; second, from systems theory, Habermas takes the language of systems so as to embed tradition in its real social carriers; and third, from historical materialism, Habermas takes the idea of reflexively self conscious history as evolution. Overall, and linked-up to the idea of critique, we get this: tradition is expressed in social systems that are evolving and the critical social theoretic enquiry into distortions of communication can assist evolution. As regards criticisms of the formal core of the work, the formal core is presented via debates with hermeneutics, systems theory and Marx, and so these exchanges must be noted. On Marx: remarks on Habermas's treatment of Marx are made above and not repeated here. On systems theory: it is odd that Habermas should prefer language of systems theory to the language of political economy when addressing business of real world carriers of tradition. Many commentators have found the use of systems theoretic machineries unexpected and unpersuasive. McCarthy[98] reports that Habermas borrows from systems theory and does not properly digest it and this contributes to over-generality of later work. Held[99] makes the same observation; there are intellectual slides to the general consequent upon the use of systems theoretic concepts. Giddens[100] thinks the use of systems is hopeless. On hermeneutics: McCarthy[101] identifies a de-emphasizing of hermeneutics in favour of systems theory as a contribution to the unhelpful shift to abstract general level of later work. At the same time Bernstein[102] takes Habermas's grounded hermeneutics as a way to get beyond Gadamer's relativism. It is true that Habermas's use of hermeneutics is problematic: Habermas often seems close to the hermeneutics line of thought but his preoccupation with relativism skews debate; Habermas's view that Gadamer is relativistic is unhelpful, and when the systems theory stripped away from Habermas then both theorists can be seen to have very similar interests in language.

In respect of deploying and grounding the work: critical theoretic interventions in the super-structural sphere will be in the nature of exercises in ideology critique; and critical theoretic materials will endeavour to illuminate the restrictive cultural circumstances of particular social groups with a view to fostering emancipatory action. Such ideology critiques will be open-ended, dialogic and discursively redeemed; and thus finally grounded, cognitively and ethically, in human language. On dialogue: first, with whom; second, what if they do not want to hear; third, what if they hear and misunderstand; fourth, what if the proffered message is taken over and misrepresented; and fifth, what if circumstances block hearing messages (censorship, repression, etcetera). All of these are problems that can be addressed, but it must be noted that the overall project of culture critique is very loosely textured. On ideology critique: first, is this any different to the rest of the humanist Marxian line or other lines, thus Fay[103] speaks of distinguishing critical theory from critical social science and then he adds there are lots of specimens of critical social science (familiarly, social criticism); and second, Habermas seems to make this the key, but development theory has offered lessons to the effect that political economic analysis of economic-social-political systems is vital. On grounding: it might be that critical theory does not need to be grounded. Habermas sees himself as overcoming the relativism of hermeneutics by lodging the cognitive and ethical base of the enterprise in language, this argument from the truth-transmitting character of language is powerful, if abstract, others doubt that the effort succeeds,[104] others that it is necessary.[105]

As regards Habermas's substantive analysis: it is argued that contemporary industrial capitalism is marked by a distinctive technocratic culture which reserves decisions for the sphere of putative experts and resists the involvement of the wider population. The system is liable to crises of legitimation, to the withdrawal of wide societal consent, and it is in need of a thoroughgoing democratization. The position is of considerable interest. *The Structural Transformation of the Public Sphere* sketches the historically anticipated and desired goal; the material of *Towards a Rational Society* contributes to the ideology critique of contemporary culture of capitalism and *Legitimation Crisis* sketches a mechanism of change. The model of a rational discursive democratic society has found many admirers, as have the critiques of modern political life, but as regards the theory of a legitimation crisis, Held[106] remarks that he doesn't believe a word of it. However, there are now extensive social scientific examinations of the dynamics of the cultural sphere. As regards the overall position: a defence of reason and an affirmation of democracy in the face of contemporary industrial capitalism's technical rationalization seems wholly proper and useful. And in respect of the debate on Habermas generally: the summary judgement could be that the work is an ambiguous continuation of the Frankfurt School tradition, but deservedly influential.[107]

An unfolding project

Habermas's work continues to unfold; it has been developed over many years; it has extended to many areas of philosophical, social scientific and political reflection; and whilst it can be read as an extension of the classical tradition of European social theory the body of work resists easy labelling. There are difficulties in slotting the work into the tradition, thus the rejection of political economy, the structuralist argument and the generality of the later material on communication, but, for the moment, it can be concluded that critical theory is efficiently grounded in language and that the repertoire of concepts assembled is enough to allow the critical emancipatory analysis of contemporary society. In brief, it is a persuasive argument from the nature of political community. It also adopts, evidently, a favourable position in respect of the prospects for the project of modernity; many commentators find this laudable whilst others have their doubts.

Sceptical responses to the modernist project

A number of sceptical responses to the late nineteenth century high tide of positivistic optimism have been recorded;[108] a sense of cultural malaise; a concern for consciousness; a concern for values; a deepening appreciation of the complexity of the social world and the difficulties of attempts at explanation on the model of the sciences; and a deeper concern for ways of characterizing human kind and establishing knowledge of these matters. In the event the cultural world of early twentieth century Europeans collapsed around their heads; ruin, division and cold war followed; the subsequent recovery was ordered in part in terms of 'liberal-democracy' relatedly in terms of its co-definer 'state-socialism'; nonetheless, the recovery was successful, with the construction of domestic welfare states and the overarching machinery of the European Union. It might have been understood as a period of high achievement and future optimism; a view many analysts took; but not all, and from both the political right wing and the left new diagnoses of problems emerged; and what these critiques had in common was a scepticism about the advertised success of contemporary modernity. In the latter years of the twentieth century one expression took the form of claims to a novel 'post-modernity', others were not so sure and some, it seemed, didn't care either way.

The turn of the twenty-first century has seen shifting structural patterns within the global system: the collapse of the Soviet Union, coupled to a stream of subsequent debate ('we won' or 'the end of history' or 'the new global order'); the uni-polar moment of the ascendancy of the USA, coupled to a stream of subsequent commentary ('hyper-power' or 'empire' or 'full-spectrum dominance'); and the deepening integration of the international economy ('globalization' or 'regionalization' or 'hubs' or 'market-states'). And, at the same time as these debates were unfolding, an ambitious diagnosis of the entire package of changes was presented, 'postmodernism'. This diagnosis comprised numerous strands, often rather disparate:[109] first, aesthetic – changes within the world of art, a reaction against the austerity of the 'international style' in architecture and the claims of the modern more generally and a preference for playfulness, pastiche and the non-serious; second, productive – changes in the nature and operation of contemporary industrial capitalism as new technologies generated ever greater flows of consumer goods – scarcity was replaced by abundance (for the burgeoning numbers of the fortunate); and third, philosophical – where sceptical post-structural thought undermined received ideas about the surety of scientific knowledge.

These arguments have been debated. David Harvey[110] unpacks the issue of production change in terms of the distinction between 'fordist' and 'post-fordist' production: the former being the archetypal mass production (production lines making identical products – famously, 'any colour you like so long as its black'); and the later resting on new technologies allowing the multiplication of variations of a basic theme such that consumer choice is taken to proliferate ('any colour you like, just tell us, and we'll order it for you'). This line of thought has been pursued in the territory of celebratory globalization (less, the emergence of post modernism, more the untrammelled victory of late twentieth century American corporate capitalism). Harvey records his doubts that anything very new is happening, save maybe in the fields of finance and credit.[111] In a similar vein, Frederick Jameson[112] argues that there is no new form of life, rather a novel consumer capitalism has developed and theorists need to take it seriously. It celebrates the ephemeral pleasures of consumption, it celebrates 'choice' and it has considerable ideological impact as a consequence, binding-in the modestly successful whilst branding the poor as failures. More speculatively, Harvey follows the aesthetic line into the arts, architecture and city planning, where the austere simplicity of modernism is challenged by a new penchant for decoration and display (thus the fashion for adorning buildings with decorative iron-work, as in Singapore's upgraded housing blocks, or adding lighting schemes to buildings, as with Hong Kong's harbour side office buildings, or just riding modern computer assisted engineering in order to build any shape you like, thus Beijing's new 'twisted trousers' television centre, or Bangkok's 'elephant building' office block).

J.F. Lyotard[113] pulled these disparate strands of debate and criticism together. A package was proposed, postmodernism. The ideas in respect of unfolding change are turned against the inherited ideas of reason and claims to universality must be abandoned. The contemporary world is a relativistic, provisional and fragmented social world, where received meta-discourses of progress have to be abandoned as familiar patterns-of-life structured by industrial capitalism give way to life-style creation within the knowledge-based global system of post-industrial society. At the same time, received patterns of social theoretical argument are in need of radical renewal; the familiar confidence of our culture in respect of historical dynamics of progress can no longer be sustained; and in place of the experience of continuous intelligible progress, the experienced world of post-modernity has become one of partial truths and relativistic subjective perspectives. In our ordinary lives we are invited to select from proffered consumer alternatives in order to construct a life-style, and in the realm of social theorizing we are similarly enjoined to reject received traditions aspiring to universal knowledge in favour of the local, the partial, the contingent, the gestural.

Such arguments generated many responses; Bauman affirmed a sceptical modernity; he distinguished legislators and interpreters,[114] and suggested that the former role was no longer tenable but – against fashionable despair[115] or acquiescent indifference[116] – the later role remained available and could decipher the shifting relationships of contemporary global industrial capitalist consumerism; against the intellectual adventures of postmodernism, the modernist project was thus reaffirmed, albeit in the full knowledge of its historical and cultural context dependence: universal claims are untenable; our sciences are not an ahistorical model, a clear benefit to mankind, rather they are an ambiguous social product;[117] our received traditions are diverse, so too those of other cultures; and thus the notion of dialogue moves into the foreground. And, with equal vigour, MacIntyre[118] suggested that the modern world of liberal democracy lacked any notion of community, that environment within which people could make their lives and with reference to which they could understand moral precepts and the nature of human practical wisdom. Instead, the social world had cast aside religious ideas (which did involve ideas of community) in favour of an implausible individualism (autonomous asocial selves) in pursuit of satisfactions where such egoistic behaviour was to be regulated by abstract moral rules and bureaucratic rational state machineries. The upshot, argued MacIntyre, was an emotivist culture which saw individual claims to rights confronting both the claims of others and the claims to utility of bureaucratic managers, where such claims were buttressed by further claims to social scientific knowledge. MacIntyre argued that the claims to managerial expertise were untenable, mere covers for the pursuit of elite and corporate goals, whilst the former jumble of claims to rights merely illustrated the condition of a disintegrated moral realm. The solution, if there was one, would be found in an appropriate return to a pre-enlightenment ideal of community.

However, not all commentators offer a sharp choice of either enthusiasms for, or reactions against, the present. Richard Rorty recommends the stance of liberal ironist; the world is what it is, so we might usefully celebrate what we take to be good whilst trying to mitigate the bad. It might be said that Rorty[119] takes the idea of 'contingency' seriously. Centrally, language is social, it has no ground in the facts, nor any ground in our innermost selves, it is social through and through, and thus the familiar empiricist/positivist and equally familiar Kantian informed theses about the grounds of language are in error. After Wittgenstein, language games run through forms of life; it is not possible to step outside language; and our conceptual apparatuses and our ethics are all internal to the language game we inhabit. Rorty goes on to argue that the self is contingent; it has no base in either material drives or quasi-ethical assertions; it is social; aspirations to self-knowledge will uncover how we fit within the world; that is, it will help us avoid dancing to other people's tunes, but no more; and our re-descriptions of ourselves will never be final, they will merely stop with our deaths. Rorty goes on to note that the liberal community with which we are familiar is also contingent; there are no extra-social grounds for preferring our liberal society; the tradition asserts the values of tolerance and debate; Rorty rejects Foucault's pessimism in respect of costs of social discipline, and rejects Habermas' attempts to ground our social world in communication; and instead grants their contingency and affirms the values anyway; it is the stance of the liberal ironist. Rorty distinguishes a private-self and public-self; for former, reflection is upon who we find ourselves to be; for later, it celebrates the goals our tradition of tolerance and debate. All this is contingent; it has no ground, it is just the tradition we inherit and inhabit.

****

It is true that social theorizing is routinely practically engaged; it is also true that social theorizing is context-bound; the issue of grounding remains open; but, for the moment, it is enough to note that claims to the scientificity of the social sciences require much more than either an appeal to the received model of the natural sciences or the invocation of the language carried nature of human social life; social theorizing rests between the demands/concerns of context, the interests/skills of the theorist and the needs/wishes of the audience and this requires that the engaged practicality of theorizing be acknowledged; social theorists make arguments in order to inform action in the world.

Political community and social theorizing

Social theorists are engaged agents lodged within the social relationships they seek to characterize; and so the idea of critique is crucial, from Kant, Hegel and Marx. The early formulations within the Marxist tradition of the idea of critique are both intelligible in the early Marx and obscured by the scientistic versions of Marx promulgated after his death and which culminate in an official scientific state socialism. A reaction comes from Georg Lukacs, Karl Korsch and Antonio Gramsci who one way or another reassert: first, the central role of the early Marx who used strategies of Hegelian critique; second, deny the empiricist/positivist ideas found in both orthodox social science and later official Marxism; third, stress the importance of the realms of culture, in general, and the particular sphere of popular culture (as it opens up a way of dealing with systematic mis-understandings or 'false consciousness'); and, fourth, go on to stress the need for a thoroughgoing critique of popular culture as a precondition for any political advance on behalf of progressive/democratic political groups. The Frankfurt School's theorists continue with the idea of critique; at first they work within readily identifiable Marxist framework; in the 1930s Max Horkheimer, Theodor Adorno along with Herbert Marcuse[120] and Eric Fromm[121] all continue with intellectual novel engaged work; however, later, progressively, they become more abstract, general and with Horkheimer and Adorno, finally pessimistic; indeed, eventually, they come to look not merely pessimistic but irrelevant. Jurgen Habermas revives the Frankfurt School with his ambitious politics adequate for the present, an affirmation of the democracy partially generated by the bourgeoisie and guaranteed in language; the critique of ideology is the key to evolutionary change overcoming the present dominance of industrial capitalism and its associated technocratic thought forms; and the notion of a critical social science is thereby re-worked and re-deployed.

In summary, arguments from political community to the nature, value and utility of social theorizing are familiar; in recent years, through a long exchange with available notions of both the social sciences and the realm of political life, theorists have re-presented a long-established counter-tradition to empiricist/positivist tales. Critical social theorizing centres on the interpretive-critical elucidation of patterns of complex change in the unfolding process of the shift to the modern world, entails valuation and prescription, where such matters are necessary elements of the procedural logic of social scientific theorizing, and this position may be summarized as the contemporary social scientific affirmation of the modernist project, a sceptical, context-bound, dialogic form of the tradition.

5
Language, Tradition and Practice

Making sense of the social world is an activity generic to humankind, intrinsic to forms-of-life, a mundane, practical and routine social accomplishment; such understandings range from the materials of little traditions found in common sense, folk wisdom and the words of witch doctors, shamans, politicians and so on, through to great traditions carried in the work of priests, artists and philosophers. The sphere of formal social theorizing is one more attempt; it evidences a diversity of practical efforts to read local circumstances in the light of the intellectual materials of received tradition. After Ludwig Wittgenstein, it comprises a family of loosely related attempts to make sense of the social world; each a circumstance-sensitive problem-specific deployment of the intellectual machineries of received tradition; each with an audience in view; each with an expectation of a particular sort of action built into the analytical machineries which carry the argument; each a distinctive mode of engagement. The European tradition of social theorizing revolves around the modernist project; diverse agents read and react to enfolding circumstances in the process of the ongoing shift to the modern world;[1] thus scholarly social theorizing is a particular mode of engagement, other agents have different agendas and make their arguments accordingly.

This text has looked at formal debates cast in terms of the received model of natural science, reflections on the nature of language/understanding and affirmations of the ineluctably practical/political nature of social life and come to the summary view that social theorizing as understood within the European tradition is grounded in language, located in tradition and deployed in practice in the form of discrete modes of engagement in order to grasp an ever shifting agenda of issues. Here arguments will be recalled which illuminate the formal core of the tradition; these will be augmented by noting the practical business of social theorizing, its diverse engaged character plus its substantive preoccupations and emergent agendas. Various ways of grasping the diversity within received tradition will be reviewed. And additionally, the issue of other traditions will be broached; it is true that scholars inhabit received tradition, but Euro-centrism, the banal affirmation of the resources of an inherited intellectual repertoire as universal in its relevance and reach, is not tenable; the world is home to multiple traditions. Some idea of the nature of the exchange of received tradition and ideas/practice cast in terms of other traditions is needed (a formal and substantive requirement). By way of a final word, it will be recalled (once again) that social theorizing is a practical activity, its character best revealed in the context of the production and deployment of arguments on behalf of particular audiences. And here it might be noted that as social theorizing is suffused with the contextual and prospective demands of practice, one contemporary sphere of concern is the unfolding dynamic of the European Union within the contemporary global system; it is an urgent issue and in recent years has been the subject of a wealth of scholarly reflection. Overall, it can be confidently asserted that the classical European tradition of social theorizing offers a rich stock of cognitive, ethical and practical argument; the tradition remains vigorous, the project unfolding.

Language: ontology, practice and ethic

Language is central to human social life and whilst reflection upon the nature of language is not new, social theorists have considered the implications for social theorizing and these can be summarized thus: language is the ontology of humankind, medium of social life and location of a minimum ethic. The theorists considered in this text cut into the issue of language in different ways; tradition (history), practice (anthropology), signs (semiotics) and community (politics). Hans-Georg Gadamer argues that tradition-bound language is the ontology of humankind; Ludwig Wittgenstein explicates the subtle social nature of language; Ferdinand de Saussure's formal analysis of language illuminates the arbitrary social nature of the sign; and Jurgen Habermas finds a minimum democratic ethic lodged in language itself.

Gadamer remarks that 'Being that can be understood is language';[2] the key is tradition; carried in language it embraces us, the means to hermeneutic dialogue. The notion of tradition is crucial, the set of ideas which we inhabit; history and culture vehicled in language are sedimented in our minds. Tradition is neither fixed nor unavailable to its inhabitants, it is continuously remade and reinterpreted and reflexive critical hermeneutic enquiry can decipher received tradition; human beings are knowledgeable inhabitants of culture and history. Humankind inhabits a language-carried history and culture. Tradition comprises the language-carried stock of knowledge/meaning given to us in the present as history and culture. Tradition is internally structured; the ordinary world of routine social life is meaningful and persons and groups move through this world perfectly smoothly; it all works, actors are knowledgeable agents. These webs of meaning are structured: horizontally in the reach of ideas (fashions, zeitgeists and the formal positions of institutions); vertically in the linkages of self, society and epoch; and longitudinally in history, the stock, source and repository of meanings. Gadamer explicitly gives us the idea that language is the ontology of humankind; we construct the social world we inhabit by drawing on culture and history. This tradition is present for us in language and is fluid and flexible. Interpretive enquiry into received tradition is thus dialogic in form and orthodox ideals of objectivity – accommodating to the given world – are set aside. All interpretation is internal to language because there is no outside to which appeals can be directed. It is in this sense that Gadamer characterizes language as the ontology of humankind.

Wittgenstein considers the nature of language: it is a human social construct, embedded in ordinary social practice, language-games vehicle forms-of-life. Wittgenstein argues that to understand a language-game is a matter of learning how language works in a particular social context and the crucial idea is a rule;[3] human behaviour is intelligible when it is rule governed; such rule following will be social, carried in the medium of ordinary language. Rules have to be social; one cannot set and obey one's own rules; language/social life is fundamentally trans-individual. Wittgenstein argues that language-games are the vehicle for forms-of-life; sets of concepts constitute social practices which are discrete and separate from each other; they are finite,[4] contained, each a sphere of use or activity, there is no essence waiting to be unpacked. Wittgenstein calls attention to the intimate linkage of patterns of language use with actual social practices so as to offer a strategy of the therapeutic dissolution of philosophical puzzles; any problem can be resolved by a close-textured report on how ordinary language uses the problematical words or formulations. Wittgenstein is not offering a social philosophy, yet the discussion of language does illuminate the nature of social life, and offers the basis for a non-natural science referring strategy of social theorizing; the focus is given social practices, what people or groups actually do in routine social life.

Turning to the work of Saussure, here the appeals to history and ordinary life are eschewed in favour of the formal analysis of the machineries of language; these systems of signs are radically social; they are carried in routine practice; and they serve to 'slice up the world'[5] we inhabit. Linguistics works with a distinction between speech and language; every act of speaking both invokes and reproduces the rules of the language being used; once again, the social nature of human language and thinking is underscored.

Work in critical theory provides a final element derived from language: a minimum ethic. Habermas argues that any language carried act of speech carries within it the requirement for the practical condition of free rational communication. The nature of language itself carries these requirements; they are inherent characteristics. Language carries a minimum epistemology; any move from the realm of taken-for-granted ideas to discourse invokes the regulative ideal-speech situation, matters are resolved by free debate where language acts to transmit truth, uncovering the best argument. Language carries a related minimum ethic; the ideal-speech situation implies the requirement for open dialogue free of constraints in order to find the best argument. These ideas form elements of a complex critical theory: these claims are lodged within received European culture but they make minimal universal claims, a base for dialogue, a route to deploying these ideas outside their received cultural sphere.

The analysis of language illuminates the nature of human social being and offers the means to ground social theorizing: it is formally interpretive-critical, practical and engaged; it is widely dispersed in terms of its substantive concerns.

Tradition: received contexts/resources

Grounded in language, dispersed in practice, any exercise in social theoretic engagement will involve an elaborate exchange of context, theorist and audience where the context comprises shifting circumstances and the stock of resources carried in tradition available to social theorizing.

The business of making sense is generic to humankind. Language is the key to humankind. The social world we inhabit – the dense patterns of social interaction and understanding – is constituted in and carried by language. The social world is open to extensive reflection;

we interact and we reflect upon interaction. The process of reflection generates a diverse spread of ways of making sense of the social world; all these forms of reflection carry knowledge claims; all are ways of reflecting upon action and interaction. We can speak of little traditions: routine, habit, common sense, oral tradition or folk knowledge. We can speak of great traditions: the realms of the arts or religious traditions. We can speak also about science, one more way of making sense; natural science and social science, the former the key to modern industrial society, the latter an extensively developed body of systematic and critical reflections upon patterns of life. The realm of formal social scientific argument is diverse. The social sciences inhabit tradition, the materials are available for practical use and the work of practitioners constitutes that tradition. All exercises in social theorizing are lodged within tradition: making an argument entails affirming conception/intent, it is a practical task; so too is critical commentary, unpacking the dialectic of context, theorist and audience. Social theorizing is located in tradition and within shifting contemporary circumstances and what counts as social theorizing is given by tradition.

The shift to the modern world radically remade the worlds which Europeans had inhabited and presented theorists with a daunting task of understanding: the interlinked sweeping changes had to be interpreted from the inside (the changes embraced theorists as they did everyone else), with little idea of the end point (the changes were unique) and with no very great idea of the appropriate set of intellectual machineries. As the sequence of changes unfolds down the years, with a series of geographical centres, a body of work is accumulated centred on the analysis of complex change: it can be characterized as the classical European tradition of social theorizing; the attempt to critically elucidate the dynamics of complex change in the ongoing shift to the modern world.

In the European tradition social theorizing is an embedded/active process; reflexive critical commentary can illuminate a series of aspects of the situated dynamic: the context/resources of theorizing, the commitments/concerns of the theorist and the expectations/responses of audiences. First, the *tradition* can be disaggregated; it provides the context for exercises in theorizing (discipline – resources, restriction and possibility); it is not all of a piece; it is diverse. The history of ideas reveals great richness and the history of practice reveals similar richness.[6] The diversity of the tradition can be ordered; reflection systematized. Yet received tradition is but one amongst many: others might be expected to evidence different resources, agents and audiences; they offer potential partners in dialogue. Second, the *activity* of theorizing can be disaggregated; it is generic to human kind, it is diverse in practice. Social theorists make arguments for audiences and we can assemble a collection of examples, an external description. Any argument will evidence a mix of conception (how arguments should be made) and intention (the use to which they are expected to be put); and the commitments of the theorist in these matters can be described, an analytical unpacking. Any exercise in social theorizing, argument deployed to some end, will affirm a model of humankind; the model shapes theorizing, it feeds into the expectations of the theorist, and it can be analytically recovered, spelled out. The work of any particular theorist can be located, placed in relationship to diverse received tradition. Tradition is the start point of theorizing; it is flexible, it is not fixed and final, nor, as noted, is it singular as there are multiple traditions, each carrying resources and one aspect of which will determine how theorizing works (persons, institutions, addressees and limits/responsibilities). Third, the nature of the *audiences* variously addressed can be disaggregated; how they are conceived shapes theorizing: hence, for example, target groups, co-inhabitants or cultural sophisticates. Audience as target group points to social groups: it requires assumed models of society (who is *there* to be addressed); it projects responses (*why* address them) and it assumes relative status distinctions (audience addressed *how*). Audience as co-inhabitants: theorizing must engage; then dialogue, scholarly validation and popular authentication.[7] Audience as cultural sophisticates: theorizing must attend to rhetoric and narratives in persuasion.[8] As before, European tradition social theorizing has a received stock of audiences, it has a stock of current audiences and styles of address have been extensively worked on, strategies are available.

The analysis of tradition illuminates the stock of resources – cognitive, moral and practical – available to social theorists in their various practical engagements.

Practice I: the record of working social scientists

The central locus of reflection upon the nature of social science lies with the philosophy of social science; a further source is available in the routine practice of social scientists; we can say something about the nature of social science by attending to the activities of practising social scientists; but this is not to say we can undertake an inductive procedure which aggregates the experience of practising social scientists, rather that reflection upon the mundane details of practice will further illuminate theoretical enquiry – the realm of practice offers us a rich 'stock of examples' of arguments in action.

Acknowledging the practical nature of the work of social scientists, the subtle mix of context, agent and audience, opens up a number of problems: first, the significance of the social context of theorizing; second, the extent to which the work of agents could/should escape/ transcend their given contexts; and third the manner in which social scientific work could be received by those for whom it might be prepared. One popular strategy for dealing with these questions has been the appeal to the received model of the natural sciences, the pursuit of objective value-free knowledge is affirmed. And as the familiar objectivist package within the social sciences separates the theorist from the social realm under investigation, then questions of context, agent and audience are answered/elided (depending on one's overall position). If this stance is rejected the question of how to deal with the issues of context, agent and audience within social scientific enquiry is raised and a series of answers have been given: some appeal to procedural artifice (context-given values help select topics of enquiry, but research thereafter is scientific and audiences receive reliable technical knowledge); some appeal to profession (scholarship is a vocation, and its practitioners can be trusted to strive for reliable knowledge); and some in contrast embrace the given-ness of the specified problems and the formal necessity of critical reflexivity. Here, however, for the moment, attention can be turned to the tradition which carries all this work; there is, it might be said, a practical answer to these questions carried in the record of substantive work undertaken; it reveals what counts as social theorizing.

Recalling the nature of the classical tradition: urgent, engaged and critical

Against the restricted claims to the nature of social science affirmed by the orthodox consensus,[9] it is clear that the theorists of the nineteenth century routinely offered robust, engaged and practical analyses.[10] Their work drew on multiple sources, addressed urgent issues and proposed action be taken by particular key social groups. One might summarize as follows: Marx, argued on behalf of the proletariat, Durkheim on behalf of the developing progressive French middle classes and Weber on behalf of the liberal German bourgeoisie.[11] Noting these materials, Ernest Gellner[12] argues: first, that social theorists work perforce from inside those social processes which they try to decipher; second, that the scope and demanding urgency of the work of the theorists of the nineteenth century, the tradition which we inherit, is recalled in the work of contemporary development theorists; and third, that the centrality of the politics of being and becoming industrial are underscored by the work in development. Gellner reads the attempt to theorize development as a learning experience for all social theorists; that is, what we find in development theorizing is something akin to a restatement of the core concern of the classical European tradition of social theorizing with the analysis of complex change in pursuit of the modernist project.

Development theorizing has been an area of intense social scientific activity following the dissolution of formal European, American and Japanese empires which took place after the end of the Second World War; most of these territories became independent states within the international system; and where the elites of these new states were variously committed to the pursuit of growth and welfare, the elites of the metropolitan countries were anxious to maintain extant economic links. The coincidence of interest came to revolve around the idea of development, which quickly received attention from politicians, policy analysts and scholars. Theorizing the nature of development quickly became an industry; macro-theories and micro-studies were produced for international and national-level planning bureaucracies; multiple arguments were made for an equally large and diverse set of audiences; and the exchange between theorists and those theorized was thoroughly tangled, one noted theorist referred to 'battlefields of knowledge',[13] indicating that the out-turn of development work was as much to do with politics as any plausible claims to expertise. An immense amount of work was undertaken, much of it focused on practical detail, however, one characteristic or intellectual habit was the production of general theory; such argument is distinctive; the role of such general theory is to serve as a preliminary cashing of a moral stance, that is, they offer a summary statement about how the world is when read from a particular engaged (ethical/political) position; and such general theories can frame subsequent analyses in respect of any number of particular issues (formal and substantive). It might be noted that these general theories are routinely mis-understood by proponents of the orthodox consensus as programmatic announcements of large-scale empirical projects (needing 'more research'); nonetheless, development theory work has produced a wealth of such general theories.[14] An influential example was the 1950/60s confection of modernization theory[15] which vehicled the political concerns of the USA in the late 1950s and early 1960s: bipolarity, containment and aid-donor competition in the Third World. The social scientific material can be taken to comprise a package deal which specifies the fundamental logic of industrial society, argues that capitalism and socialism will converge as this logic drives the global system forward, indicates how non-industrial societies might be expected to modernize, and suggests that the system will produce widespread prosperity with a consequent end of ideological debates.[16] The position was very influential. It was heavily criticized.

Overall, in the early years following decolonization, much of the development theory produced in the metropolitan centres of the global system took the form of general theories, often cast in technical, value-neutral interventionist terms. However, over the years the intensely political nature of development theorizing has been widely granted, and here work attains a high degree of intellectual sophistication; and the issue has seen the production of a rich stock of examples of theory-in-action. The context-bound practicality of social theorizing is amply illustrated in the varied work of development theorists; the field has also, as will be noted, seen material produced outside the sphere of the putatively advanced countries; other voices have been raised.[17]

Recent prospective analysis: further engaged analyses of macro-change

The production of social scientific statements dealing with broad patterns of change has continued. One might say that the quality of the material has fallen away in recent years,[18] but the overall concern to grasp the fundamental logics of historical dynamics has continued. The end of the cold war has generated more examples, further insights into social theorizing. The long era of the cold war involved economic, political and military competition. An elaborate public/official rhetoric developed. The end of the cold war saw the collapse of these rhetorics, the extensively elaborated talk of the competition between the free world and the soviet block, and there has been a plethora of proposed replacement theories. The notion of globalization has been particularly popular.

The cold war was integral to the American elite's political project to construct a global liberal trading regime.[19] It came to have an elaborate apparatus, economic, political and military. In the public/official political sphere it functioned as the overarching frame within which global politics were understood. It was an official truth, an agreed discourse, a way of seeing a deeper sense in local actions/decisions, a way of ordering activity. The events of 1989–91 made the discourse redundant. A number of responses were made, in particular amongst policy analysts, think tanks and the media (an elite public sphere). A series of readings of the new situation were presented – we won – the end of history – the clash of civilizations – victory in the long war,[20] and globalization. This last noted has provoked extensive debate. It looks like a term designed to vehicle continuing (or, expanding) American priority within the global system. The idea has been criticized,[21] in particular with reference to the notion of regionalism. A vigorous debate is in process. Again we can see how arguments are made for audiences, again we can see how argument entails action and again we can see how social theorizing is something other than singular, neutral and scientific. The recent concern for globalization is in large measure a reaction, an attempt to find an official truth (to vehicle a new political project) in the wake of the end of the cold war; but many would hazard that the better idea is regionalism.

The European Union – new agendas

The construction of the European Union has attracted the attention of scholars; once again, the issue of theorizing complex change has come to the fore, and it has generated a wealth of novel social scientific thinking. The debates surrounding the unfolding creation of the European Union have been vigorous and practical political conflict has been mirrored by intense theoretical debate. The political project is novel and the theoretical debates have produced similarly novel material. And, of course, none of this is settled, neither the politics nor the theory.

European politics can be thought of in terms of the domestic and international concerns of a number of long-established nation-states: the 1648 Treaty of Westphalia created a system of sovereign states; thereafter the idea of nation was invented in order to express the unity that was supposed to exist (and later on did exist) within their boundaries and to legitimate elite claims to popular obedience; thus nation states; perfectly familiar, wholly contingent. Elites of nation states competed and moved against non-European cultures; nationalism and claims to the superiority of Europeans flourished as the continent became richer than any previous civilization. Yet in the twentieth century the empire/capitalist system entered a general crisis which saw economic, social and political breakdown. The final catastrophe of the Second World War meant that most of Europe from the Atlantic Ocean all the way through to Leningrad and Moscow was ruined by warfare; the continent was occupied and divided into two halves, 'East' and 'West'; the former group of countries were organized by the USSR and sought to build 'state socialism' whereas the latter group were organized by the USA, styled themselves 'the free world' and sought to build 'liberal democracy'; and the division was not overturned until 1989/91.

These events – modernity, empire, war, division and occupation – have shaped contemporary European political thinking, and there are many lessons: a rejection of empire; a rejection of the utility of war; a distinct preference for peaceful co-existence; and a somewhat inchoate desire for unification within Europe. The experience of the general crisis feeds directly into the impetus to build the European Union; the elites of Europe, in particular, France and Germany resolved to settle their long standing conflicts; the early moves begin with the 1952 European Coal and Steel Community (ECSC); the 1957 Treaty of Rome brings the European Economic Community into being; there are further treaties including the 1985 Single Market Treaty and the 1992 Maastricht By 2008 the European Union has twenty-seven members, a population of around 480 million and a gross domestic product of around $10.5 trillion;[22] it is a global economic super-power and it has significant cultural 'soft power', however it is not a global political/diplomatic super-power.

There has been a long debate amongst theorists about the nature of the European Union; in particular, there have been debates amongst international relations theorists and political scientists.[23] Several approaches are identifiable: first, federalism, a European political movement with pre-war origins which inspired early figures in the European Union; second, functionalism, a European political ideal from pre-war which identified a role for non-political agents in running key functional elements of modern industrial society and which inspired early figures in European Union; third, neo-functionalism, which found formal expression in the 1950s (with a strong US input) and which generates ideas of specific functional responsibilities, technical advances plus spill-over; fourth, inter-governmentalism, an international relations perspective (also influenced by American thinking) derived from realism and stressing the importance of the practical interests of states (state (security) and market (trade) versions are available); fifth, governance and policy making, a social science approach which looks at political processes, rather than formal institutions and law; sixth, deep regionalism, an approach drawing on international political economy themes and speaking of the European Union as a region within the global system; and seventh, social constructivist ideas about the role of ideas in making a European identity.

Once again, the issue of change is placed at the forefront of the intellectual agendas of European social theorists; once again, the issues are urgent; once again thoroughly practical; and once again a diverse spread of voices contribute to debate.

Diversity of engagements: particular arguments for particular audiences

The lessons of these examples of social theorizing in action for more abstract reflections revolve around the engaged nature, intellectual robustness and practicality of social theorizing; those who engage in social theorizing do so in order to address directly, or indirectly, problems in the real world. It would be possible to track back and forth through the work of the classical tradition, development theory and the more recent exercises in the analysis of the European Union and generate a large stock of examples of social theorizing in action, political, policy and scholarly; however, a more systematic survey can reveal something of the sheer diversity of available modes of engagement.

Practice II: engagements, diverse

The instances of social theoretic engagements are many and diverse; after Wittgenstein we could accumulate examples unsystematically but received intellectual tradition, specificity in engagements and family resemblance all help order the diversity. In particular, tradition is flexible but it is not infinitely tractable; it embraces continuity; it specifies what counts as social theorizing; and it comprises a body of resources available to theorists. There are numerous ways in which tradition can flow through the social world and any exercise in social theorizing can be analysed by attending to the fine grain of argument making; its assumptions, structure and strategies of embedding in received tradition. These issues can be investigated in a number of inter-related ways: the presentation of exemplars drawn from the social theoretic tradition; the preparation of an ideal-typical framework; and the piecemeal accumulation of a stock of examples of social theorizing in practice. Ordering the diversity of available modes of social theoretic engagement permits theorists to more accurately locate their own efforts, to be clear just what game they are playing; it permits commentators to more accurately characterize the efforts of those whose work they consider, to be clear what is and is not at issue; and thus in both cases it fosters better argument making and more effective criticism.

Grasping the diversity 1: exemplars

The history of social scientific practice in Europe is complex, with many agents involved and numerous lines of argument addressed to a bewildering variety of audiences. The evident diversity can be ordered by specifying exemplars;[24] noting the 'great names' whose work constitutes an intellectual tradition and exemplifies its practices.[25]

It can be argued that there is a classical European tradition of social theorizing which centres on the elucidation of the dynamics of complex change in the unfolding shift to the modern world. In the nineteenth and early twentieth centuries theorists sought to grasp change in order to inform practice. As noted earlier, the contribution of Karl Marx was turned to the political economic elucidation of progressive historical dynamics (arguments on behalf of the international proletariat), later Emile Durkheim offered the functional analysis of the dynamics of the division of labour (arguments on behalf of the progressive French bourgeoisie) and towards the end of this period Max Weber tackled the dialectic of system rationalization and willed action (arguments on behalf of the liberal German bourgeoisie). Around the turn of the twentieth century and in the years before the Great War, doubts were raised, the costs of progress noted. And later, in the years of crisis,[26] attention turned to grasping the reasons, for example in the work of the Frankfurt School, and proposing lines of possible solution, as with the work of J.M. Keynes and other planner/bureaucrats. And more recently, following the Second World War, the strains of recovery and success have commanded attention in discussions of the emergence of the European Union, its intrinsic logic and its place in a regionalized global system.

The tradition can be disaggregated. As social theorizing is embedded within the changing social world, analysis reveals an intermingled set of national trajectories which provide important environments for social theorizing and in place of individual theorists several discrete sub-traditions can be identified. There are national strands of social theorizing: in France a republican statist polity, affirming citizenship, reason and celebrating intellectual life; in Britain an oligarchic liberal polity, affirming subject-hood, accumulative pragmatics and relegating intellectual life to closed circles of the elite; and in Germany a democratic polity, affirming law, the public sphere and the possibility of rational political/social life. The European tradition finds different expression within these particular, restricting environments; stereotypes are available,[27] so too detailed histories.[28] The tradition is not unitary and the history is discontinuous, but the tradition generates new responses to the various demands associated with unfolding national and regional trajectories. The exemplars evidence social theoretic engagements, they can be systematized and they constitute the tradition we inhabit; thus understood they offer a way of locating contemporary exercises in social theorizing.

Grasping the diversity 2: ideal typical modes of engagement

The empiricist/positivist ideal typical mode of engagement reproduces within the sphere of the social the supposed relationship of natural scientist to their particular object realm, that is, technical manipulative authoritative knowledge. Social scientific enquiry is at base a matter of the accurate representation of a given social world; it is true that the peculiarities of that social world present problems, thus humans both answer back and resist being made the subject of controlled experiment, but these are manageable; it is also true that the peculiar status of the social scientist as both observer and unavoidably participant also create problems of observation, but these too are manageable; it is also true that the results of social science might thus far be described as meagre, but this is a problem of the relative immaturity of these disciplines and moreover where procedures of quantification and mathematization are advanced so too is the intellectual status of these areas, most obviously, mainstream economics; and thus overall the social sciences can be regarded as a growing and increasingly reliable body of technical, authoritative knowledge in respect of the social world, available, therefore, to knowledge users such as states, corporations and citizen groups within the broad social world.

The mainstream empiricist/positivist tale has been criticized; many social theorists find the claims of its proponents to a quasi-natural scientific status in respect of procedures and results to be absurd; others, however, note that these styles of enquiry have been embraced within discipline carried discourses and that characterizing those who work within and with reference to such discourses as in error is not enough; what is needed is a much richer grasp of the exchange of circumstances, theorist and audience. Zygmunt Bauman[29] has spoken in terms of legislators and interpreters; earlier, Karl Mannheim[30] distinguished ideological and utopian thinking and reserved a particular role for free floating intellectuals; and, earlier still, in this reflexive line, Max Horkheimer and Theodor Adorno[31] distinguished positive and negative thinking, the former passive, the latter, prospective and engaged. Such stylized characterizations of the range of ideal-typical modes of engagement could be multiplied; and an accumulation of such examples could serve to underscore the already realized diversity; but they are of restricted utility in ordering our reflections; such ideal typical characterizations needs must be relatively simple, lest they hinder rather than help.

Thus a simpler strategy is available: the historical experience of theorists working within the classical European tradition can be summarized as ideal typical modes of engagement: politics, policy and scholarship.[32] In this simple schema, the arguments of political agents are shaped by structural patterns, balances of forces and immediate problems; the arguments of policy analysts are shaped by institutional locations, organizational contexts and contemporary problems; and the arguments of scholars are shaped by cultural traditions, intellectual disciplines and current concerns. Exercises in social theorizing can be allocated to one of these categories, their arguments unpacked and thereafter evaluated; the classificatory scheme admits of further elaboration as necessary; it is a strategy of simple preliminary characterization and commentary. The task of mapping via exemplars requires detailed knowledge of the location from which the model is taken and similar knowledge of the location where the lessons learned are applied, but, in contrast, the systematic frame is abstract and it useful for grasping in a preliminary fashion the work of newly encountered thinkers.

Grasping the diversity 3: accumulating a stock of examples

Accumulating a stock of examples,[33] after the style of Wittgenstein's philosophical analysis, each revealing something of the exchange of context, theorist and audience, is a further strategy: it is the pure strategy, evidencing diversity at the same time as accessing it, however once again tradition constrains what might reasonably/intelligibly be understood to be social theoretic engagement. And whilst it would be possible to track back and forth amongst the output of social scientists and produce a wide range of examples of social theoretic arguments in action, the resources of the core tradition offer convenient ways of ordering available materials. Three sets of examples will be considered, each a distinctive mode of engagement: the *political writer* (a species of political agent); the *administrator/scholar* (a species of state or corporate bureaucrat-planner); and the *critical engaged scholar* (a species of scholarship).

(a) Political writers

In the European tradition with its commitment to the public sphere one distinctive way of making arguments can be captured in the notion of the political writer.[34] The claims of political writing are shaped by the immediate context; the political writer puts a distinctive politically engaged view to the fore; and work is thereafter organized so as to persuade the audience of the correctness of their view, such work is typically polemical.[35] Political writing is turned to face the demands of the present. Such work is not all of a piece and a number of versions of political writing can be identified; first, those who write out of their own *commitments* for the public sphere, a matter of moral or ideological conviction; second, those who write out of their own *experience* of politics, a matter of personal careers, in a banal form, the memoirs of politicians, in a richer fashion, the work of émigrés, those displaced by circumstances;[36] and third, those who write as a *profession* within the contemporary burgeoning world of media, members of the commentariat, print and electronic.[37]

Many figures and debates could be offered as illustrations. But one pervasive theme in recent European political writing has been that of war and identity – how might Europeans deal with the 1914–45 years of violent catastrophe and the subsequent 1945–89 years of division and occupation (plus more recent events, 2001–08): here, George Orwell and Gunter Grass; the political world is variously unpacked as both write from experience and commitment, from the assertion of an available simplicity of political discourse which might be readily accessed by decent minded people, through to a long-drawn out public engagement with the difficulties of dealing with historical memory.

Eric Blair's background and early career are conventional: a conservative 1930s middle class background; a public schoolboy; a colonial official; a policeman; and, thereafter, unusually, travels in London, Paris and Spain. The two elements, background and travels as a young man, together shape his approach to politics; substantively, so to say, he is successively a pacifist, an anarchist, a socialist, a patriot and finally a cold war liberal; there are common themes; politics as choice;[38] a preference for action, male-ness[39] and a habit of patronizing those populations with whom he claimed a political affinity (colonial subjects, the working classes and indeed the English). After the experience of travel, Blair reinvents himself as George Orwell and becomes a writer, both novels, successively, light romantic fiction, political allegory and science fiction political satire, plus extensive work as a journalist.

Orwell wanted to be treated as a political writer; the middle class background, a clear and distinct class location in pre-war Britain, was disguised in a process of self-invention; that is, as a writer he constructed an elaborate persona around the theme of plain, direct, speech; an honest language user. Blair invented Orwell as a straight speaking reliable man. Orwell exhibits the style of political writing, thus the work is engaged, the audience invited to identify with the ideas of the author. In Orwell's case, the author's perspective is the only moral perspective (judgements are not explained, they are asserted or assumed and they centre on the notion of 'decency'); the author is presented as decent, thus the audience can safely identify as invited with the proffered views; the author can see the failings of others, which are pointed out, and the audience is invited to participate in condemnation. Orwell also invented himself as a man of the left, a witness to the civil war in Spain and to domestic poverty in England; later, in the context of the Second World War, he reinvented himself as a patriot, still, ostensibly on the political left. Orwell's politics are cast as an appeal to common sense; the stance is conservative. Later, Orwell reinvents himself once again, now as a key propagandist of the political right with two novels widely taken as key texts of the cold war: *Animal Farm* and *1984*; these were used as critiques of totalitarianism by cold war liberals. Orwell was also taken up by the British Labour Party, a subaltern conservative party whose animating ethos has long been obedience to the status quo, respectability and decency.

Orwell continues to attract attention;[40] biographies are written;[41] his name is routinely invoked in the British press; recently in the context of the war against 'Islamic-fascism'; the style of plain, direct speech has been adopted as an exemplar of political speech but in truth it was anti-intellectual, quietist and reactionary;[42] he has become part national treasure, part cliché, nonetheless, usefully, his work illustrates one quite distinctive mode of social theoretic engagement.

Gunter Grass[43] has made extensive interventions in public discussion around the theme of German history, society and politics in the wake of the 1930s collapse into National Socialism and its subsequent reconstruction within the fame of the 'West'. These issues have been pursued in novels. The sequence of books includes: the *Tin Drum* 1959 chronicles the fall of pre-war Danzig and the start of the Second World War; *My Century* 1999 reviews the politics of the continent; and *Crabwise* 2002 opens up the issue of German suffering in the Second World War. This last noted opens up the crucial issue of addressing some sixty years after the end of the Second World War in Europe the losses suffered by the German people and does so via a text, part *novel*, part *recollection* and part *political commentary*, which revolves around the loss and memorialization in right wing web-sites of the *Wilhelm Gustloff*, a pre-war holiday cruise ship named after a murdered Swiss National Socialist and sunk by a Soviet submarine in the Baltic in the closing weeks of the war. Grass acknowledges the losses of the German people in a striking image of thousands of drowned children, their life belts working to make them float upside down, and makes the point that if centre/left don't speak of it the right wing will. It is a resonant image and the point is well made. Others have raised analogous issues: refugees from the east, victims of aerial bombing.[44] Such writing contributes to public debate, not merely in one country but in others too; thus, more broadly, the slow uneven unification of Europe requires that the Allied scheme of history[45] be revisited, a task likely to be uncomfortable, drawn-out and public.

And so, in an analogous fashion, by way of a note, French political and intellectual life confronted a sequence of problems: the catastrophe of defeat and occupation was followed by the difficulties of reconstruction, decolonization and the task of locating France as a nation within Europe. A number of crucial debates took place; the nature of the wartime Vichy regime and the response of ordinary French men and women; the wars of colonial withdrawal, in Indo-China and then Algeria; and the relationship with Germany and the business of the European Union.[46] In regard to the war, the collapse of French forces in May 1940, the collaborationist regime in Vichy and the wartime resistance were the subject of anxious debate. Famously, the episode is examined in J.P. Sartre's[47] *Roads to Freedom* trilogy, affirming the role of individual resistance, a matter of conscience or personal moral self-affirmation. Such issues were revisited in the period of the end of empire, a fraught period, as it was with other European empires, with catastrophic wars in Indo-China and in Algeria. The later produced extensive political violence, not merely in the colony but also in metropolitan France, and the situation was famously analysed by Franz Fanon[48] in *Black Skin, White Masks* and *The Wretched of the Earth*; trained as a psychiatrist, witness to the damage caused by colonialism and colonial medicine, he unpacked the damage in terms of the thinking of those involved, matters of cultural and personal deformation. Others similarly influenced included Albert Camus and in different vein Pierre Bourdieu; there were long drawn out debates undertaken by French writers and intellectuals in respect of the country's extensive mid-century catastrophes.

The mode of engagement of the political writer is distinctive; it has developed alongside the interrelated cultural spaces of the public sphere and civil society; and political writing is turned to the ideal of rational consensus secured via critical public dialogue. Other political cultures work differently, placing different demands on those disposed to participate in the ordered political life of their communities. More immediately, one line of objection is frequently brought, cast in terms of a distinction between politics and administration, the later, it is said, is the more reliable.[49]

(b) Administrator-scholars: colonial, metropolitan and international

Max Weber's rational bureaucrat is an important if largely mythic denizen the European tradition of social theory; introduced in the context of reflections upon the particular dynamics of German society in the late nineteenth and early twentieth centuries, one of a quartet of ideal-types of action and authority, the figure was subsequently absorbed into American social science, and popularized after the Second World War, part cultural criticism, part theory of the middle range,[50] a further instance of a trans-Atlantic cultural trade which burgeoned in the middle twentieth century as European collapse modulated into a novel yet broadly expressed pre-eminence for the United States of America. However, against orthodox claims to straightforward neutral technical-rational expertise, the substance of this mode engagement (as Weber knew full well, given his extensive engagement in the politics of the day) involves multiple roles, part rational administration, part organizational politics and part national and international political activity.[51] The mode of engagement is familiar; bureaucrat-planners inhabit much of the institutional and organization structures of contemporary industrial capitalism, state and corporate, and their claims to expertise are routine, so too effective criticism. However, a variant form of this mode of engagement can be identified; the administrator-scholar; part official, part political animal and part scholar; here examples of the ways in which their arguments are made for their various audiences: T.S. Raffles and J.S. Furnivall.

Raffles[52] was active in Southeast Asia around the turn of the nineteenth century; an official of the East India Company, he is credited with establishing Singapore. A number of roles are evident in his career and in each a different practical mode of engagement is required as he deals with different audiences to secure various objectives: researcher (a nineteenth century style collector he accumulated a vast stock of specimens of local fauna and flora); diplomat (involved in initiating discussions and negotiating treaties with local Johor-Riau political agents); strategist (manœuvring for British trading advantage against the Dutch who dominated the archipelago); and politician (manœuvring for advantage in respect of the project of a base on Singapore against both the EIC headquartered in India and London). Raffles is remembered in Singapore as the official founder; but as indicated, the truth is more complex and the record admits of description not merely in glowing terms but also in the multiple shades of grey appropriate to the colonial world.

Furnivall was an administrator-scholar in colonial Malaya; had socialist sympathies, links with Burmese independence groups and came to argue for a socialist commonwealth to succeed empire.[53] The colonial world had distinctive economies, societies and polities. The economies were organized for the colonial power, first, sugar, spices, tea/coffee and opium, and later, as the metropolitan economies advanced, plantations, mines, ports and so on. The societies were complex race/class hierarchies; theories of racial difference were common, so too stereotyping;[54] the European elite ordered masses comprising the diverse locals (with indigenous families, kin groups and clans) plus (as the colonial powers encouraged/ allowed migration within their empire territories) multiple minorities, sometimes low status labourers, sometimes higher status minor functionaries, plus those communities generated by inter-marriage, mixed race groups with ambiguous statuses. All these groups/gradations were found in and reflected[55] in the colonial cities. The polities were divided along lines of class and ethnicity; the outsider elites controlled the state and economy; local elites were co-opted/created; the local masses provided labour to the market sector and subsisted within the traditional sector; they had no access to the state; the colonial powers adopted direct rule/indirect rule, the former via colonial officials, the latter via traditional rulers. The cultures of colonial territories comprised a melange of diverse cultural resources, new perspectives and ideas of home for the colonialists.[56] It was in this context that Furnivall published *Netherlands India*.[57] The work is political–economy of the Dutch East Indies. The analysis is constructed against the standard liberal market theories and the economy is characterized as a series of discrete economic spheres (economic activities coincided with ethnic identities); there is no unified society; there is therefore no unified market; there was therefore no possibility of a self-regulated market. Furnivall argues that in a plural society the co-inhabitants meet economically in the marketplace and in the absence of common culture their exchanges are asocial, narrowly economic, and the general situation offers a role for the colonial power and its administrators: to hold the ring, to oversee the system.[58]

The mode of engagement of the administrator-scholar is distinctive; intellectual resources are put to work in a practical fashion; part politics, part administration and part scholarship. What is important here is to note that the engagement is specific; it does not admit of reduction to any simple model of quasi-natural scientific technical expertise neutrally deployed; these figures were not textbook-style 'rational bureaucrats', rather, these agents were actively engaged with their social worlds.

(c) Critical engaged scholars

Engagement is the key; familiar core professional commitments to scholarship can provide the occasion for interventions in wider debates; scholarly work is intertwined with clear political and ethical stances, and these are presented in the public sphere. Such work is ordered around the ideal of rational public discourse, implicit or explicit; yet there are no guarantees; insight is sought, error is quite possible. It is a distinctively European image of a possible political life; celebrated, or perhaps mythologized, in the guise of the informal conversations of the coffee shop,[59] it has found its most explicit theorist and practitioner in the inheritor of the mantle of the Frankfurt School, Jurgen Habermas. Commentators have characterized the work as a pedagogic politics, one deeply informed by the experience of Germany and firmly oriented towards a discourse democracy carried in the rational debates of the public sphere. Habermas is well known, not simply a matter of his brilliant scholarship, but also an appreciation of his particular environment, that of Germany recovering from the catastrophe of war and National Socialism.

Other figures – also offering critical scholarship – have moved within different environments; they have followed other trajectories, and fought other battles and produced, in their turn, distinctive interventions in public debate. Here, two can be cited, both, in contrast to Habermas, liberals, one located in the environment of cold war, the other, a participant in those debates, but latterly a more detached figure.

Ernest Gellner was an anthropologist, philosopher and controversialist; engaged vigorously with a variety of thinkers and issues; adopted a species of Popperian inflected liberalism and resisted contemporary work in an iconoclastic manner.[60] One text, *Thought and Change* reveals the ways in which engaged scholarship works: the author is self-consciously aggressive; the intellectual resources of available tradition are turned to urgent practical problems; thus the tradition is characterized as centred on the issues of being and becoming industrial; in turn, these are central issues in contemporary politics and scholarly reflection; and a key role is made for the enlightened elite, those who can grasp and order these enfolding processes of sweeping structural change. The combative tone is usually maintained in Gellner's work; social scientific argument counted, so it was worth pursuing with seriousness and vigour.

Richard Rorty engages with the work of Wittgenstein, Heidegger and Dewey in order to represent pragmatism both as an intellectual disposition (the role of liberal ironist) and as informing a reformist line of political activity; the former position is informed by an embrace of contingency,[61] in respect of language, self-hood and the familiar realm of liberal society; the later, looks to the model of American liberal reformism, a tradition shaped by the New Deal, sustained in the post-Second World War period up until the conflicts of the sixties and in need of urgent reanimation.[62] The two strands are run-together: a matter of private irony (contingency entails a scepticism that can only be sustained by ironic detachment) and public liberal hope (arguing for the best in the culture into which one happens to have been born). Much of the intellectual disposition is unpacked in reflections on the nature of language, the history of philosophy and the role of philosophical reflection/engagement. The later work is recalled in a later text noting the battles of the post-war American scene. Rorty stresses conversation; as debates run down through time, the best we can hope for is to participate in some interesting conversations; these are open ended, a matter of edification, not the pursuit of any specified final intellectual/moral condition.

The mode of engagement of critical scholars is once again quite distinctive; their work is not turned to immediate unfolding political events (the concerns of political writers), nor are they engaged in the pragmatics of administrative debate/action, rather they are concerned to unpack deep-seated patterns of structural change, uncovering the logics of events and looking to the future.

Diversity is a given

Exercises in social theorizing are multiple, diverse and entirely routine; this diversity can be mapped; the procedure allows participants to orient themselves; to be clear what sort of an argument, addressed to what sort of audience and with what end in view they are making. It permits commentators to better identify what is at issue in the work or practices they consider. However, given the variety of locations and ends of theorizing, it would be wrong to assume that all participants welcome clarity. Many might prefer un-clarity; in policy analysis, it might be argued, manipulative intentions require obfuscation; and in politics, it might be said, agents run multiple conversations with a range of interlocutors and clarity might well be functionally unhelpful. However, in contrast, in scholarship, concerned, after Habermas, with making arguments on behalf of humankind,[63] clarity is required, thus, given the evident diversity, it can be asserted that reflexivity[64] is a necessary condition of scholarship (and contrariwise, eschewal of reflexivity entails that the arguments being made, whatever they are, are not scholarship); and such clarity aids not only the production of better arguments and the more effective criticism of those already on offer but also recalls that the business is a mundane, everyday, routine practical activity.

This position affirms certain core ideas and generates some further questions. Any exercise in argument making instances an exchange of context, theorist and audience; each is discrete but they have family resemblances; these exchanges can be analysed, their logics unpacked. Such analyses illuminate the business of making arguments, however reflexively they can be assimilated to broader claims about the fundamental nature of European social theorizing. A double claim can illuminate the issue: first, social theorizing works within deep contexts, the immediate situation (the groups or communities served or advised or studied) is addressed using the resources of intellectual tradition, that tradition is itself lodged within ordered political communities, these too can be located within wider social systems, and in turn lodged within unfolding historical development trajectories; second, the European tradition of social theorizing finally revolves around the ideal of reason, the modernist project.

Within the European tradition a particular model of the polity is affirmed; an ideal typical triangular arrangement of state, private realm and public sphere where the political world is suffused by the demands of reason. The political ideal is one of rational consensus secured by dialogue in the public sphere, and political agents, policy makers and scholars all work with reference to this ideal.[65] The tradition provides the intellectual/ethical context of social theorizing; the multiple resources upon which theorists draw in order to fashion arguments for audiences, and the result, as noted above, is a multiplicity of modes of social theoretic engagement, after Wittgenstein, a family of activities. But tradition is not fixed, it is a live resource put to work to grasp unfolding circumstances and its expressions change; Bauman distinguishes legislators and interpreters, tendencies within social theorizing, more or less prominent at different times within the modern history of Europe.[66] As Europe emerges from war, collapse and occupation, it may be that prospective work is required in both idioms.

Thus an appreciation of the deeply socially embedded nature of social theorizing opens up one further question: not the future of European theorizing, rather the nature of work produced outside the cultural bubble of Europe. It might be asked: what is the nature of the practice of other cultures, of other communities of social theorists. And it might be asked: how might European scholars access the work of those dwelling within other cultures.

Practice III: the engagements of others

Making sense of the social world is a routine human achievement; social theorizing is one variant; it is diverse and many engagements can be envisioned; it centres on the activities and understandings of ordered political communities, polities. The resources of the European tradition are the basis for engagements with the denizens of other traditions;

one cannot step outside the culture one inhabits, as there is nowhere to step to, and in dealing with other cultures the baggage of one's own is not merely an inconvenience but the inevitable starting point of enquiry; thereafter, we can look for analogues in other traditions of social theorizing centred on political life, the sphere of prudential understandings.[67]

Accessing the practices of another culture is awkward; the resources available are those of the theorist's own culture; multiple preconceptions suffuse enquiry; here three domain assumptions[68] might be noted: theorizing is context-bound, turned to the practical tasks of polities and might be accessed in dialogue. These generate an approach; inviting a search for analogues to European practice, they encourage the discovery of dialogue partners.[69]

Locating other traditions, polities and social theorizing

All social theorizing is embedded within a definite social world; the practice can be thought of as layered whereby a series of contexts shape the efforts of the theorists: any exercise in social theorizing will be shaped by the specific exchange of context, theorist and audience; any exchange will be shaped by available intellectual and moral resources; any set of available resources will be shaped by the historical trajectory of the polity; and any trajectory will be shaped by contingent dealings with other polities in the global system. Any exercise in social theorizing will be marked by this deep context; and in accessing other cultures a first task is to grasp the one inhabited.

(a) *Stepping outside the bubble of received assumptions*

This is the first task: two ideas can serve as starting points: the distinction between local and universal models,[70] where, against those who suppose that the former belong to restrictedly local cultures and the later to the universalistic developed West, universal models are just another form of local model; and the proposal that accumulating detail about multiple discrete forms of life via thick description is the way to reach some understanding of how they work.[71] Or, after Andy Kershaw,[72] who suggested disregarding western commercial pop music in favour of 'world music', the rich diversity of authentic local music made around the planet, a 'world politics' might be envisioned; thus there are diverse forms of political life carried in tradition, specific in their logics, the multiple environments of various styles of social theorizing. Acknowledging that 'our' model is local, instead of asking how other political cultures differ (familiarly cast in un-reflexive comparative terms, specifying how they meet, match, surpass or, more often than not, fail to live up to received standards), enquiry can turn to how they got the way they are, what ideas/ practices constitute them and what ethics are embedded within their routine practices.

(b) Affirming the resources of received local tradition

Reflexive self-embedding in unfolding contingent processes entails acknowledging the embeddedness of social theorizing; that is, theorists make sense of their world from the inside. The intellectual resources available are part of the familiar world; the resources of received culture, tradition. The idea of complex change lies at the heart of the classical European tradition of social theorizing; it points to unfolding patterns of change in economic, social, cultural and political structures, to the ways in which agent groups read and react to these changes (how they understand) and to the projects they formulate (the actions they take); shifting structural patterns can be described, the ways in which agent groups read and react to the changes enfolding their lives can be elucidated and the actions they take can be detailed. The historical development experience of any country can be tracked; the detail of the form of life of the country (as it shifts and changes down through time) can be spelled out; and the detail of ways of understanding (as they shift and change) can be unpacked. These ideas are the basis of possible dialogues with others.

(c) Surveying other trajectories

After Wittgenstein, one might recall that 'what has to be accepted, the given so to say, are forms of life'; such forms would embrace the collective pursuit-of-livelihood; patterns of relationships between persons-in-the-world; and the ways in which these are understood and ordered. These forms of life are the contingent; the outturns of unfolding trajectories; and patterns of ordering will be contingent. Or, put another way, different communities have different political logics and as a consequence they will have different conceptions of the nature and role of social theorizing (and the focus here is on the political side).

A gesture can be made towards the substantive general theory implied in this orientation towards the nature of social theorizing in the form of a macro-survey, unpacking a view from within the frame of received European tradition. Thus different polities have sketched out different historical trajectories in their still unfolding shift to the modern world; these trajectories are the out turn of elite responses to shifting structural circumstances; these historical processes generate distinct polities; such polities will affirm a national past, sketching past, characterizing present and indicating the ideal future; such polities will identify a role for social theorists (or their analogues); such trajectories are intermingled; the contemporary global system is the contingent outturn; and in all this change is given, the whole is fluid; there is no definitive end point.

The modern world took shape in Europe; conventionally, from the sixteenth century onwards; the rise of science, the accidental invention of capitalism; the domestic demands of the system for intensification; and the external demands of the system for expansion. It is a familiar story; the Europeans expanded outwards, came into contact with existing cultures and over a period of several centuries more or less remade these societies as they were drawn into a metropolitan centred system of empires; these empires reached their apogee in the years before the Great War; thereafter, inter-imperial rivalry, metropolitan calls for empire reform, the rise of a multiplicity of peripheral, indigenous elite nationalisms, plus finally, the Second World War damaged these empires beyond repair; and through the episode of the cold war the contemporary world of sovereign states emerged. The sequence of expansion/retreat embraces the Americas, the Middle East, South Asia, Southeast Asia, East Asia and Africa; it is through the experience of colonial rule with its characteristic mix of exploitation and development that hitherto existing civilizations are remade and enter the modern world. These trajectories have a family resemblance, but they are distinct, they have created distinctive economic, social and political logics and these provide the environment and resources for social theorizing.[73]

Social theorizing is embedded in deep context; theorists work with reference to traditions, these are carried in polities, themselves lodged in societies, in turn located in unfolding historical trajectories. And, at this point, case studies could illuminate further the specificity of theorizing.[74] Case studies complement the macro-survey material; they produce detail and open more chances for dialogue, they are the outcome of what a sociologist would call participant observation.[75] There are multiple polities, the out turn of particular historical trajectories and they have their own logics, and these inform their social theorizing. And, the key for present purposes is the systematic difference in understandings of relations between persons-in-the-world and the ways such understandings inform the particular sphere of social scientific reflection; thus, illustratively: persons as responsible individuals (Britain);[76] persons as members of families/communities (Japan);[77] persons as members of families/communities oriented towards a collective national project (Singapore);[78] persons as members of family, kin and clan (China);[79] and persons as rational/moral members of the public sphere (Germany).[80] Each associates with a domestic style of social theorizing: in Britain, liberal economics conjoined with ameliorist welfarism; in Singapore, policy work, oriented towards unpacking elite specified national directions; or in Germany, a strong commitment to the scientific value of social science within the public policy sphere.

(d) The nature of the patterns of life and ideas of others

As the majority of humankind do not dwell within the cultural confines of the rich first world, other cultures must be characterized; the general theory sketched directs attention to the historical trajectories of territories within the global system, illuminating the great diversity of patterns of life. Illustratively, a starting point can be found in the nature of the pre-modern global system: the medieval European world was poor, insecure, local, filled with spirits/gods and was ordered as a shifting series of agrarian kingdoms subject to Latin Christendom;[81] in East Asia the Sino-centric system included the middle kingdom, Korea, Japan and Vietnam with various agrarian feudalisms built around family and clan and ordered by Confucian, Buddhist and Taoist folk religious traditions;[82] in the Malay world of Southeast Asia agrarian, fishing and trading economies supported fluid local polities informed by the great traditions of Islam Hinduism;[83] in Australasia, aboriginal groups sustained stone-age patterns of life/belief;[84] in South Asia agrarian, manufacturing and trading kingdoms with the great traditions of Islam and Hinduism;[85] in the Arab world clan based civilization centred on Islam;[86] in Africa, tribal/kin groups;[87] in North America native American hunter/gathers and agriculturalists ordered in tribe/kin groups affirming folk religions; and in Latin America, native peoples evidenced both tribal groups and ordered civilizations.[88] A great diversity of cultures existed;[89] thereafter, the accidental invention of the capitalist form of life reordered the global pattern.[90] Science, industry and democracy underpinned the rise of the capitalist modern world.[91] It was a dynamic system:[92] domestic intensification and overseas expansion fostered the slow creation of a global system as cultures were drawn into the modern world; the idea of empire became popular. Yet reaction was not slow in coming: the 1911 Chinese Revolution and the 1917 Soviet Revolution encouraged anti-colonial politics and the chaos of the Second World War undermined the system leaving replacement elites engaged in state making and nation-building, establishing a series of new trajectories running down to the present day, each with its distinctive pattern of life.

As with patterns of life, so with ideas, there are other views of the social world; yet all societies have to order themselves, raising issues of political-cultural identity, the ways in which people locate themselves within ordered political communities.[93] One aspect is illuminated by the distinction great/little tradition: in the former the broadest elite cultural commitments are made, enshrined in arts, literature, religion and official ideologies they may be carried by particular institutions or there may be particular sites which exemplify the great tradition ideas,[94] whereas little tradition points to the intellectual/moral resources of ordinary life which may be used in resisting the elites.[95] In total, the rich ideas/practices, accumulated over time, shifting, which constitute political communities.

(e)　Other futures can be identified

On the basis of these trajectories, other futures can be imagined. The shift to the modern world entailed intensification, expansion, declonization and reconstruction; more recently the rhetoric of cold war obscured changes; the end of the cold war ushered in a rethink; American pre-eminence was no longer obvious; attempts at reassurance were made, but it was clear that the world had other centres of power, other communities, envisioning other futures. Two exercises in theorizing might be noted; both work to theorize the historical trajectories of regions outside the metropolitan heartland of global industrial capitalism; both utilize a mix of indigenous and indigenized theory; respectively, Latin American dependency theory and the ideas associated with the East Asian developmental state.

Dependency theory was a specific reading of the historical trajectory of the countries of Latin America; the proponents of dependency theory stressed: first, the importance of considering both the historical experience of peripheral countries and the phases of their involvement within wider encompassing systems; second, the necessity of identifying the specific economic, political and cultural linkages of centres and peripheries; and third, the requirement for active state involvement in the pursuit of development. The dependency theorists argued that the relevant context within which the historical development of the countries of Latin America could appropriately be analysed was the global industrial capitalists system. It proved influential, as politics, policy and scholarship.

East Asia's distinctive historical trajectory has produced a number of theories[96] which revolve around the idea of the developmental state. The initial example was Japan, joined thereafter by the Asian Tigers (South Korea, Taiwan, Hong Kong and Singapore) and since Deng Xiao Ping's 1978 reforms, China. Theorists have identified an elite commitment to the pursuit of national economic development ordered via the machineries of state level corporate style planning; critics speak of neo-mercantile strategies, others of the developmental state. It is the record of East Asia in particular, that has encouraged the broadening discussions amongst theorists from various parts of the world of the notion of regionalism.[97]

(f) The world that we have

The global system comprises a pattern of relationships: its constituents are diverse forms of life; each has its internal logic, there are dense patterns of accumulated inter-linkages and all this generates the actual historical pattern. The global system is the contingent outturn of the history that we have had; it is not a system, it has no single coherent logic, it is not ordered according to any extra-social principles (no essence, no teleology), nor is it anarchical, the inter-linkages are many and deep. It comprises many polities, there are inter-locking and over-lapping jurisdictions;[98] it comprises many markets, interlocking and overlapping; it comprises many societies and it comprises many cultures. The order is not planned, nor spontaneously generated, it is a contingent accumulation of institutions, competencies and jurisdictions; it is the world that we have. The contingent global system centres on discrete forms of life; they have trajectories, a mix of domestic logics and external relationships (shifting structural contexts). These trajectories and relationships are contingent; the overall pattern – the world that we happen to have at any one time – is the contingent outturn of these intermingled trajectories.

The available ethical/political ideal for Europeans is an order secured via dialogic democracy; yet we are not the model; our responsibility for others is restricted; there are other polities; they have their own logics; the task of a world politics is to identify and characterize extant polities as it is here that we find the environments of a multiplicity of social theoretic engagements.

In brief, labouring the point (once again), social theoretic engagement is practical; the centre of gravity is practical understanding; not *episteme* or *techne*, rather *phronesis*; it is not natural science; it is not singular; modes of social theoretic engagement are diverse: they are diverse within the framework of familiar European modernist political culture; and they are diverse within the forms of life outside the bubble, in world politics.

Final words

A desire to make sense of the social world is intrinsic to humankind; no-one has to be taught; it comes with the territory; and it takes multiple forms, ranging from the un-remarked common sense of particular communities, through the claims of experts of one sort or another and then to the institutional truths of organizations, states and international organizations. The realm of formal, self-conscious, social scientific theorizing is but one more way of making sense. Social theorizing is not a variant form of natural science; it does not deal in terms of causes/effects operating within a material realm; rather, it deals with the world of people; thus social theorizing is interpretive, critical and engaged. Social theorists make arguments on behalf of a wide variety of audiences, proposing action of various sorts. Such exercises in argument making might be more or less detached but they are not context-less, quite the reverse, the work of social theorists is shaped by contexts and audiences; and each exercise in theorizing is finite in its aspirations and intellectual reach. Social scientific arguments are diverse; there are many theorists, many contexts and many audiences; but the spread of work is constrained; social scientific work is lodged within tradition, which it thereby constitutes through practice; and the classical European tradition of social theorizing is concerned with the elucidation of the dynamics of complex change in the unfolding process of the construction of the modern world. Social theorizing is always practical, an unfolding process; thus the classical European tradition of social theorizing is central to our form of life, it is vigorous and continues to unfold in extensive practical engagements.

Notes

Chapter 1

1 Hans Georg Gadamer 1979 2nd ed. *Truth and Method*, London, Sheed and Ward
2 The film was part of a television series entitled *Building Sights*; reproduced in book form by Ruth Rosenthal and Maggie Toy (eds) 1995 *Building Sights*, Academy Editions
3 Anthony Giddens 1979 *Central Problems in Social Theory*, London, Macmillan
4 Alasdair MacIntyre 1985 2nd ed. *After Virtue*, London, Duckworth, pp.106–7
5 Peter Winch 1958/1990 2nd ed. *The Idea of a Social Science and Its Relation to Philosophy*, London, Routledge
6 C.B. Macpherson 1973 *Democratic Theory: Essays in Retrieval*, Oxford University Press
7 MacIntyre 1985
8 Thomas McCarthy 1984 *The Critical Theory of Jurgen Habermas*, Cambridge, Polity
9 Zygmunt Bauman 1987 *Legislators and Interpreters*, Cambridge, Polity, caught the shift nicely in his now well known distinction of social roles
10 Perhaps, most obviously, in the realm of political life downstream from the end of the cold war, the unfolding project of the European Union: on the history, see Tony Judt 2005 *Post-war: A History of Europe Since 1945*, New York, The Penguin Press; on the history of the European Union see Alasdair Blair 2005 *The European Union Since 1945*, London, Longman; and on the Brussels machineries, see Jeremy Richardson (ed.) 2001 2nd ed. *European Union: Power and Policy Making*, London, Routledge

Chapter 2

1 Norman Davies 2000 *Europe: A History*, London, Pimlico
2 An overview of the philosophy of science is offered by Samir Okasha 2002 *Philosophy of Science: A Very Short Introduction*, Oxford University Press
3 The convenient notion of 'the orthodox' is from a trio of essays: Anthony Giddens 1979 'The prospects for social theory today' in *Central Problems in Social Theory*, London, Macmillan; Anthony Giddens 1982 'Classical social theory and the origins of modern sociology' in *Profiles and Critiques in Social Theory*, London, Macmillan; Anthony Giddens 1987 'Nine theses on the future of sociology' in *Social Theory and Modern Sociology*, Cambridge, Polity
4 William Outhwaite 1975 *Understanding Social Life: The Method Called Verstehen*, London, Allen and Unwin, chapter four
5 Zygmunt Bauman 1978 *Hermeneutics and Social Science*, London, Hutchinson

6   Ted Benton 1977 *Philosophical Foundations of the Three Sociologies*, London, Routledge; Richard Kilminster 1979 *Praxis and Method: A Sociological Dialogue with Lukacs, Gramsci and the Early Frankfurt School*, London, Routledge and Kegan Paul; see also the neo-pragmatist Richard Rorty 1999 *Philosophy and Social Hope*, London, Penguin, who characterizes the legacy of Darwin and Dewey as 'naturalist'

7   Paradigmatically, French; analysed by Immanuel Kant in *What is Enlightenment?* See Roy Porter 2001 2nd ed. *The Enlightenment*, London, Palgrave; Gertrude Himmelfarb 2005 *The Roads to Modernity: The British, French and American Enlightenments*, New York, Vintage

8   In particular: J. Passmore 1970 *The Perfectibility of Man*, London, Duckworth; S. Pollard 1971 *The Idea of Progress*, Harmondsworth, Penguin; C.B. Macpherson 1962 *The Political Theory of Possessive Individualism*, Oxford University Press; Porter 2001 Himmelfarb 2005; plus others as cited

9   T.L. Hankins 1985 *Science and the Enlightenment*, Cambridge University Press, p.9

10 A.F. Chalmers 1982 2nd ed. *What is this Thing Called Science?*, Milton Keynes, Open University Press, pp.67–75

11 Passmore 1970

12 Pollard 1971

13 Macpherson 1962

14 Alasdair MacIntyre 1967 *A Short History of Ethics*, London, Routledge; Martin Hollis 1977 *Models of Man*, Cambridge University Press

15 Jane Rendall 1978 *The Origins of the Scottish Enlightenment*, London, Macmillan; A.C. Chitnis 1976 *The Scottish Enlightenment: A Social History*, London, Croom Helm; and David Daiches, Peter Jones and Jean Jones (eds) 1986 *A Hotbed of Genius: The Scottish Enlightenment 1730–1790*, Edinburgh University Press

16 Pollard 1971; Porter 2001, see also Ian Buruma 1999 *Voltaire's Coconuts: Or Anglomania in Europe*, London, Weidenfeld and Nicolson, chapter two in particular; John Plamenatz 1963 *Man and Society Vol. 1*, London, Longman

17 Raymond Aron 1968 *Main Currents in Sociological Thought Vol. 1*, Harmondsworth, Pelican

18 This is a simplification of complex debates, see Barrington Moore 1967 *The Social Origins of Dictatorship and Democracy*, London, Allen Lane

19 Pollard 1971

20 Aron 1968

21 Greta Jones 1980 *Social Darwinism and English Thought*, Brighton, Harvester; J.W. Burrow 1966 *Evolution and Society*, Cambridge University Press

22 Geoffrey Hawthorn 1976 *Enlightenment and Despair*, Cambridge University Press, chapter five

23 Stephan Collini 1979 *Liberalism and Sociology: L T Hobhouse and Political Argument in England 1880–1914*, Cambridge University Press; Philip Abrams 1968 *The Origins of British Sociology*, Chicago University Press

24 Richard Rorty 1998 *Achieving Our Country: Leftist Thought in Twentieth-Century America*, Harvard University Press, chapter one

25 Anthony Giddens 1971 *Capitalism and Modern Social Theory: An Analysis of the Writings of Marx, Durkheim and Max Weber*, Cambridge University Press, chapter five

26 R.J. Evans 1997 *Re-reading German History: From Unification to Reunification 1800–1996*, London, Routledge; progressive ideas about social reform mix with ideas of hygiene, race and race-competition and these inform the National Socialist goal of colonial empire in Eastern Europe – on this see Andreas Hilgruber 1981 *Germany and the Two World Wars*, Harvard University Press

27 Benedict Anderson 1983 *Imagined Communities*, London, Verso; Ernest Gellner 1983 *Nations and Nationalism*, Oxford, Blackwell

28 Robert Nisbet 1970 *The Sociological Tradition*, London, Heinemann, chapter one

29 Raymond Williams 1963 *Culture and Society 1780–1950*, Harmondsworth, Penguin

30 H. Stuart Hughes 1959 *Consciousness and Society: The Reorientation of European Social Thought 1890–1930*, London, MacGibbon and Kee

31 Zygmunt Bauman 1987 *Legislators and Interpreters*, Cambridge, Polity

32 P.W. Preston 1996 *Development Theory: An Introduction*, Oxford, Blackwell

33 Giddens 1982

34 Dasgupta 1985 *Epochs of Economic Theory*, Oxford Blackwell, pp.138–50

35 Collini 1979; Hawthorn 1976 chapter nine; Richard Swedberg 1987 'Economic Sociology Past and Present' in *Current Sociology*

36 Hawthorn 1976 chapter six, seven and ten

37 Anthony Giddens 1972 *Politics and Sociology in the Thought of Max Weber*, London, Macmillan; Swedberg 1987; Fred Block 1990 *Post Industrial Possibilities: A Critique of Economic Discourse*, University of California Press

38 Martin Jay 1973 *The Dialectical Imagination*, Boston, Little Brown

39 For example, in economics, with J.M. Keynes; in sociology, with Karl Mannheim; and in international relations, with E.H. Carr

40 See Sahotra Sarkar (ed.) 1996 *Science and Philosophy in the Twentieth Century: Basic Works of Logical Empiricism: Vol. 6 The Legacy of the Vienna Circle*, New York, Garland Publishing, the 'Series Introduction' notes a long list of major advances

41 Allan Janik and Stephen Toulmin 1973 *Wittgenstein's Vienna*, New York, Simon and Shuster, chapter two

42 Alastair Bonnett 2004 *The Idea of the West: Culture, Politics and History*, London, Palgrave, chapter one

43 C.A. Bayly 2004 *The Birth of the Modern World 1780–1914*, Oxford, Blackwell, pp.312–22

44 Christopher Bryant 1985 *Positivism in Social Theory and Research*, London, Macmillan

45 Christian Brandstatter (ed.) 2006 *Vienna 1900 And the Heroes of Modernism*, London, Thames and Hudson; Peter Gay 2008 *Modernism: The Lure of Heresy*, New York, Norton

46 For a sense of the confusions amongst which politicians, intellectuals and ordinary people moved, see Mark Mazower 1998 *Dark Continent: Europe's Twentieth Century*, London, Allen Lane, chapter two

47 Allan Janik 2001 *Wittgenstein's Vienna Revisited*, New Brunswick, Transaction, p.199

48 Oswald Hanfling 1981 *Logical Positivism*, Oxford, Blackwell, Introduction; see also Marx W. Wartofsky 1996 'Positivism and Politics: The Vienna

Circle as a Social Movement' in Sahotra Sarkar (ed.) 1996 *Science and Philosophy in the Twentieth Century: Basic Works of Logical Empiricism: Vol. 6 The Legacy of the Vienna Circle*, New York, Garland Publishing

49   Ray Monk 1991 *Ludwig Wittgenstein: The Duty of Genius,* London, Vintage, chapter twelve

50   Karl Popper 1974 5th ed. *Conjectures and Refutations*, London, Routledge, chapter one; M.H. Hacohen 2000 *Karl Popper: The Formative Years 1902–1945*, Cambridge University Press; there are social tensions, see David Edmonds and John Edinow 2001 *Wittgenstein's Poker*, London, Faber; see also W.W. Bartley 1986 *Wittgenstein*, London, The Cresset Library (the text is regarded as scurrilous by some of Wittgenstein's admirers (Monk 1991 pp.581–6) and Avrum Stroll 2002 *Wittgenstein*, Oxford, Oneworld, suggests the issues alluded to are unimportant)

51   Janik 2001 p.202

52   Bryant 1985, chapter four

53   Janik 2001 p.199

54   Bryant 1985 pp.109–16; the participants adopted different emphases and Janik 2001 pp.202–4 distinguishes strong/weak

55   The manifesto is reprinted in Sahotra Sarkar (ed.) 1996 *Science and Philosophy in the Twentieth Century: Basic Works of Logical Empiricism: Vol. 1 The Emergence of Logical Empiricism*, New York, Garland Publishing, pp.321–41

56   A concern of Otto Neurath; see N. Cartwright, Jordi Cat, Lola Fleck and Thomas Uebel 1996 *Otto Neurath: Philosophy Between Science and Politics*, Cambridge University Press

57   This is derived from Hanfling 1981

58   Ludwig Wittgenstein 1953 *Philosophical Investigations,* Cambridge University Press

59   Giovanna Borradori 1994 *The American Philosopher*, University of Chicago, see chapter one, a conversation with Quine

60   A.J. Ayer 1971 *Language, Truth and Logic,* Harmondsworth, Penguin, Introduction to 1946 edition

61   See Ayer 1971, Preface to 1936 edition

62   Ayer 1971 pp.139–40

63   Ayer 1971 pp.141–2

64   Ayer 1971 p.143

65   Ayer 1971 pp.148–9

66   Perry Anderson 1992 *English Questions*, London, Verso, pp.60–4; Daniel Snowman 2003 *The Hitler Émigrés: The Cultural Impact on Britain of Refugees from Nazism*, London, Pimlico

67   Janik 2001, p.202, speaks of a 'virtual methodological "reign of terror" in countries like America'

68   See Perry Anderson 2004 'Deringolade' *London Review of Books* Vol. 26.17; Perry Anderson 2004 'Union Sucree' *London Review of Books* Vol. 26.18

69   Hacohen 2000, Epilogue

70   There is also an evolutionary theory of objective structures, real, social and cognitive, World Three, see Bryan Magee 1973 *Popper*, London, Fontana; and in recent years the reformist strand has found a celebrant in George Soros' *Open Society Institute*

71   See Karl Popper 1974 5th ed.

72 Popper 1974 5th ed. pp.33–9 explains that part of his motivation was to separate science from Marxism and psychoanalysis

73 McCarthy 1984

74 Passmore 1970, see chapter ten, scientific method cannot guarantee social progress, theorists wedded to the idea of progress must identify a *social mechanism*

75 Marjorie Greene 1966 *The Knower and the Known*, London, Faber and Faber

76 T. Tudor 1982 *Beyond Empiricism*, London, Routledge, p.144

77 Karl Popper 1945 *The Open Society and Its Enemies*, London, Routledge and Kegan Paul; Karl Popper 1957 *The Poverty of Historicism*, London, Routledge and Kegan Paul

78 Perry Anderson 1992 *English Questions*, London, Verso, pp.60–5; Snowman 2003; reviewed by Eric Hobsbawm (2005) 'Benefits of Diaspora' in *London Review of Books*, Vol. 27.20

79 Paul Diesing 1991 *How Does Social Science Work: Reflections on Practice*, University of Pittsburgh Press, chapter two, argues that Popper does not follow his own advice about falsification; that is, it is dogmatic

80 Thomas Uebel 2008 'The Vienna Circle' in *The Stanford Encyclopaedia of Philosophy*, Edward N. Zalta (ed.) http://plato.stanford.edu/archives/fall2008/entries/vienna-circle/

81 W.V.O. Quine and J.S. Ullian 1970 *The Web of Belief*, New York, Random House

82 W.V.O. Quine 1953 *From a Logical Point of View*, New York, Harper, chapter two

83 Quine 1953 p.36

84 Quine 1953 p.42

85 Quine and Ullian 1970

86 R.J. Anderson, J.A. Hughes and W.W. Sharock 1986 *Philosophy and the Human Sciences*, London, Croom Helm, chapter seven; see also William Outhwaite 1987 *New Philosophies of Social Science: Realism, Hermeneutics and Critical Theory*, London, Macmillan

87 Rorty 1998

88 Gerard Delanty and Piet Strydom (eds) 2003 *Philosophies of Social Science: The Classical and Contemporary Readings*, Maidenhead, Open University Press, p.19

89 Ernest Nagel 1961 *The Structure of Science*, London, Routledge and Kegan Paul

90 Stephen Gudeman 1986 *Economics as Culture*, London, Routledge; P.W. Preston 1996 *Development Theory: An Introduction*, Oxford, Blackwell, chapter fourteen

91 Thomas Kuhn 1970 2nd ed. *The Structure of Scientific Revolutions*, University of Chicago; Richard Bernstein 1979 *The Restructuring of Social and Political Theory*, London, Methuen

92 Giddens 1979 pp.238–40

93 Richard Bernstein 1983 *Beyond Objectivism and Relativism: Science, Hermeneutics and Praxis*, Oxford, Blackwell

94 Paul Feyerabend 1988 Revised ed. *Against Method*, London, Verso

95 Paul Feyerabend 1978 *Science in a Free Society*, London, New Left Books

96   See David Bloor 1991 *Knowledge and Social Imagery*, Chicago University Press; Bruno Latour 1987 *Science in Action*, Harvard University Press; Bruno Latour 1999 *Pandora's Hope*, Harvard University Press

97   Ulla Segerstrale (ed.) 2000 *Beyond the Science Wars: The Missing Discourse about Science and Society*, State University of New York

98   E. Gellner 1964 *Thought and Change*, p.179, London, Weidenfeld

99   P.W. Preston 1994 *Discourses of Development*, Aldershot, Avebury, chapter five

100 Terrel Carver (ed.) 1975 *Karl Marx Texts On Method*, Oxford, Blackwell, characterizes classical political-economy as intellectually catholic and resolutely practical

101 A.K. Dasgupta 1985 *Epochs of Economic Theory*, pp.90–5, Oxford, Blackwell

102 Swedberg 1987 argues that it is from this period that the Anglo-Saxon world inherits the institutional and thus disciplinary division between economics, the hard science of the social, and sociology, the vague moralistic study of the leftovers

103 It was to become a key text in the monetarist attack on Keynes, see David Smith 1987 *The Rise and Fall of Monetarism*, Harmondsworth, Penguin; the ideology is made explicit in Milton Friedman 1962 *Capitalism and Freedom*, University of Chicago Press; Milton Friedman and Rose Friedman 1980 *Free to Choose*, London, Secker

104 Milton Friedman 1953 *Essays in Positive Economics*, p.4, University of Chicago Press

105 Geoffrey Hodgson 1988 *Economics as Institutions*, Cambridge, Polity, points to the dearth of discussions about the social institutional nature of markets

106 Ken Cole, John Cameron and Chris Edwards 1991 *Why Economists Disagree*, London, Longman; Roger Backhouse 2002 *The Penguin History of Economics*, Harmondsworth, Penguin; or more controversially, Paul Ormerod 1994 *The Death of Economics*, London, Faber and Faber

107 John Pheby 1988 *Methodology and Economics: A Critical Introduction*, London, Macmillan; see also Philip Mirowski 1988 *Against Mechanism: Protecting Economics from Science*, New Jersey, Rowman and Littlefield; see also M. Hollis and E.J. Nell 1975 *Rational Economic Man*, Cambridge University Press

108 Fredric Jameson 1991 *Postmodernism: The Cultural Logic of Late Capitalism*, London, Verso, notes that self-conscious ideology and social reality intermingle

109 Hodgson 1988; Martin Staniland 1985 *What is Political Economy*, Yale University Press

110 Gudeman 1986; John Clammer 1985 *Anthropology and Political Economy*, London, Macmillan; Swedberg 1987; on consumption, see the journal *Theory, Culture and Society* cited as intellectually novel by Martin Albrow 'The Changing British Role in European Sociology' in Nedelmann and Sztompka 1993

111 Preston 1996; Kyoko Sheridan (ed.) 1998 *Emerging Economic Systems in Asia*, St. Leonards, Allen and Unwin

112 See Mathew Watson 2005 *Foundations of International Political Economy*, London, Palgrave

113   See Donald N. McClosky *If You are So Smart: The Narrative of Economic Expertise*, University of Chicago Press

114   See discussions in *Financial Times* and *Economist*, August 2008

115   Geoffrey Hawthorn 1976 *Enlightenment and Despair*, Cambridge University Press; Birgitta Nedelmann and Piet Sztompka (eds) 1993 *Sociology in Europe: In Search of an Identity*, Berlin, Walter de Gruyter

116   An odd exchange: in the 1930s European ideas flow across the Atlantic and they are read into the American scene and then after the war in the late 1940s re-exported back across the Atlantic – but the messages get garbled in the process – it seems that not until the 1960s did European sociologists look to their own traditions

117   Giddens 1979, see chapter seven

118   Robert Merton 1968 (enlarged edition) *Social Theory and Social Structure*, New York, The Free Press – see Part One, in particular, sections two and three

119   Merton 1968 p.39

120   Merton 1968 pp.70–2; then section three 'Manifest and Latent Functions'

121   Andrew Vincent 2004 *The Nature of Political Theory*, Oxford University Press

122   Colin Hay 2002 *Political Analysis: A Critical Introduction*, London, Palgrave; see also Dave Marsh and Gerry Stoker (eds) 1995 *Theory and Methods in Political Science*, London, Macmillan

123   Hay 2002

124   Kenneth Waltz 1959 *Man, State and War*, Columbia University Press

125   Michael Cox, *Introduction* to E.H. Carr 1939 (2001) *The Twenty Year Crisis*, London, Palgrave

126   John Haslam 1999 *The Vices of Integrity: E.H. Carr 1892–1982*, London, Verso

127   C. Jones 1998 *E H Carr and International Relations: A Duty to Lie*, Cambridge University Press

128   Jones 1998 p.160

129   B.M.A. Crawford 2000 *Idealism and Realism in International Relations*, London, Routledge

130   Charles Taylor 1967 'Neutrality in Political Science' in P. Laslett and W.G. Runciman (eds) *Philosophy, Politics and Society Third Series*, Oxford, Blackwell

131   Richard Rorty 1982 *The Consequences of Pragmatism*, University of Minnesota Press, in particular, chapter twelve

132   The distinction between 'Anglo-American analytic philosophy' and 'Continental philosophy' is familiar; Rorty, as noted, sees and regrets the division, Borradori 1994 also notes the division; others either deny it or dismiss the Continental – see Simon Critchley 2001 *Continental Philosophy: A Very Short Introduction*, Oxford University Press

133   Richard Rorty 1989 *Contingency, Irony and Solidarity*, Cambridge University Press

134   Bauman 1987

135   Critchley 2001

Chapter 3

1   D. Robey (ed.) 1973 *Structuralism: An Introduction*, Oxford University Press – otherwise, semiotics

2   David Pears 1971 *Wittgenstein*, London, Fontana, pp.25–41

3   Ray Monk 1991 *Ludwig Wittgenstein: The Duty of Genius*, London, Vintage, offers an intellectual biography

4   Allan Janik and Stephen Toulmin 1973 *Wittgenstein's Vienna*, pp.196–201, New York, Simon and Shuster

5   A 'third Wittgenstein' has been identified who finally grounds claims to knowledge in ways of acting; the key text is Ludwig Wittgenstein 1974 *On Certainty*, Oxford, Blackwell; see D. Moyal-Sharrock (ed.) 2004 *The Third Wittgenstein: The Post-Investigation Works*, Aldershot, Avebury; see also A. Stroll 2002 *Wittgenstein*, Oxford, One World; see also A. Stroll in R.H. Popkin 1999 *The Pimlico History of Western Philosophy*, London, Pimlico, pp.640–1 which hints at a new foundationalism, a sort of realism (the given are the material world and human communities), which seems misleading given Wittgenstein's stress on the social nature of life/language

6   Stroll 2002 p.1 remarks that there are around 7,000 pieces dealing with his work

7   Peter Winch 1958/1990 2nd ed. *The Idea of a Social Science and Its Relation to Philosophy*, London, Routledge; also in contrast Ernest Gellner 1959 *Words and Things*, London, Routledge; also T.P. Uschanov 2002 'Ernest Gellner's criticisms of Wittgenstein and ordinary language philosophy' in G. Kitching and N. Pleasants (eds) 2002. *Marx and Wittgenstein: Knowledge, Morality and Politics*, London, Routledge

8   Janik and Toulmin 1973 report that contemporary thinkers viewed it as decadent – not so Karl Popper as late Hapsburg was tolerant, precisely the place for an assimilated liberal Jew – see M.H. Hacohen 2000 *Karl Popper: The Formative Years 1902–1945*, Cambridge University Press

9   Janik and Toulmin 1973 report that educated Viennese paid attention to science

10 Janik and Toulmin 1973 p.24

11 Monk 1991 pp.197–217, on the publication of *Tractatus*

12 The mix of art, science, social experimentation and establishment connections of the Bloomsbury Group recalls the position of family Wittgenstein in Vienna – see Peter Gay 2008 *Modernism: The Lure of Heresy*, pp.194–214, New York, Norton

13 P.M.S. Hacker 1996 *Wittgenstein's Place in Twentieth Century Analytical Philosophy*, Oxford, Blackwell

14 Avrum Stroll 1999 'Twentieth Century Analytic Philosophy' in Richard P. Popkin (ed.) *The Pimlico History of Western Philosophy*, London, Pimlico

15 H. Stuart Hughes 1959 *Consciousness and Society*, London, MacGibbon and Kee, sees them as re-presenting positivism in contrast to *fin de siecle* romanticism

16 The ethics/politics differ from those of Wittgenstein, a different strand of 'centre/left' opinion; on the social reformers, Hacohen 2000; N. Cartwright, J. Cat, L. Fleck and T. Uebel 1996 *Otto Neurath: Philosophy Between Science and Politics*, Cambridge University Press

17   Oswald Hanfling 1981 *Logical Positivism*, Oxford, Blackwell

18   A.J. Ayer 1985 *Wittgenstein*, Harmondsworth, Penguin

19   This seems to have particularly attracted some of his British adherents: see Monk 1991; and Brian McGuiness 1988 *Wittgenstein: A Life 1889–1921*, Harmondsworth, Penguin, who notes acquaintances remarking on Wittgenstein's fastidiousness and ethically self-critical style with some apparently viewing him as a saint

20   Janik and Toulmin 1973; see also Simon Critchley 2001 *Continental Philosophy: A Very Short Introduction*, Oxford University Press, who argues that United Kingdom based philosophers read mainland work into their own concerns; thus 'two cultures' and anti-European prejudices; and thus mis-read the material; see also Giovanna Borradori 1994 *The American Philosopher*, pp.5–9, University of Chicago Press, who reports this as an American prejudice

21   Janik and Toulmin 1973; for wider scene, Critchley 2001; Hacohen 2000

22   Janik and Toulmin 1973 see an essential continuity beneath changes in emphasis, pp.222–5 – however, it is noticeable how little they say about the *Investigations*

23   R.J. Anderson, J.A. Hughes and W.W. Sharock 1986 *Philosophy and the Human Sciences*, London, Croom Helm

24   K.O. Apel 1980 *Towards a Transformation of Philosophy*, London, Routledge, remarks that the theory of language/reality in the *Tractatus* is quasi-Leibnizian, that is, an abstract general metaphysics

25   The *Investigations* acknowledges the Italian Marxist political economist Piero Sraffa; in Kitching and Pleasants (eds) 2002 K. Sharpe 'Sraffa's Influence on Wittgenstein: A Conjecture' and J. B. Davies 'A Marxist Influence of Wittgenstein via Sraffa' consider the issue with the former speculating that Sraffa may have objected to the *Tractatus'* asocial view of language and opened up anthropology, whilst the later speculates that Sraffa may have fed an influence from Gramsci into Wittgenstein's thinking, in particular, the idea of critique, which implies contextualization; Monk 1991 pp.260–1 mentions this line of influence but does not pursue it

26   Anthony Kenny 1973 *Wittgenstein*, p.14, Harmondsworth, Penguin

27   Jonathan Culler 1976 *Saussure*, London, Fontana

28   Clifford Geertz 2000 *Available Light: Anthropological Reflections on Philosophical Topics*, Princeton University Press, p.xi

29   Pears 1971 p.168

30   Winch 1958/1990; Colin Lyas 1999 *Peter Winch*, Teddington, Acumen, p.4 remarks that Winch influenced the hermeneutics of both K.O. Apel and Jurgen Habermas

31   Winch 1958/1990 p.15

32   Anthony Giddens 1976 *New Rules of Sociological Method*, London, Hutchinson, pp.44–51 suggests that the notion of rule governed does too much work – but Winch (following Wittgenstein) recalls attention to the experiential depth of human social life whereas Giddens looks to the matter of concrete historical social formations

33   Winch 1958/1990 p.43 argues sociology is 'misbegotten epistemology' having wrongly taken the job of elucidation of the nature of the social to be an empirical question

34 Some might disagree; the 1960s saw the rise of 'anti-psychiatry', for an example see R.D. Laing 1965 *The Divided Self: An Existential Study in Sanity and Madness*, Harmondsworth, Penguin; R.D. Laing 1970 *Knots*, London, Tavistock; today one might want to find a better example of 'having no rules'

35 Winch 1958/1990 p.72

36 Giddens 1976

37 Richard J. Bernstein 1979 *The Restructuring of Social and Political Theory*, pp.63–74, London, Methuen (also Richard J. Bernstein 1983 *Beyond Objectivism and Relativism: Science, Hermeneutics and Praxis*, Oxford, Blackwell), criticizes the claim, suggesting that just as the concepts clustering around meaningfulness are richly elaborated then perhaps there should be a similar cluster developed around cause; Winch acknowledges the point in the Preface to the Second Edition – however, the sets of social regularities with which any individual is simply confronted can be grasped in terms of structures – this would be a better way of getting at what we tag in casual conversation as 'cause'

38 Winch 1958/1990 p.122

39 Giddens 1976 chapter two

40 Alasdair MacIntyre 1962 'A mistake about causality in social science' in P. Laslett and W. G. Runciman (eds) *Politics, Philosophy and Society Second Series*, Oxford, Blackwell

41 Alasdair MacIntyre 1971 'The idea of a social science' in *Against the Self Images of the Age*, London, Duckworth

42 Alasdair MacIntyre 1985 2nd ed. *After Virtue: A Study in Moral Theory*, London, Duckworth, chapter eight

43 MacIntyre 1962 p.52

44 Anthony Giddens 1972 *Politics and Sociology in the Thought of Max Weber*, London, Macmillan; see also Dennis Smith 1991 *The Rise of Historical Sociology*, Cambridge, Polity

45 MacIntyre 1962 pp.60–1

46 MacIntyre 1962 p.63

47 MacIntyre 1962 p.69

48 Lyas 1999 pp.64–5 takes the view that MacIntyre's concerns can be accommodated

49 MacIntyre 1985; for a conversation with MacIntyre, see Borradori 1994

50 Stephen Lukes 1973 *Individualism*, Oxford, Blackwell

51 MacIntyre 1985 pp.106–7

52 Peter McMylor 1994 *Alasdair MacIntyre: Critic of Modernity*, London, Routledge, chapter five

53 Pears 1971 p.168

54 On objectivism/subjectivism see Bernstein 1983

55 David Bloor 1983 *Wittgenstein: A Social Theory of Knowledge*, London, Macmillan

56 Pears 1971 pp.173–4

57 Pears 1971 p.174

58 Thus, famously, Bertrand Russell; see also Pears 1971 and Ayer 1985

59 Bloor 1983; also David Bloor 1997 *Wittgenstein: Rules and Institutions*, London, Routledge

60 Lyas 1999 pp.63–4 suggests that asking Wittgenstein to produce an empirical social science is rather beside the point

61 Bloor 1983 pp.140–9

62 Apel 1980; Lyas 1999 pp.90–2

63 Ferdinand de Saussure 1990 *Course in General Linguistics*, London, Duckworth

64 Zygmunt Bauman 1978 *Hermeneutics and Social Science*, London, Hutchinson

65 Josef Bleicher 1980 *Contemporary Hermeneutics: Method, Philosophy and Critique*, London, Routledge, chapter one; Bauman 1978 pp.23–31

66 Bauman 1978

67 Charles Taylor 1971 'Interpretation and the science of man' in *Review of Metaphysics* 25

68 William Outhwaite 1975 *Understanding Social Life: The Method Called Verstehen*, London, Allen and Unwin

69 Taylor 1971; Bauman 1978; Bleicher 1980; Josef Bleicher 1982 *The Hermeneutic Imagination: Outline of a Positive Critique of Scientism and Sociology*, London, Routledge

70 Hughes 1959

71 Hans Georg Gadamer 1994 *Heideggers's Ways*, State University of New York, chapters one and two

72 H.A. Hodges 1944 *Wilhelm Dilthey An Introduction*, London, Kegan Paul, Trench, Trubner and Co

73 H.P. Rickman 1976 *Wilhelm Dilthey Selected Writings*, Cambridge University Press; Rickman reports that his selections represent only about five percent of Dilthey's published work and the Hegelian material is preferred; all the references to Wilhelm Dilthey 1914 *Collected Works*, Leipzig, are as cited in Rickman

74 Dilthey 1914 Vol. 1 pp.xv–xix

75 Dilthey 1914 Vol. 1 pp.xv–xix

76 Dilthey 1914 Vol. 1 pp.xv–xix

77 Dilthey 1914 Vol. III pp.79–88

78 Dilthey 1914 Vol. III pp.79–88

79 Dilthey 1914 Vol. VII pp.130–66

80 Dilthey 1914 Vol. VII pp.130–66

81 Dilthey 1914 Vol. VII pp.130–66

82 Dilthey 1914 Vol. VII pp.189–200

83 Dilthey 1914 Vol. V pp.317–37

84 Including, not only Dilthey but also Friedrich Nietzsche, Georg Simmel and Henri Bergson

85 The relationship is tangled and not always happy – see, for example, Thomas Sheehan 2006 'Reading a Life: Heidegger and Hard Times' in Charles B. Guignon (ed.) 2006 *The Cambridge Companion to Heidegger*, Cambridge University Press

86 On the phases of Husserl's work, see J.N. Mohanty 1995 'The Development of Husserl's Thought' in Barry Smith and David Woodruff Smith (eds) 1995 *The Cambridge Companion to Husserl*, Cambridge University Press

87 Giddens 1976

88   The implications of Heidegger's short membership of the National Socialist's are much debated: Richard Wolin 1990 *The Politics of Being: The Political Thought of Martin Heidegger*, New York, Columbia University Press; also Richard Wolin 1992 *The Terms of Cultural Criticism: The Frankfurt School, Existentialism and Poststructuralism*, Columbia University Press; also Julian Young 1997 *Heidegger, Philosophy and Nazism*, Cambridge University Press; the former author argues the membership is implicated in the philosophy which is therefore undermined; the later thinks the philosophy stands and Heidegger's politics are an extrinsic banal recycling of nationalist ideas – 'the ideas of 1914' – and the membership of the party an error; the later argument is the more plausible; see also Gadamer 1994 p.20 who writes of a 'political folly'; see also Richard Rorty 1999 *Philosophy and Social Hope*, London, Penguin, chapter thirteen, who comments that junking the philosophy in the light of a mistake made in the 1930s would be absurd; an interesting insight comes from Elzbieta Ettinger 1995 *Hannah Arendt and Martin Heidegger*, Yale University Press

89   Martin Heidegger 1996 *Being and Time*, State University of New York

90   Jurgen Habermas 1997 *A Berlin Republic*, University of Nebraska Press, p.39, remarks, apropos contemporary Germany that it would be a mistake to return to '…that Teutonic mix of muddy and deep thought that once seemed to Heidegger to be our "most authentic" quality'

91   David Couzens Hoy 2006 'Heidegger and the Hermeneutic Turn', in Guignon (ed.) 2006, who points to Sections 31 and 32 of *Being and Time* as marking the turn to hermeneutics

92   Andrew Vincent 2004 *The Nature of Political Theory*, Oxford University Press, chapter eight offers a critical commentary

93   On the occasion for mis-celebrating method, see Joel Weinsheimer 1985 *Gadamer's Hermeneutics: A Reading of Truth and Method*, Yale University Press

94   Hans Georg Gadamer 1979 *Truth and Method*, London, Sheed and Ward

95   Georgia Warnke 1987 *Gadamer: Hermeneutics, Tradition and Reason*, Cambridge, Polity, chapter one

96   Warnke 1987 chapter three

97   Gadamer 1979 p.345

98   Gadamer 1979 p.347

99   Gadamer 1979 p.349

100   Gadamer 1979 p.408

101   Gadamer 1979 p.432

102   Richard Kearney (ed.) 1996 *Paul Ricoeur: The Hermeneutics of Action*, London, Sage

103   And nor is the 'problem of relativism' as there is no 'outside' to appeal to; see Geertz 2000, chapter 3

104   Taylor 1971; Bernstein 1983 pp.1–50 discuses 'objectivism' and 'relativism'

105   Charles Taylor 1980 'Understanding in human science' in *Review of Metaphysics* 34

106   Anthony Giddens 1979 *Central Problems in Social Theory*, London, Macmillan, pp.257–9 – advances the strategy of 'dual rethinking'

107   Bernstein 1983, in particular Part One pp.1–50

108 Paul Feyerabend remarks somewhere that natural science does not need a philosophical mummy and daddy to get their methods straight because science is a form of life, it works – the argument recalls Richard Rorty 1989 *Contingency, Irony and Solidarity*, Cambridge University Press, chapter one, who remarks that philosophers are not auxiliaries to scientists – or, one might say, not 'armchair lab-technicians'

109 Brian Fay 1975 *Social Theory and Political Practice*, London, Allen and Unwin

110 Brian Fay 1987 *Critical Social Science*, Cambridge, Polity, separates critical social science from critical theory which is then dismissed; a more general interpretive line is offered in Brian Fay 1996 *Contemporary Philosophy of Social Science*, Oxford, Blackwell

111 Bauman 1978

112 Roy Harris 1990 *Language, Saussure and Wittgenstein: How to Play Games with Words*, London, Routledge

113 R.J. Anderson, J.A. Hughes and W.W. Sharock 1986 *Philosophy and the Human Sciences*, London, Croom Helm

114 Ferdinand de Saussure 1990 *Course in General Linguistics*, London, Duckworth – the book was first published in 1913, after his death, from notes taken by students of lectures given in 1907–11

115 Culler 1976 p.22

116 Culler 1976 p.91

117 Anderson *et al.* 1986, chapter five

118 Alan Sheridan 1980 *Michael Foucault The Will to Truth*, London, Tavistock; Paul Rabinow (ed.) 1984 *The Foucault Reader*, Harmondsworth, Penguin; J.G. Merquior 1985 *Foucault*, London, Fontana; John Sturrock 1986 *Structuralism*, London, Palladin

119 Michel Foucault 1970 *The Order of Things: An Archaeology of the Human Sciences*, London, Tavistock

120 Michel Foucault 1973 *The Birth of the Clinic*, New York, Vintage; Michel Foucault 1977 *Discipline and Punish*, New York, Pantheon; Rabinow 1984; also David Macey 1993 *The Lives of Michel Foucault*, London, Vintage

121 The formal work is rooted a sophisticated knowledge of philosophy; the substantive work is contemporary with anti-psychiatry (R.D. Laing, Thomas Szasz and David Cooper) and work on sexuality (Herbert Marcuse, Wilhelm Reich)

122 A list of the key structuralist ideas might include the following: appearance and reality are distinguished (the method reveals the reality at back of appearance); surface configuration and underlying reality are distinguished (again, analysis aims to uncover hidden underlying reality); form and content are distinguished (applied to cultural phenomena by structuralists in order to get at forms underlying appearances); individuals versus networks of relationships are distinguished (the key theme now applied to persons, otherwise, the de-centring of the individual); the part/whole distinction is affirmed (the structuralist method lodges particulars in relevant contexts); the idea of unity in diversity is affirmed (diversity is a surface thing and unity is structural); and the focus of analysis is therefore on totality, elements, parts and internal relations.

123 Anderson *et al.* 1986 p.109

124 Anderson *et al.* 1986 p.110

125   Derived from Anderson *et al.* 1986
126   Christopher Norris 1987 *Derrida*, London, Fontana
127   An anxiety evident in Vincent 2004; but see Geertz 2000
128   From the final paragraph of R.D. Laing 1967 *The Politics of Experience and The Bird of Paradise*, Harmondsworth, Penguin, p.155
129   Rorty 1989

Chapter 4

1   P.W. Preston 1996 *Development Theory: An Introduction*, Oxford, Blackwell, chapter one, p.7
2   C.B. Macpherson 1973 *Democratic Theory: Essays in Retrieval*, Oxford University Press; also Raymond Plant 1991 *Modern Political Thought*, Oxford, Blackwell, chapter nine
3   Sidney Pollard 1971 *The Idea of Progress*, Harmondsworth, Penguin
4   Ernest Gellner 1964 *Thought and Change*, London, Wiedenfeld, chapters two and eight
5   H. Stuart Hughes 1959 *Consciousness and Society: The Reorientation of European Social Thought 1890–1930*, London, MacGibbon and Kee
6   Zygmunt Bauman 1987 *Legislators and Interpreters*, Cambridge, Polity
7   Martin Hollis 1977 *Models of Man*, Cambridge University Press
8   Robert Nisbet 1970 *The Sociological Tradition*, London, Heinemann
9   Arno Mayer 1981 *The Persistence of the Old Regime*, New York, Croom Helm; also Mark Mazower 1998 *Dark Continent: Europe's Twentieth Century*, London, Allen Lane; Eric Hobsbawm 1994 *The Age of Extremes: The Short Twentieth Century 1914–1991*, London, Michael Joseph
10   J.L. Gaddis 1998 *We Know Now: Rethinking Cold War History*, Oxford University Press; also Chalmers Johnson 2004 *The Sorrows of Empire: Militarism, Secrecy and the End of the Republic*, London, Verso
11   A. Vincent 2004 *The Nature of Political Theory*, Oxford University Press, pp.145–54 on Michael Oakeshott's conservatism
12   C.A. Bayly 2004 *The Birth of the Modern World 1780–1914*, Oxford, Blackwell, see chapter eight; also Peter Worsley 1984 *The Three Worlds: Culture and World Development*, London, Weidenfeld
13   C.B. Macpherson 1962 *The Political Theory of Possessive Individualism*, Oxford University Press; also Stephen Lukes 1973 *Individualism*, Oxford, Blackwell
14   John Passmore 1970 *The Perfectibility of Man*, London, Duckworth, argues that liberalism affirmed the ethically unprecedented idea of the rationality of the pursuit of unlimited wants
15   See Alasdair MacIntyre 1988 *Whose Justice, Which Rationality?*, London, Duckworth, chapters one and twelve to sixteen
16   Roy Porter 2000 *Enlightenment: Britain and the Creation of the Modern World*, London, Allen Lane
17   Ian Buruma 1999 *Voltaire's Coconuts: Or Anglo-Mania in Europe*, London, Weidenfeld and Nicolson
18   Anatol Lieven 2004 *America Right or Wrong: An Anatomy of American Nationalism*, London, HarperCollins

19 See Karl Popper 1945 *The Open Society and Its Enemies*, London, Routledge and Kegan Paul; Karl Popper 1974 5th ed. *Conjectures and Refutations: The Growth of Scientific Knowledge*, chapter sixteen, London, Routledge and Kegan Paul; see also MacIntyre 1985 chapters seven and eight

20 David Held 1987 *Models of Democracy*, Cambridge, Polity

21 Benedict Anderson 1983 *Imagined Communities*, London, Verso

22 Famously, Edmund Burke's 1790 *Reflections on the Revolution in France*

23 Mayer 1981; Anderson 1983; Ernest Gellner 1983 *Nations and Nationalism*, Oxford, Blackwell

24 Hobsbawm 1994

25 Paul Hirst and Grahame Thompson 1999 2nd ed. *Globalization in Question*, Cambridge, Polity; also Anthony Payne (ed.) 2004 *The New Regional Politics of Development*, London, Palgrave

26 Hughes 1959, chapter two

27 David Kellner 1989 *Critical Theory, Marxism and Modernity*, p.9, Cambridge, Polity

28 Richard Rorty 1989 *Contingency, Irony and Solidarity*, Cambridge University Press, chapter one; Richard Rorty 1999 *Philosophy and Social Hope*, Introduction, London, Penguin

29 Max Horkheimer 1937 'Traditional and Critical Theory', reprinted in Paul Connerton (ed.) 1976 *Critical Sociology*, Harmondsworth, Penguin; also Brian Fay 1987 *Critical Social Science*, Cambridge, Polity, chapter one

30 Martin Jay 1973 *The Dialectical Imagination*, Boston, Little Brown; Peter Hamilton 1974 *Knowledge and Social Structure*, London, Routledge and Kegan Paul; Richard Kilminster 1979 *Praxis and Method: A Sociological Dialogue with Lukacs, Gramsci and the Early Frankfurt School*, London, Routledge and Kegan Paul; Tom Bottomore 1984 *The Frankfurt School*, London, Ellis Horwood

31 Georg Lukacs 1971 *History and Class Consciousness*, London, Merlin

32 Martin Jay 1984 *Marxism and Totality*, Cambridge, Polity

33 Lukacs 1971 p.13

34 Lukacs 1971 pp.20–1

35 Lukacs 1971 pp.197–209

36 See David Held 1980 *Introduction to Critical Theory: Horkheimer to Habermas*, p.20, London, Hutchinson

37 See Chris Jenks 1993 *Culture*, pp.77–80, London, Routledge

38 Karl Korsch 1970 *Marxism and Philosophy*, London, New Left Books

39 Fred Halliday 1970 'Introduction' to Karl Korsch *Marxism and Philosophy*, p.13; Bottomore 1984 *The Frankfurt School*, p.1 records that Felix Weil ran a seminar in summer 1922 – attended by Lukacs and others – which was in part devoted to discussing Korsch's text

40 Korsch 1970 p.51

41 Korsch 1970 p.54

42 Korsch 1970 p.84

43 Antonio Gramsci (ed. Q. Hoare and G. Nowell Smith) 1971 *Selections from the Prison Notebooks*, London, Lawrence and Wishart

44 Made clear in the Hoare and Nowell Smith 1971 – Introduction

45 The political life of Gramsci is detailed in the introduction (Hoare and Nowell Smith 1971) to Antonio Gramsci 1971

46   Leonardo Salamini 1974 'Gramsci and Marxist sociology of knowledge' in *The Sociological Quarterly 15*, p.365

47   Discussed in an essay entitled 'The Intellectuals' reprinted in the *Prison Notebooks*

48   See Salamini 1974; Leonardo Salamini 1975 'The specificity of Marxist sociology in Gramsci's theory' in *The Sociological Quarterly 16*; also Leonardo Salamini 1981 *The Sociology of Political Praxis: An Introduction to Gramsci's Theory*, London, Routledge; also Renate Holub 1992 *Antonio Gramsci: Beyond Marxism and Postmodernism*, London, Routledge

49   Role is often debated; see Jeremy Jennings and A. Kemp-Welch (eds) 1997 *Intellectuals in Politics: From the Dreyfus affair to Salman Rushdie*, London, Routledge; Carl Boggs 1993 *Intellectuals and the Crisis of Modernity*, State University of New York Press; Frank Furedi 2004 *Where Have All the Intellectuals Gone: Confronting 21st Century Philistinism*, London, Continuum

50   Hobsbawm 1994 chapters two to five

51   Jay 1973 p.61

52   Hughes 1959 chapter two; John Passmore 1957 *A Hundred Years of Philosophy*, Harmondsworth, Penguin, chapter five, makes a link to pragmatism

53   Horkheimer 1937 (page references to Connerton) p.206

54   Horkheimer 1976 p.212

55   Horkheimer 1976 p.221

56   Horkheimer 1976 p.222

57   Horkheimer 1976 p.223

58   Thomas McCarthy 1984 *The Critical Theory of Jurgen Habermas*, Cambridge, Polity; William Outhwaite (ed.) 1996 *The Habermas Reader*, Cambridge, Polity

59   This text focuses on phase one, for an overview of phase two see J.G. Finlayson 2005 *Habermas: A Very Short Introduction*, Oxford University Press

60   Jurgen Habermas 1974 *Theory and Practice*, London, Heinemann; Jurgen Habermas 1971 *Knowledge and Human Interests*, Boston, Beacon; Jurgen Habermas 1971 *Towards a Rational Society*, London, Heinemann; and Jurgen Habermas 1976 *Legitimation Crisis*, London, Heinemann

61   See annex to *Knowledge and Human Interests*

62   The reformulated programme is inaugurated in Jurgen Habermas 1979 *Communication and the Evolution of Society*, Boston, Beacon

63   Jurgen Habermas 1984 *The Theory of Communicative Action: Vol. 1: Reason and the Rationalization of Society*, London, Heinemann; Jurgen Habermas 1987 *The Theory of Communicative Action: Vol. 2: The Critique of Functionalist Reason*, Cambridge, Polity

64   See Habermas 1974 pp.10–13

65   This brief overview draws on McCarthy 1984, in particular chapter one

66   Citing Greek philosophical ideas – *phronesis, techne* and *scientia* – but modern Europe is rooted in sixteenth century Italy, Rhine valley, France and the Low Countries – the reference back to Greece dates from later – Jacques Darras and Daniel Snowman 1990 *Beyond the Tunnel of History*, London, Macmillan

67 Habermas 1974 pp.41–81
68 Habermas 1974 pp.142–69
69 Habermas 1974 pp.170–94
70 Habermas 1974 pp.195–252
71 Habermas 1974 pp.253–82
72 Max Horkheimer and Theodor Adorno 1972 *Dialectic of Enlightenment*, London, Allen Lane
73 Perry Anderson 1983 *In the Tracks of Historical Materialism*, London, Verso
74 Jurgen Habermas 1988 *On the Logic of the Social Sciences*, Cambridge, Polity, surveys the field arguing that the split between natural and social sciences should not be enshrined in positivism or idealist hermeneutics but overcome in the construction of a 'theory of the present'
75 Habermas 1988, chapter eight; reprinted as 'A review of Gadamer's *Truth and Method*' in Fred R. Dallymar and Thomas A. McCarthy 1977 *Understanding and Social Enquiry*, University of Notre Dame Press; also Robert C. Holub 1991 *Jurgen Habermas Critic in the Public Sphere*, London, Routledge, chapter three
76 R.J. Anderson, J.A. Hughes and W.W. Sharock 1986 *Philosophy and the Human Sciences*, London, Croom Helm, chapter three
77 See Anderson *et al.* 1986 chapter three
78 McCarthy 1984 chapter three
79 Habermas 1971 essay three
80 Habermas 1974 essay six
81 Habermas 1971 essay two
82 Habermas 1971 essays ten, eleven and twelve
83 Zygmunt Bauman 1976 *Towards a Critical Sociology*, London, Routledge and Kegan Paul, distinguishes 'scholarly validation' and 'dialogic authentication'
84 Habermas 1971
85 Habermas 1971
86 Jurgen Habermas 1997 *A Berlin Republic: Writings on Germany*, University of Nebraska Press; Jurgen Habermas 2001 *The Postnational Constellation: Political Essays*, MIT Press; Jurgen Habermas 2006 *The Divided West*, Cambridge, Polity; Giovanna Borradori (ed.) 2003 *Philosophy in a Time of Terror: Dialogues with Jurgen Habermas and Jacques Derrida*, University of Chicago Press
87 Holub 1991
88 Andrew Vincent 2004 *The Nature of Political Theory*, Oxford University Press, pp.278–80, notes this as a possibly emerging area of exegetical debate on the unity or otherwise of the body of work
89 Perry Anderson 1983 *In the Tracks of Historical Materialism*, pp.57–67, London, Verso
90 McCarthy 1984 p.357
91 Richard Bernstein (ed.) 1985 *Habermas and Modernity*, pp.12–25, Cambridge, Polity
92 Much further work followed *Theory of Communicative Action* as formal elements were detailed, see Finlayson 2005
93 Anderson 1983
94 Bernstein 1985
95 Anderson 1983
96 Carver 1975

97   See Lewis Carrol 1965 *Alice in Wonderland*, London, Dent
98   McCarthy 1984 chapter five
99   Held 1980
100   Anthony Giddens 'Labour and Interaction' in John B. Thompson and David Held (eds) 1982 *Habermas: Critical Debates*, London, Macmillan
101   McCarthy 1984 chapter five
102   Bernstein 1983
103   Fay 1987
104   See John B. Thompson 'Universal pragmatics' in Thompson and Held (eds) 1982; H. Ottman 'Cognitive Interests and Self-reflection' in Thompson and Held (eds) 1982; Thomas McCarthy 'Rationality and Relativism: Habermas's Overcoming of Hermeneutics' in Thompson and Held (eds) 1982
105   Rorty in Bernstein 1985
106   David Held 'Crisis Tendencies, Legitimation and the State' in Thompson and Held (eds) 1982
107   David Held 1980 *Introduction to Critical Theory*, London, Hutchinson, offers further general criticisms
108   Hughes 1959 pp.14–24
109   Alex Callinicos 1989 *Against Postmodernism: A Marxist Critique*, Cambridge, Polity, see Introduction
110   David Harvey 1989 *The Condition of Postmodernity*, Oxford, Blackwell
111   Harvey 1989 p.196
112   Frederick Jameson 1991 *Postmodernism: Or, the Cultural Logic of Late Capitalism*, London, Verso
113   J.F. Lyotard 1979 *The Postmodern Condition*, Manchester University Press
114   Bauman 1987
115   Anthony Woodiwiss 1993 *Postmodernity USA*, London, Sage
116   Zygmunt Bauman 1988 *Freedom*, Milton Keynes, Open University Press
117   Zygmunt Bauman 1989 *Modernity and the Holocaust*, Cambridge, Polity; Zygmunt Bauman 1991 *Modernity and Ambivalence*, Cambridge, Polity; Zygmunt Bauman 1992 *Intimations of Modernity*, London, Routledge
118   MacIntyre 1985
119   Richard Rorty 1989 *Contingency, Irony and Solidarity*, Cambridge University Press
120   Herbert Marcuse 1964 *One Dimensional Man*, Boston, Beacon; Herbert Marcuse 1969 *Eros and Civilization*, London, Sphere; Herbert Marcuse 1972 *An Essay on Liberation*, Harmondsworth, Penguin; on 'the sixties' see Tony Judt 2005 *Post-War: A History of Europe Since 1945*, New York, The Penguin Press, chapter twelve
121   Erich Fromm 1942 *Fear of Freedom*, London, Routledge

Chapter 5

1   Ernest Gellner 1964 *Thought and Change*, London, Weidenfeld, has a good discussion of the business of theorizing social change from inside the system – unsettling, unclear and uncertain
2   Hans-Georg Gadamer 1979 *Truth and Method*, p.432, London, Sheed and Ward

3 Peter Winch 1958/1990 2nd ed. *The Idea of a Social Science and Its Relation to Philosophy*, London, Routledge
4 David Bloor 1983 *Wittgenstein: A Social Theory of Knowledge*, London, Macmillan, presents the idea of finitism – arguments are tools, they do specific finite jobs
5 J. Culler 1976 *Saussure*, London, Fontana
6 There are different ways of writing histories, but see for example: John Plamenatz 1963 *Man and Society* (2 vols), London, Longman; Raymond Plant 1991 *Modern Political Thought*, Oxford, Blackwell; Ian Hampshire-Monk 1992 *A History of Modern Political Thought*, Oxford, Blackwell; James Tully (ed.) 1988 *Meaning and Context: Quentin Skinner and his Critics*, Cambridge, Polity
7 Zygmunt Bauman 1976 *Towards a Critical Sociology*, London, Routledge and Kegan Paul
8 Maureen Whitebrook 2001 *Identity, Narrative and Politics*, London, Routledge; Fred Inglis 1993 *Cultural Studies*, Oxford, Blackwell
9 Anthony Giddens 1979 *Central Problems in Social Theory*, London, Macmillan
10 See Irving Zeitlin 1968 *Ideology and the Development of Sociological Theory*, New York, Prentice Hall
11 Anthony Giddens 1971 *Capitalism and Modern Social Theory*, Cambridge University Press; also P.W. Preston 1996 *Development Theory*, Part Two, Oxford, Blackwell
12 Gellner 1964 chapters 2 and 6
13 Norman Long and Ann Long (eds) 1992 *Battlefields of Knowledge*, London, Routledge
14 P.W. Preston 1996 *Development Theory: An Introduction*, p.339, Oxford, Blackwell
15 Preston 1996 chapter 9
16 Clark Kerr *et al.* 1973 *Industrialism and Industrial Man*, Harmondsworth, Pelican; also Alasdair MacIntyre 1971 *Against the Self-Images of the Age*, London, Duckworth
17 Bjorne Hettne 1995 2nd ed. *Development Theory and the Three Worlds*, London, Longman; Anthony Payne (ed.) 2004 *The New Regional Politics of Development*, London, Palgrave
18 MacIntyre 1971
19 Gabriel Kolko 1968 *The Politics of War: US Foreign Policy 1943–45*, New York, Vintage; J.L. Gaddis 1998 *We Know Now: Rethinking Cold War History*, Oxford University Press; Chalmers Johnson 2004 *The Sorrows of Empire*, London, Verso
20 Philip Bobbit 2002 *The Shield of Achilles*, New York, Knopf
21 Paul Hirst and Grahame Thompson 1999 2nd ed. *Globalization in Question*, Cambridge, Polity
22 In comparison, the United States figures are population around 400 million and a gross domestic product of around $10.4 trillion, and East Asia has a larger population of around two billion and a similar aggregate economic strength
23 Jeremy Richardson (ed.) 2001 2nd ed. *European Union: Power and Policy Making*, London, Routledge; Alasdair Blair 2005 *The European Union Since 1945*, London, Longman; see also Thomas Christiansen, Knud Erik Jorgensen and Antje Wiener (eds) 2001 *The Social Construction of Europe*, London, Sage; also Tony

Judt 2005 *Post-War: A History of Europe Since 1945*, New York, The Penguin Press

24   Easy for sociologists of my generation, we looked to Anthony Giddens 1971 *Capitalism and Modern Social Theory: An Analysis of the Writings of Marx, Durkheim and Max Weber*, Cambridge University Press

25   W.W. Sharock, J.A. Hughes and P.J. Martin 2003 *Understanding Modern Sociology*, London, Sage, remark rather reluctantly that their discussion of classical theory does not imply accepting the unfashionable idea of a 'canon', sociology (specifically) they say is 'an argument rather than a knowledge subject' (p.203), but even so many texts offer lists as ways of grasping unfolding tradition; see, for example, P. Belharz 1991 *Social Theory: A Guide to Central Thinkers*, London, Allen and Unwin, or in different vein, John Lechte 1994 *Fifty Key Contemporary Thinkers: From Structuralism to Post-modernity*, London, Routledge

26   A sequence can be identified: the shift to the modern world; the general crisis 1914–45/89; and recovery/success 1945–2003; the idea of general crisis is Antonio Gramsci's as discussed by Arno Mayer 1988 *Why did the Heavens Not Darken: The 'Final Solution' in History*, New York, Pantheon

27   Thus: French rationalism; British empiricism; and German idealism

28   In respect of sociology, see Geoffrey Hawthorn 1976 *Enlightenment and Despair*, Cambridge University Press; Birgitta Nedelmann and Piotr Sztompka (eds) 1993 *Sociology in Europe: In Search of an Identity*, Berlin, Walter de Gruyter

29   Zygmunt Bauman 1987 *Legislators and Interpreters*, Cambridge, Polity

30   Karl Mannheim 1936 *Ideology and Utopia*, London, Routledge

31   Max Horkheimer and Theodor Adorno 1972 *Dialectic of Enlightenment*, London, Allen Lane

32   Preston 1996; Preston 1985

33   P.W. Preston 1987 *Rethinking Development*, London, Routledge

34   Self description reported in Bernard Crick 1980 *George Orwell*, Harmondsworth, Penguin, p.15; also Scott Lucas 2003 *Orwell: Life and Times*, London, Haus Publishing; also Stefan Collini 2003 'No Bullshit Bullshit' in *London Review of Books* 25.02 23 January 2003

35   Bernard Williams 2005 *In the Beginning Was the Deed: Realism and Moralism in Political Argument*, Princeton University Press, argues that moral judgements are always bound by context and use, thus 'morals-in-practice'

36   In the case of Europe, the rise of fascism, the disaster of war and the absurdity of cold war all produced such figures: see Eric Hobsbawm 2002 *Interesting Times: A Twentieth Century Life*, London, Abacus; generally, Daniel Snowman 2003 *The Hitler Émigrés: The Cultural Impact on Britain of Refugees from Nazism*, London, Pimlico

37   Not pursued here, but see, for example, Hugo Young 1998 *This Blessed Plot: Britain and Europe from Churchill to Blair*, London, Papermac; Christopher Hitchens 1990 *Blood, Class and Nostalgia: Anglo-American Ironies*, London, Vintage – Hitchens has recently presented controversial views in respect of the 'global war on terror'

38   Giovanna Borradori 2003 *Philosophy in a Time of Terror: Dialogues with Jurgen Habermas and Jacques Derrida*, University of Chicago Press, distinguishes 'political activism' from 'social critique' (pp.4–8) – Orwell would fall into the first noted category

39 A point rehearsed in Lucas 2003 p.127

40 Richard Rorty 1989 *Contingency, Irony and Solidarity*, Cambridge University Press, chapter eight

41 Terry Eagleton 2003 'Reach Me Down Romantic' in *London Review of Books* 25.12 19 June 2003

42 E.P. Thompson in Raymond Williams (ed.) 1974 *George Orwell: A Collection of Critical Essays*, Englewood Cliffs, Prentice Hall, p.82, suggested he was 'a man raw down one-side and numb down the other'

43 Gunter Grass 1962 *The Tin Drum*, London, Secker and Warburg; Gunter Grass 1990 *Two States, One Nation*, London, Secker and Warburg; Gunter Grass 1999 *My Century*, London, Faber and Faber; Gunter Grass 2002 *Crabwalk*, London, Faber and Faber

44 A related discussion looks at the aerial bombing of Germany: Sven Lindqvist 2002 *A History of Bombing*, London, Granta; also W. G. Sebald 2004 *On the Natural History of Destruction*, Harmondsworth, Penguin; also Jorg Friedrich 2006 *The Fire: The Bombing of Germany 1940–1945*, Columbia University Press; the British response is hesitant, recently discussed by A.C. Grayling 2006 *Among the Dead Cities*, London, Bloomsbury

45 Norman Davies 1997 *Europe: A History*, pp.39–42, London, Pimlico

46 Robert Gildea 2002 'Myth, Memory and Policy in France since 1945' in Jan-Werner Muller (ed.) *Memory and Power in Post-War Europe*, Cambridge University Press

47 J.P. Sartre *The Age of Reason*, *The Reprieve* and *Iron in the Soul*; some context for these works is given by Rod Kedward 2006 *La Vie en Bleu: France and the French Since 1900*, London, Penguin, chapters ten to sixteen

48 Franz Fanon 1967 *Black Skin, White Masks*, New York, Grove Press; Franz Fanon 1967 *The Wretched of the Earth*, Harmondsworth, Penguin

49 A familiar trope in public discourse; see Alasdair MacIntyre 1985 2nd ed. *After Virtue*, London, Duckworth

50 Dennis Warwick 1974 *Bureaucracy*, London, Longman; also Martin Albrow 1970 *Bureaucracy*, London, Macmillan

51 H.H. Gerth and C. Wright Mills 1948 *From Max Weber: Essays in Sociology*, London, Routledge and Kegan Paul; also David Beetham 1985 *Max Weber and the Theory of Modern Politics*, Cambridge, Polity

52 Remembered in various ways – his wife's biography – vaguely in popular British memory – actively by people in Singapore; also S.H. Alatas 1971 *Thomas Stamford Raffles: Schemer or Reformer*, Sydney, Angus and Robertson

53 Christopher Bayley and Tim Harper 2004 *Forgotten Armies: The Fall of British Asia 1941–45*, London, Allen Lane, pp.xxi, 9, 355; Orwell was in Burma at the same time as Furnivall, see Adrian Vickers 2004 'The Classics of Indonesian Studies: J.S. Furnivall's *Netherlands India*' in proceedings of 15th *Biennial Conference of Asian Studies Association of Australia*, Canberra 29 June 2004

54 S.H. Alatas 1977 *The Myth of the Lazy Native*, London, Frank Cass; also Alastair Bonnet 2004 *The Idea of the West: Culture, Politics and History*, London, Palgrave; also Rana Kabbani 1994 *Imperial Fictions: Europe's Myths of Orient*, London, Pandora; also Ian Buruma 1996 *The Missionary and the Libertine: Love and War in East and West*, London, Faber and Faber

55   Anthony D. King 1990 *Urbanism, Colonialism and the World Economy*, London, Routledge

56   On the end of empire, see Anthony Burgess 1972 *The Malayan Trilogy*, Harmondsworth, Penguin; on the pleasures, see David Canadine 2001 *Ornamentalism*, London, Allen Lane; and on the nostalgia of expatriates, see Roger Scruton 2001 *England: An Elegy*, London, Pimlico

57   J.S. Furnivall 1939 *Netherlands India: A Study of a Plural Economy*, Cambridge University Press

58   J.M. Keynes was roughly a contemporary; much more familiar; a key figure in inter-war and post-war British public life; academic economist of distinction at Cambridge, member of the Bloomsbury group and a key figure in Whitehall. See Robert Skidelsky 2004 *John Maynard Keynes 1883–1946*, London, Pan Macmillan

59   George Steiner 1992 'Culture: The Price You Pay' in Richard Kearney (ed.) *Visions of Europe*, Dublin, Wolfhound Press

60   Ernest Gellner 1959 *Words and Things*, London, Routledge

61   Richard Rorty 1980 *Philosophy and the Mirror of Nature*, Oxford, Blackwell; Richard Rorty 1989 *Contingency, Irony and Solidarity*, Cambridge University Press

62   Richard Rorty 1998 *Achieving Our Country: Leftist Thought in Twentieth-Century America*, Harvard University Press

63   Lest this sound absurdly pious, it might be noted that social theorists are just as prone as any one else to error, foolishness, self-delusion, enthusiasm and so on, however, the critical community acts – we hope – to weed out the nonsense over the longer run

64   P.W. Preston 1985 *New Trends in Development Theory*, London, Routledge, chapter five, the idea can be unpacked in various ways; it is a theme in the work of Bourdieu, see Pierre Bourdieu 2007 *Sketch for a Self Analysis*, Cambridge, Polity

65   Mark Mazower 1998 *Dark Continent: Europe's Twentieth Century*, London, Allen Lane, who details recent *practice*

66   Zygmunt Bauman 1988 *Legislators and Interpreters*, Cambridge, Polity

67   Bent Flyvbjerg 2001 *Making Social Science Matter: Why Social Enquiry Fails And How It Can Succeed Again*, Cambridge University Press

68   Michael Polanyi 1962 *Personal Knowledge*, London, Routledge

69   At which point, the argument of the text takes a quite particular turn – reflexive claims about the nature of social theorizing entail claims about the social world that has been the sustaining environment of that theorizing – hence the talk about the development of the modern world – however, now, attention turns to the category of 'others' – those who dwell outside the received sphere of practice and theory – but it is the theory which posits these others – it is the theory which gives rise to the enquiry – this exchange cast in terms of language philosophy and social theory is noted by Barbara Fultner 2001' Do Social Philosophers need a Theory of Meaning? Social Theory and Semantics after the Pragmatic Turn' in William Rehg and James Bohman 2001 (eds) *Pluralism and The Pragmatic Turn: The Transformation of Critical Theory*, Massachusetts Institute of Technology

70   Stephen Gudeman 1986 *Economics as Culture*, London, Routledge

71 Clifford Geertz 1993 *The Interpretation of Cultures*, London, Fontana, chapter one

72 Andy Kershaw on BBC Radio plays 'world music' – diverse instances of a generic human disposition to music-making where there is no authoritative standard; the idea of world politics does similar work; on 'relativism' see Clifford Geertz 2000 *Available Light: Anthropological Reflections on Philosophical Topics*, Princeton University Press, chapter three

73 By way of specimen discussions: on the USA, see Anatol Lieven 2004 *America Right or Wrong: An Anatomy of American Nationalism*, London, HarperCollins; on Latin America, see F.H. Cardoso and E.H. Faletto 1979 *Dependency and Development in Latin America*, University of California Press; on Islam, see Karen Armstrong 2002 *Islam: A Short History*, London, Weidenfeld; on South Asia, see Stuart Corbridge and John Harriss 2000 *Reinventing India*, Cambridge, Polity; on Southeast Asia, see Carl A. Trocki 1990 *Opium and Empire: Chinese Society in Colonial Singapore, 1800–1910*, Cornell University Press on China, see Jonathan Spence and Annping Ching 1996 *The Chinese Century: A Photo History*, London, HarperCollins; on Africa, see Basil Davidson 1994 *The Search for Africa*, London, James Currey

74 Flyvbjerg 2001 stresses case study; in abstract terms, so does Wittgenstein; see P.W. Preston 2000 *Understanding Modern Japan: A Political Economy of Development, Culture and Global Power*, London, Sage; P.W. Preston 2007 *Singapore in the Global System: Relationship, Structure and Change*, London, Routledge Curzon – the crucial point here is that both polities are coherent, functioning, subtle and successful and they are not simple variants (successful or otherwise) on the European modernist model – nor are they specimens of an involuted cultural autarchy – they have their own historical trajectories, societies, polities and modes of social theoretic engagement

75 These illustrations are drawn from places with which I have direct familiarity – I have lived and worked in four of these places – thus what sociologists would call 'participant observation' – my experience of China is Hong Kong plus the cities of Beijing and Shanghai

76 On this recall C.B. Macpherson's analysis of Hobbes and Locke; recall also A MacIntyre's analysis of emotivist Western ethico-political culture; note also that this autonomous rational individual figures in much Anglo-American social theorizing (thus, neo-classical economics' 'rational economic man', see Watson 2005). See also Martin Hollis 1977 *Models of Man*, Cambridge University Press

77 See John Clammer 1995 *Difference and Modernity*, London, Kegan Paul International; John Clammer 1997 *Contemporary Urban Japan: A Sociology of Consumption*, Oxford, Blackwell; a distinctive style of theorizing is available in 'Nihonjinron' work, investigations of the special-ness of the Japanese, see Kosaku Yoshino 1992 *Cultural Nationalism in Contemporary Japan*, London, Routledge

78 See Chua, B.H. 1995 *Communitarian Ideology and Democracy in Singapore*, London, Routledge; on 'Singaporean sociology' see John Clammer 2001 'The Dilemmas of the Over Socialized Intellectual' in *Inter-Asia Cultural Studies* 2.2

79 See Norman Stockman 2000 *Understanding Chinese Society*, Cambridge, Polity

80 On Habermas see Holub 1991

81 Norman Davies 1997 *Europe: A History*, London, Pimlico
82 Barrington Moore 1967 *The Social Origins of Dictatorship and Democracy*, London, Allen Lane
83 Nicholas Tarling (ed.) 1992 *The Cambridge History of Southeast Asia Vol. 1*, Cambridge University Press
84 Henry Reynolds 1990 *The Other Side of the Frontier*, Ringwood Victoria, Penguin; also Robert Hughes 1988 *The Fatal Shore*, London, Pan; also Gillian Whitlock and David Carter (eds) 1992 *Images of Australia*, University of Queensland Press
85 Mark Tulley 1992 *No Full Stop in India*, Harmondsworth, Penguin; also Corbridge and Harriss 2000
86 Karen Armstrong 2002
87 Basil Davidson 1974 *Africa in Modern History*, London, Paladin; also Davidson 1994
88 F.H. Cardoso and E.H. Faletto 1979 *Dependency and Development in Latin America*, University of California Press
89 The disciplines of anthropology, linguistics, archaeology, history and so on are attempts to characterize these patterns of life – what exists today has been altered by long exchange with the modern world; see Peter Worsley 1984 *The Three Worlds: Culture and World Development*, London, Weidenfeld; see also C.A. Bayly 2004 *The Birth of the Modern World 1780–1914*, Oxford, Blackwell
90 A.G. Frank 1998 *Reorient: Global Economy in the Asian Age*, University of California Press; also Kenneth Pomeranz 2000 *The Great Divergence: China, Europe and the Making of the Modern World Economy*, Princeton University Press; also J.M. Hobson 2004 *The Eastern Origins of Western Civilization*, Cambridge University Press
91 Roy Porter 2000 *Enlightenment: Britain and the Creation of the Modern World*, London, Allen Lane
92 Karl Marx and Friedrich Engels 1848 *The Manifesto of the Communist Part*, in Karl Marx and Fredrich Engels; *Selected Works*, London, Lawrence and Wishart
93 Pursued in P.W. Preston 1997 *Political/Cultural Identity: Citizens and Nations in a Global Era*, London, Sage
94 Patrick Wright 1985 *On Living in an Old Country*, London, Verso, speaks of 'auratic sites' – exemplifying the identity of the polity
95 James C. Scott 1985 *Weapons of the Weak*, Yale University Press; see Ben Kerkvliet 1977 *The Huk Rebellion: A Study of Peasant Revolt in the Philippines*, University of California Press; also Kevin O'Brien and Li Lianjiang 2006 *Rightful Resistance in Rural China*, Cambridge University Press
96 Thus – the idea of Asian Values – the idea of Confucian capitalism – the idea of rational authoritarianism – the idea of economic nationalism
97 Anthony Payne (ed.) 2004 *The New Regional Politics of Development*, London, Palgrave; also Mark Beeson 2007 *Regionalism and Globalization in East Asia*, London, Palgrave
98 Geertz 2000, chapter ten

Bibliography

Abrams, P. 1968 *The Origins of British Sociology*, Chicago University Press

Acharya, A. 2000 *The Quest for Identity: International Relations of Southeast Asia*, Oxford University Press

Alatas, S.H. 1971 *Thomas Stamford Raffles: Schemer or Reformer*, Sydney, Angus and Robertson

Alatas, S.H. 1977 *The Myth of the Lazy Native*, London, Frank Cass

Albrow, M. 1970 *Bureaucracy*, London, Macmillan

Anderson, B. 1983 *Imagined Communities*, London, Verso

Anderson, P. 1983 *In the Tracks of Historical Materialism*, London, Verso

Anderson, P. 1992 *English Questions*, London, Verso

Anderson, P. 2004 'Deringolade', *London Review of Books* Vol. 26.17

Anderson, P. 2004 'Union Sucree', *London Review of Books* Vol. 26.18

Apel, K.O. 1980 *Towards a Transformation of Philosophy*, London, Routledge and Kegan Paul

Armstrong, K. 2002 *Islam: A Short History*, London, Weidenfeld

Aron, R. 1968 *Main Currents in Sociological Thought Vol.1*, Harmondsworth, Pelican

Aron, R. 1970 *Main Currents in Sociological Thought Vol.2*, Harmondsworth, Penguin

Ayer, A.J. 1971 *Language, Truth and Logic*, Harmondsworth, Penguin

Ayer, A.J. 1985 *Wittgenstein*, Harmondsworth, Penguin

Backhouse, R. 2002 *The Penguin History of Economics*, Harmondsworth, Penguin

Bartley, W.W. 1986 *Wittgenstein*, London, The Cresset Library

Bauman, Z. 1976 *Towards a Critical Sociology*, London, Routledge and Kegan Paul

Bauman, Z. 1978 *Hermeneutics and Social Science*, London, Hutchinson

Bauman, Z. 1987 *Legislators and Interpreters*, Cambridge, Polity

Bauman, Z. 1988 *Freedom*, Milton Keynes, Open University Press

Bauman, Z. 1989 *Modernity and the Holocaust*, Cambridge, Polity

Bauman, Z. 1991 *Modernity and Ambivalence*, Cambridge, Polity

Bauman, Z. 1992 *Intimations of Modernity*, London, Routledge

Bayley, C. and Harper, T. 2004 *Forgotten Armies: The Fall of British Asia 1941–45*, London, Allen Lane

Bayly, C.A. 2004 *The Birth of the Modern World 1780–1914*, Oxford, Blackwell

Beetham, D. 1985 *Max Weber and the Theory of Modern Politics*, Cambridge, Polity

Belharz, P. 1991 *Social Theory: A Guide to Central Thinkers*, London, Allen and Unwin

Benton, T. 1977 *Philosophical Foundations of the Three Sociologies*, London, Routledge and Kegan Paul

Bernstein, R. 1979 *The Restructuring of Social and Political Theory*, London, Methuen

Bernstein, R. 1983 *Beyond Objectivism and Relativism: Science Hermeneutics and Praxis*, Oxford, Blackwell

Bernstein, R. (ed.) 1985 *Habermas and Modernity*, Cambridge, Polity

Blair, A. 2005 *The European Union Since 1945*, London, Longman

Bleicher, J. 1980 *Contemporary Hermeneutics: Method, Philosophy and Critique*, London, Routledge

Bleicher, J. 1982 *The Hermeneutic Imagination: Outline of a Positive Critique of Scientism and Sociology*, London, Routledge

Block, F. 1990 *Post Industrial Possibilities: A Critique of Economic Discourse*, University of California Press

Bloor, D. 1983 *Wittgenstein: A Social Theory of Knowledge*, London, Macmillan

Bloor, D. 1991 *Knowledge and Social Imagery*, Chicago University Press

Bloor, D. 1997 *Wittgenstein: Rules and Institutions*, London, Routledge

Boggs, C. 1993 *Intellectuals and the Crisis of Modernity*, State University of New York Press

Bonnet, A. 2004 *The Idea of the West: Culture, Politics and History*, London, Palgrave

Borradori, G. 1994 *The American Philosopher*, University of Chicago

Borradori, G. 2003 *Philosophy in a Time of Terror: Dialogues with Jurgen Habermas and Jacques Derrida*, University of Chicago Press

Bottomore, T. 1984 *The Frankfurt School*, London, Ellis Horwood

Brandstatter, C. (ed.) 2006 *Vienna 1900 and the Heroes of Modernism*, London, Thames and Hudson

Brewer, A. 1980 *Marxist Theories of Imperialism*, London, Routledge

Bryant, C. 1985 *Positivism in Social Theory and Research*, London, Macmillan

Burgess, A. 1972 *The Malayan Trilogy*, Harmondsworth, Penguin

Burke, E. 1790 *Reflections on the Revolution in France*

Burrow, J.W. 1966 *Evolution and Society*, Cambridge University Press

Buruma, I. 1996 *The Missionary and the Libertine: Love and War in East and West*, London, Faber and Faber

Buruma, I. 1999 *Voltaire's Coconuts: Or Anglo-Mania in Europe*, London, Weidenfeld and Nicolson

Callinicos, A. 1989 *Against Postmodernism: A Marxist Critique*, Cambridge, Polity

Canadine, D. 2001 *Ornamentalism*, London, Allen Lane

Cardoso, F.H. and Faletto, E.H. 1979 *Dependency and Development in Latin America*, University of California Press

Carr, E.H. 1939 (2001) *The Twenty Year Crisis*, London, Palgrave

Carrol, L. 1965 *Alice in Wonderland*, London, Dent

Cartwright, N., Cat, J., Fleck, L., and Uebel, T. 1996 *Otto Neurath: Philosophy Between Science and Politics*, Cambridge University Press

Carver, T. (ed.) 1975 *Karl Marx Texts On Method*, Oxford, Blackwell

Chalmers, A.F. 1982, 2nd ed. *What is this Thing Called Science?*, Milton Keynes, Open University Press

Chitnis, A.C. 1976 *The Scottish Enlightenment: A Social History*, London, Croom Helm

Cipolla, C. 1996 *Guns, Sails and Empire*, New York, Pantheon

Clammer, J. 1985 *Anthropology and Political Economy*, London, Macmillan

Clammer, J. 1995 *Difference and Modernity*, London, Kegan Paul

Clammer, J. 1997 *Contemporary Urban Japan: A Sociology of Consumption*, Oxford, Blackwell

Clammer, J. 2001 'The Dilemmas of the Over Socialized Intellectual', in *Inter-Asia Cultural Studies 2.2*

Cole, K., Cameron, J., and Edwards, C. 1991 *Why Economists Disagree*, London, Longman

Colley, L. 1992 *Britons: Forging the Nation 1707–1837*, Yale University Press

Collini, S. 1979 *Liberalism and Sociology: L T Hobhouse and Political Argument in England 1880–1914*, Cambridge University Press

Collini, S. 2003 'No Bullshit Bullshit' in *London Review of Books* 25.02 23 January 2003

Connerton, P. (ed.) 1976 *Critical Sociology*, Harmondsworth, Penguin

Corbridge, S. and Harriss, J. 2000 *Reinventing India*, Cambridge, Polity

Crawford, B.M.A. 2000 *Idealism and Realism in International Relations*, London, Routledge

Crick, B. 1980 *George Orwell*, Harmondsworth, Penguin

Critchley, S. 2001 *Continental Philosophy: A Very Short Introduction*, Oxford University Press

Culler, J. 1976 *Saussure*, London, Fontana

Cummings, B. 1997 *Korea's Place in the Sun*, New York, Norton

Daiches, D., Jones, P., and Jones, J. (eds) 1986 *A Hotbed of Genius: The Scottish Enlightenment 1730–1790*, Edinburgh University Press

Dallymar, F.R. and McCarthy, T.A. 1977 *Understanding and Social Enquiry*, University of Notre Dame Press; for a commentary

Darras, J. and Snowman, D. 1990 *Beyond the Tunnel of History*, London, Macmillan

Dasgupta, A.K. 1985 *Epochs of Economic Thought*, Oxford, Blackwell

Davidson, B. 1974 *Africa in Modern History*, London, Paladin

Davidson, B. 1994 *The Search for Africa*, London, James Currey

Davies, N. 1997 *Europe: A History*, London, Pimlico

de Saussure, F. 1990 *Course in General Linguistics*, London, Duckworth

Delanty, G. and Strydom, P. (eds) 2003 *Philosophies of Social Science: The Classical and Contemporary Readings*, Maidenhead, Open University Press

Delors, J. 1992 *Our Europe: The Community and National Development*, London, Verso

Diesing, P. 1991 *How Does Social Science Work: Reflections on Practice*, University of Pittsburgh Press

Dilthey, W. 1914 *Collected Works*, Leipzig

Dunleavy, P., Kelly, P.J., and Moran, M. (eds) 2000 *British Political Science: Fifty Years of Political Studies*, Oxford, Blackwell

Eagleton, T. 2003 'Reach Me Down Romantic' in *London Review of Books* 25.12 19 June 2003

Edmonds, D. and Edinow, J. 2001 *Wittgenstein's Poker*, London, Faber

Ettinger, E. 1995 *Hannah Arendt and Martin Heidegger*, Yale University Press

Evans, R.J. 1997 *Re-reading German History: From Unification to Reunification 1800–1996*, London, Routledge

Fanon, F. 1967 *Black Skin, White Masks*, New York, Grove Press

Fanon, F. 1967 *The Wretched of the Earth*, Harmondsworth, Penguin

Fay, B. 1975 *Social Theory and Political Practice*, London, Allen and Unwin

Fay, B. 1987 *Critical Social Science*, Cambridge, Polity

Fay, B. 1996 *Contemporary Philosophy of Social Science*, Oxford, Blackwell

Feyerabend, P. 1978 *Science in a Free Society*, London, New Left Books

Feyerabend, P. 1988 Revised ed. *Against Method*, London, Verso

Finlayson, J.G. 2005 *Habermas: A Very Short Introduction*, Oxford University Press

Flyvbjerg, B. 2001 *Making Social Science Matter: Why Social Enquiry Fails and How It Can Succeed Again*, Cambridge University Press

Foucault, M. 1970 *The Order of Things: An Archaeology of the Human Sciences*, London, Tavistock

Foucault, M. 1973 *The Birth of the Clinic*, New York, Vintage

Foucault, M. 1977 *Discipline and Punish*, New York, Pantheon

Frank, A.G. 1998 *Reorient: Global Economy in the Asian Age*, University of California Press

Friedman, M. 1962 *Capitalism and Freedom*, University of Chicago Press

Friedman, M. and Friedman, R. 1980 *Free to Choose*, London, Secker

Friedman, M. 1953 *Essays in Positive Economics*, University of Chicago Press

Friedrich, J. 2006 *The Fire: The Bombing of Germany 1940–1945*, Columbia University Press

Fromm, E. 1942 *Fear of Freedom*, London, Routledge

Fukuyama, F. 1992 *The End of History and the Last Man*, London, Hamish Hamilton

Furedi, F. 2004 *Where Have All the Intellectuals Gone: Confronting 21st Century Philistinism*, London, Continuum

Furnivall, J.S. 1939 *Netherlands India: A Study of a Plural Economy*, Cambridge University Press

Gadamer, H-G. 1979 2nd ed. *Truth and Method*, London, Sheed and Ward

Gadamer, H-G. 1994 *Heideggers's Ways*, State University of New York

Gaddis, J.L. 1998 *We Know Now: Rethinking Cold War History*, Oxford University Press

Gay, P. 2008 *Modernism: The Lure of Heresy*, New York, Norton

Geertz, C. 1993 *The Interpretation of Cultures*, London, Fontana

Geertz, C. 2000 *Available Light: Anthropological Reflections on Philosophical Topics*, Princeton University Press

Gellner, E. 1959 *Words and Things*, London, Routledge

Gellner, E. 1964 *Thought and Change*, London, Wiedenfeld

Gellner, E. 1983 *Nations and Nationalism*, Oxford, Blackwell

Gerth, H.H. and Mills, C.W. 1948 *From Max Weber: Essays in Sociology*, London, Routledge and Kegan Paul

Giddens, A. 1982 *Profiles and Critiques in Social Theory*, London, Macmillan

Giddens, A. 1987 *Social Theory and Modern Sociology*, Cambridge, Polity

Giddens, A. 1971 *Capitalism and Modern Social Theory: An Analysis of the Writings of Marx, Durkheim and Max Weber*, Cambridge University Press

Giddens, A. 1972 *Politics and Sociology in the Thought of Max Weber*, London, Macmillan

Giddens, A. 1976 *New Rules of Sociological Method*, London, Hutchinson

Giddens, A. 1979 *Central Problems in Social Theory*, London, Macmillan

Giddens, A. 1984 *The Constitution of Society*, Cambridge, Polity

Goldman, L. 1969 *The Human Sciences and Philosophy*, London, Cape

Gramsci, A. (ed. Q. Hoare and G. Nowell Smith) 1971 *Selections from the Prison Notebooks*, London, Lawrence and Wishart

Grass, G. 1962 *The Tin Drum*, London, Secker and Warburg

Grass, G. 1990 *Two States, One Nation*, London, Secker and Warburg

Grass, G. 1999 *My Century*, London, Faber and Faber

Grass, G. 2002 *Crabwalk*, London, Faber and Faber

Greene, M. 1966 *The Knower and the Known*, London, Faber and Faber

Gudeman, S. 1986 *Economics as Culture*, London, Routledge

Habermas, J. 1971 *Knowledge and Human Interests*, Boston, Beacon Press

Habermas, J. 1971 *Towards a Rational Society*, London, Heineman

Habermas, J. 1974 *Theory and Practice*, London, Heinemann

Habermas, J. 1976 *Legitimation Crisis*, London, Heinemann

Habermas, J. 1979 *Communication and the Evolution of Society*, Boston, Beacon Press

Habermas, J. 1984 *The Theory of Communicative Action: Vol.1: Reason and the Rationalization of Society*, London, Heinemann

Habermas, J. 1987 *The Theory of Communicative Action: Vol.2: The Critique of Functionalist Reason*, Cambridge, Polity

Habermas, J. 1988 *On the Logic of the Social Sciences*, Cambridge, Polity

Habermas, J. 1989 *The Structural Transformation of the Public Sphere*, Cambridge, Polity

Habermas, J. 1997 *A Berlin Republic: Writings on Germany*, p. 39, University of Nebraska Press

Habermas, J. 2001 *The Postnational Constellation: Political Essays*, MIT Press

Habermas, J. 2006 *The Divided West*, Cambridge, Polity

Hacker, P.M.S. 1996 *Wittgenstein's Place in Twentieth Century Analytical Philosophy*, Oxford, Blackwell

Hacohen, M.H. 2000 *Karl Popper: The Formative Years 1902–1945*, Cambridge University Press

Hahn, H., Neurath, O., and Carnap, R. 1929 *The Scientific Conception of the World: the Vienna Circle*, Vienna, Ernst Mach Society

Halliday, F. 1989 *Cold War, Third World*, London, Hutchinson Radius

Hamilton, P. 1974 *Knowledge and Social Structure*, London, Routledge and Kegan Paul

Hamilton, P. (ed.) 1991 *Max Weber (1): Critical Assessments*, London, Routledge

Hampshire-Monk, I. 1992 *A History of Modern Political Thought*, Oxford, Blackwell

Hanfling, O. 1981 *Logical Positivism*, Oxford, Blackwell

Hankins, T.L. 1985 *Science and the Enlightenment*, Cambridge University Press

Harris, R. 1990 *Language, Saussure and Wittgenstein: How to Play Games with Words*, London, Routledge

Harvey, D. 1989 *The Condition of Postmodernity*, Oxford, Blackwell

Haslam, J. 1999 *The Vices of Integrity: E.H. Carr 1892–1982*, London, Verso

Hawthorn, G. 1976 *Enlightenment and Despair*, Cambridge University Press

Hay, C. 2002 *Political Analysis: A Critical Introduction*, London, Palgrave

Held, D. 1980 *Introduction to Critical Theory: Horkheimer to Habermas*, London, Hutchinson

Held, D. 1987 *Models of Democracy*, Cambridge, Polity

Hettne, B. 1995 2nd ed. *Development Theory and the Three Worlds*, London, Longman

Hilgruber, A. 1981 *Germany and the Two World Wars*, Harvard University Press

Himmelfarb, G. 2005 *The Roads to Modernity: The British, French and American Enlightenments*, New York, Vintage

Hindess, B. 1977 *Philosophy and Methodology in the Social Sciences*, Brighton, Harvester

Hirst, P. and Thompson, G. 1999 2nd ed. *Globalization in Question*, Cambridge, Polity

Hobsbawm, E. 2005 'Benefits of Diaspora' in *London Review of Books*, Vol. 27.20

176 *Bibliography*

Hobsbawm, E. 1990 *Nations and Nationalism Since 1780: Programme, Myth and Reality*, Cambridge University Press

Hobsbawm, E. 1994 *The Age of Extremes: The Short Twentieth Century 1914–1991*, London, Michael Joseph

Hobsbawm, E. 2002 *Interesting Times: A Twentieth Century Life*, London, Abacus

Hobson, J.M. 2004 *The Eastern Origins of Western Civilization*, Cambridge University Press

Hodges, H.A. 1944 *Wilhelm Dilthey An Introduction*, London, Kegan Paul, Trench, Trubner and Co.

Hodgson, G. 1988 *Economics and Institutions*, Cambridge, Polity

Hollis, M. 1977 *Models of Man*, Cambridge University Press

Hollis, M., and Nell, E.J. 1975 *Rational Economic Man*, Cambridge University Press

Holub, R. 1992 *Antonio Gramsci: Beyond Marxism and Postmodernism*, London, Routledge

Holub, R.C. 1991 *Jurgen Habermas Critic in the Public Sphere*, London, Routledge

Horkheimer, M. and Adorno, T. 1972 *Dialectic of Enlightenment*, London, Allen Lane

Hughes, H.S. 1959 *Consciousness and Society: The Reorientation of European Social Thought 1890–1930*, London, MacGibbon and Kee

Hughes, R. 1988 *The Fatal Shore*, London, Pan

Inglis, F. 1993 *Cultural Studies*, Oxford, Blackwell

Jameson, F. 1991 *Postmodernism: The Cultural Logic of Late Capitalism*, London, Verso

Janik, A. 2001 *Wittgenstein's Vienna Revisited*, New Brunswick, Transaction

Janik, A. and Toulmin, S. 1973 *Wittgenstein's Vienna*, New York, Simon and Shuster

Janik, A. and Veigl, H. 1998 *Wittgenstein in Vienna*, Wein, Springer

Jay, M. 1973 *The Dialectical Imagination*, Boston, Little Brown

Jay, M. 1984 *Marxism and Totality*, Cambridge, Polity

Jenks, C. 1993 *Culture*, London, Routledge

Jennings, J. and Kemp-Welch, A. (eds) 1997 *Intellectuals in Politics: From the Dreyfus affair to Salman Rushdie*, London, Routledge

Johnson, C. 2004 *The Sorrows of Empire: Militarism, Secrecy and the End of the Republic*, London, Verso

Jones, C. 1998 *E.H. Carr and International Relations: A Duty to Lie*, Cambridge University Press

Jones, G. 1980 *Social Darwinism and English Thought*, Brighton, Harvester

Judt, T. 2005 *Post-war: A History of Europe Since 1945*, New York, The Penguin Press

Kabbani, R. 1994 *Imperial Fictions: Europe's Myths of Orient*, London, Pandora

Kant, I. 1784 *What is Enlightenment?*

Kearney, R. (ed.) 1992 *Visions of Europe*, Dublin, Wolfhound Press

Kearney, R. (ed.) 1996 *Paul Ricoeur: The Hermeneutics of Action*, London, Sage

Kedward, R. 2006 *La Vie en Bleu: France and the French Since 1900*, London, Penguin

Kellner, D. 1989 *Critical Theory, Marxism and Modernity*, Cambridge, Polity

Kenny, A. 1973 *Wittgenstein*, Harmondsworth, Penguin

Kerkvliet, B. 1977 *The Huk Rebellion: A Study of Peasant Revolt in the Philippines*, University of California Press

Kerr, C. *et al.* 1960 *Industrialism and Industrial Man*, Harmondsworth, Penguin

Kilminster, R. 1979 *Praxis and Method: A Sociological Dialogue with Lukacs, Gramsci and the Early Frankfurt School*, London, Routledge and Kegan Paul

King, A.D. 1990 *Urbanism, Colonialism and the World Economy*, London, Routledge

Kitching, G. and Pleasants, N. (eds) 2002 *Marx and Wittgenstein: Knowledge, Morality and Politics*, London, Routledge

Korsch, K. 1970 *Marxism and Philosophy*, London, New Left Books

Kuhn, T. 1970 2nd ed. *The Structure of Scientific Revolutions*, University of Chicago

Laffan, B., O'Donnel, R., and Smith, M. 2000 *Europe's Experimental Union: Rethinking Integration*, London, Routledge

Laing, R.D. 1965 *The Divided Self: An Existential Study in Sanity and Madness*, Harmondsworth, Penguin

Laing, R.D. 1967 *The Politics of Experience and The Bird of Paradise*, Harmondsworth, Penguin

Laing, R.D. 1970 *Knots*, London, Tavistock

Lakatos, I. and Musgrave, A. (eds) 1970 *Criticism and the Growth of Knowledge*, Cambridge University Press

Laslett, P. and Runciman, W.G. (eds) 1962 *Politics, Philosophy and Society Second Series*, Oxford, Blackwell

Laslett, P. and Runciman, W.G. (eds) 1967 *Philosophy, Politics and Society, Third Series*, Oxford, Blackwell

Latour, B. 1987 *Science in Action*, Harvard University Press

Latour, B. 1999 *Pandora's Hope*, Harvard University Press

Lechte, J. 1994 *Fifty Key Contemporary Thinkers: From Structuralism to Post-modernity*, London, Routledge

Lieven, A. 2004 *America Right or Wrong: An Anatomy of American Nationalism*, London, HarperCollins

Lindqvist, S. 2002 *A History of Bombing*, London, Granta

Long, N. and Long, A. (eds) 1992 *Battlefields of Knowledge*, London, Routledge

Lucas, S. 2003 *Orwell: Life and Times*, London, Haus Publishing

Lukacs, G. 1971 *History and Class Consciousness*, London, Merlin

Lukes, S. 1973 *Individualism*, Oxford, Blackwell

Lukes, S. 1977 *Essays in Social Theory*, London, Macmillan

Lyotard, J.F. 1979 *The Postmodern Condition: A Report on Knowledge*, Manchester University Press

Macey, D. 1993 *The Lives of Michel Foucault*, London, Vintage

MacIntyre, A. 1967 *A Short History of Ethics*, London, Routledge and Kegan Paul

MacIntyre, A. 1970 *Marcuse*, London, Fontana

MacIntyre, A. 1971 *Against the Self Images of the Age*, London, Duckworth

MacIntyre, A. 1985 2nd ed. *After Virtue: A Study in Moral Theory*, London, Duckworth

MacIntyre, A. 1988 *Whose Justice, Which Rationality?*, London, Duckworth

Macpherson, C.B. 1962 *The Political Theory of Possessive Individualism*, Oxford University Press

Macpherson, C.B. 1973 *Democratic Theory: Essays in Retrieval*, Oxford University Press

Magee, B. 1973 *Popper*, London, Fontana

Marcuse, H. 1964 *One Dimensional Man*, Boston, Beacon

Marcuse, H. 1969 *Eros and Civilization*, London, Sphere

Marcuse, H. 1972 *An Essay on Liberation*, Harmondsworth, Penguin

Marsh, D. and Stoker, G. (eds) 1995 *Theory and Methods in Political Science*, London, Macmillan

Marx, K. and Engels, F. 1848 *The Manifesto of the Communist Party*, reprinted in Karl Marx and Fredrich Engels 1968 *Selected Works*, London, Lawrence and Wishart

Mayer, A. 1981 *The Persistence of the Old Regime*, New York, Croom Helm

Mayer, A. 1988 *Why did the Heavens Not Darken: The 'Final Solution' in History*, New York, Pantheon

Mazower, M. 1998 *Dark Continent: Europe's Twentieth Century*, London, Allen Lane

McCarthy, T. 1984 *The Critical Theory of Jurgen Habermas*, Cambridge, Polity

McClosky, D.N. 1990 *If You are So Smart: The Narrative of Economic Expertise*, University of Chicago Press

McGuiness, B. 1988 *Wittgenstein: A Life 1889–1921*, Harmondsworth, Penguin

McMylor, P. 1994 *Alasdair MacIntyre: Critic of Modernity*, London, Routledge

Menon, A. 2008 *Europe: The State of the Union*, London, Atlantic Books

Merquior, J.G. 1985 *Foucault*, London, Fontana

Merton, R. 1968 (enlarged edition) *Social Theory and Social Structure*, New York, The Free Press

Mills, C.W. 1970 *The Sociological Imagination*, Harmondsworth, Pelican

Milton, G. 1999 *Nathaniel's Nutmeg: How One Man's Courage Changed the Course of History*, London, Sceptre

Mirowski, P. 1988 *Against Mechanism: Protecting Economics from Science*, New Jersey, Rowman and Littlefield

Monk, R. 1991 *Ludwig Wittgenstein: The Duty of Genius*, London, Vintage

Moore, B. 1967 *The Social Origins of Dictatorship and Democracy*, London, Allen Lane

Moyal-Sharrock, D. (ed.) 2004 *The Third Wittgenstein: The Post-Investigation Works*, Aldershot, Avebury

Muller, J-W. (ed.) 2002 *Memory and Power in Post-War Europe*, Cambridge University Press

Nagel, E. 1961 *The Structure of Science*, London, Routledge and Kegan Paul

Nedelmann, B. and Sztompka, P. (eds) 1993 *Sociology in Europe: In Search of an Identity*, Berlin, Walter de Gruyter

Nisbet, R. 1970 *The Sociological Tradition*, London, Heinemann

Norris, C. 1987 *Derrida*, London, Fontana

O'Brien, K. and Li, L. 2006 *Rightful Resistance in Rural China*, Cambridge University Press

Okasha, S. 2002 *Philosophy of Science: A Very Short Introduction*, Oxford University Press

Ormerod, P. 1994 *The Death of Economics*, London, Faber and Faber

Outhwaite, W. 1975 *Understanding Social Life: The Method Called Verstehen*, London, Allen and Unwin

Outhwaite, W. 1987 *New Philosophies of Social Science: Realism, Hermeneutics and Critical Theory*, London, Macmillan

Outhwaite, W. (ed.) 1996 *The Habermas Reader*, Cambridge, Polity

Passmore, J. 1957 *A Hundred Years of Philosophy*, Harmondsworth, Penguin

Passmore, J. 1970 *The Perfectibility of Man*, London, Duckworth

Payne, A. (ed.) 2004 *The New Regional Politics of Development*, London, Palgrave

Pears, D. 1971 *Wittgenstein*, London, Fontana
Pheby, J. 1988 *Methodology and Economics: A Critical Introduction*, London, Macmillan
Plamenatz, J. 1963 *Man and Society* (2 vols), London, Longman
Plant, R. 1991 *Modern Political Thought*, Oxford, Blackwell
Polanyi, M. 1962 *Personal Knowledge*, London, Routledge and Kegan Paul
Pollard, S. 1971 *The Idea of Progress*, Harmondsworth, Penguin
Pomeranz, K. 2000 *The Great Divergence: China, Europe and the Making of the Modern World Economy*, Princeton University Press
Popkin, R.H. 1999 *The Pimlico History of Western Philosophy*, London, Pimlico
Popper, K. 1957 *The Poverty of Historicism*, London, Routledge and Kegan Paul
Popper, K. 1945 *The Open Society and Its Enemies*, London, Routledge and Kegan Paul
Popper, K. 1974 5th ed. *Conjectures and Refutations: The Growth of Scientific Knowledge*, London, Routledge and Kegan Paul
Porter, R. 2000 *Enlightenment: Britain and the Creation of the Modern World*, London, Allen Lane
Porter, R. 2001 2nd ed. *The Enlightenment*, London, Palgrave
Prebisch, R. 1950 *The Economic Development of Latin America*, UN Publications
Preston, P.W. 1982 *Theories of Development*, London, Routledge and Kegan Paul
Preston, P.W. 1985 *New Trends in Development Theory*, London, Routledge and Kegan Paul
Preston, P.W. 1987 *Rethinking Development*, London, Routledge
Preston, P.W. 1994 *Discourses of Development*, Aldershot, Avebury
Preston, P.W. 1996 *Development Theory: An Introduction*, Oxford, Blackwell
Preston, P.W. 1997 *Political Cultural Identity: Citizens and Nations in a Global Era*, London, Sage
Preston, P.W. 2000 *Understanding Modern Japan: A Political Economy of Development, Culture and Global Power*, London, Sage
Preston, P.W. 2004 *Relocating England: Englishness in the New Europe*, Manchester University Press
Preston, P.W. 2005 'Reading the Ongoing Changes: European Identity' in *Political Quarterly* 76.4
Preston, P.W. 2007 *Singapore in the Global System: Relationship, Structure and Change*, London, Routledge Curzon
Quine, W.V.O. 1953 *From a Logical Point of View*, New York, Harper
Quine, W.V.O. and Ullian, J.S. 1970 *The Web of Belief*, New York, Random House
Rabinow, P. (ed.) 1984 *The Foucault Reader*, Harmondsworth, Penguin
Rehg, W. and Bohman, J. (eds) 2001 *Pluralism and The Pragmatic Turn: The Transformation of Critical Theory*, Massachusetts Institute of Technology
Rendall, J. 1978 *The Origins of the Scottish Enlightenment*, London, Macmillan
Reynolds, H. 1990 *The Other Side of the Frontier*, Ringwood Victoria, Penguin
Richardson, J. (ed.) 2001 2nd ed. *European Union: Power and Policy Making*, London, Routledge
Rickman, H.P. 1976 *Wilhelm Dilthey Selected Writings*, Cambridge University Press
Robey, D. (ed.) 1973 *Structuralism: An Introduction*, Oxford University Press
Root, M. 1993 *Philosophy of Social Science: The Methods, Ideals and Politics* of Social Enquiry, Oxford, Blackwell

Rorty, R. 1980 *Philosophy and the Mirror of Nature*, Oxford, Blackwell
Rorty, R. 1982 *The Consequences of Pragmatism*, University of Minnesota Press
Rorty, R. 1989 *Contingency, Irony and Solidarity*, Cambridge University Press
Rorty, R. 1998 *Achieving Our Country: Leftist Thought in Twentieth-Century America*, Harvard University Press
Rorty, R. 1999 *Philosophy and Social Hope*, London, Penguin
Rosamund, B. 2000 *Theories of European Integration*, London, Palgrave
Rosenthal, R. and Maggie, T. (eds) 1995 *Building Sights*, Academy Editions
Rostow, W.W. 1960 *The Stages of Economic Growth: A Non-Communist Manifesto*, Cambridge University Press
Said, E. 1985 *Orientalism*, London, Peregrine
Salamini, L. 1974 'Gramsci and Marxist Sociology of Knowledge' in *The Sociological Quarterly 15*
Salamini, L. 1975 'The Specificity of Marxist Sociology in Gramsci's Theory' in *The Sociological Quarterly 16*
Salamini, L. 1981 *The Sociology of Political Praxis: An Introduction to Gramsci's Theory*, London, Routledge
Sarkar, S. (ed.) 1996 *Science and Philosophy in the Twentieth Century: Basic Works of Logical Empiricism: Vol.6 The Legacy of the Vienna Circle*, New York, Garland Publishing
Sarkar, S. (ed.) 1996 *Science and Philosophy in the Twentieth Century: Basic Works of Logical Empiricism: Vol.1 The Emergence of Logical Empiricism*, New York, Garland Publishing
Scott, J.C. 1985 *Weapons of the Weak*, Yale University Press
Scruton, R. 2001 *England: An Elegy*, London, Pimlico
Sebald, W.G. 2004 *On the Natural History of Destruction*, Harmondsworth, Penguin
Segerstrale, U. (ed.) 2000 *Beyond the Science Wars: The Missing Discourse about Science and Society*, State University of New York
Sharock, W.W., Hughes, J.A., and Martin, P.J. 2003 *Understanding Modern Sociology*, London, Sage
Sheehan, N. 1990 *A Bright and Shining Lie*, London, Picador
Sheridan, A. 1980 *Michael Foucault The Will to Truth*, London, Tavistock
Sheridan, K. (ed.) 1998 *Emerging Economic Systems in Asia*, St. Leonards, Allen and Unwin
Skidelsky, R. 2004 *John Maynard Keynes 1883–1946*, London, Pan Macmillan
Slater, P. 1977 *The Origins and Significance of the Frankfurt School*, London, Routledge and Kegan Paul
Smith, D. 1987 *The Rise and Fall of Monetarism*, Harmondsworth, Penguin
Smith, D. 1991 *The Rise of Historical Sociology*, Cambridge, Polity
Snowman, D. 2003 *The Hitler Émigrés: The Cultural Impact on Britain of Refugees from Nazism*, London, Pimlico
Sobel, D. 1998 *Longitude: The True Story of a Lone Genius Who Solved the Greatest Scientific Problem of His Time*, London, Fourth Estate
Spence, J. and Ching, A. 1996 *The Chinese Century: A Photo History*, London, HarperCollins
Staniland, M. 1985 *What is Political Economy*, Yale University Press
Steeten, P. 1972 *The Frontiers of Development Studies*, London, Macmillan
Steiner, G. 1992 'Culture: The Price You Pay' in Richard Kearney (ed.) *Visions of Europe*, Dublin, Wolfhound Press

Stone, B.L. 2000 *Robert Nisbet: Communitarian Traditionalist*, Wilmington, Delaware, ISI Books

Strange, S. 1988 *States and Markets*, London, Pinter

Stroll, A. 2002 *Wittgenstein*, Oxford, Oneworld

Sturrock, J. 1986 *Structuralism*, London, Palladin

Swedberg, R. 1987 'Economic Sociology Past and Present' in *Current Sociology*

Tarling, N. (ed.) 1992 *The Cambridge History of Southeast Asia Vol.1*, Cambridge University Press

Taylor, C. 1980 'Understanding in Human Science' in *Review of Metaphysics* 34

Taylor, C. 1971 'Interpretation and the Science of Man' in *Review of Metaphysics* 25

Thompson, J.B. and Held, D. (eds) 1982 *Habermas: Critical Debates*, London, Macmillan

Trocki, C.A. 1990 *Opium and Empire: Chinese Society in Colonial Singapore, 1800–1910*, Cornell University Press

Trocki, C.A. 1999 *Opium, Empire and Global Political Economy*, London, Routledge

Tudor, T. 1982 *Beyond Empiricism*, London, Routledge and Kegan Paul

Tulley, M. 1992 *No Full Stop in India*, Harmondsworth, Penguin

Tully, J. (ed.) 1988 *Meaning and Context: Quentin Skinner and his Critics*, Cambridge, Polity

Uebel, T. 2008 'The Vienna Circle' in *The Stanford Encyclopaedia of Philosophy*, Edward N. Zalta (ed.) http://plato.stanford.edu/archives/fall2008/entries/vienna-circle/

Vickers, A. 2004 'The Classics of Indonesian Studies: J.S. Furnivall's *Netherlands India*' in proceedings of *15th Biennial Conference of Asian Studies Association of Australia*, Canberra 29 June 2004

Vincent, A. 2004 *The Nature of Political Theory*, Oxford University Press

Waltz, K. 1959 *Man, State and War*, Columbia University Press

Warnke, G. 1987 *Gadamer: Hermeneutics, Tradition and Reason*, Cambridge, Polity

Warwick, D. 1974 *Bureaucracy*, London, Longman

Watson, M. 2005 *Foundations of International Political Economy*, London, Palgrave

Weinsheimer, J. 1985 *Gadamer's Hermeneutics: A Reading of Truth and Method*, Yale University Press

Wheatcroft, G. 2007 *Yo Blair*, London, Politico's

Whitebrook, M. 2001 *Identity, Narrative and Politics*, London, Routledge

Whitlock, G. and Carter, D. (eds) 1992 *Images of Australia*, University of Queensland Press

Williams, B. 2005 *In the Beginning Was the Deed: Realism and Moralism in Political Argument*, Princeton University Press

Williams, R. 1963 *Culture and Society 1780–1950*, Harmondsworth, Penguin

Williams, R. (ed.) 1974 *George Orwell: A Collection of Critical Essays*, Englewood Cliffs, Prentice Hall

Winch, P. 1958/1990 2nd ed. *The Idea of a Social Science and Its Relation to Philosophy*, London, Routledge

Winch, P. 1972 *Ethics and Actions*, London, Routledge

Wittgenstein, L. 1953 *Philosophical Investigations*, Cambridge University Press

Wittgenstein, L. 1974 *On Certainty*, Oxford, Blackwell

Wolin, R. 1990 *The Politics of Being: The Political Thought of Martin Heidegger*, New York, Columbia University Press

Wolin, R. 1992 *The Terms of Cultural Criticism: The Frankfurt School, Existentialism and Poststructuralism*, Columbia University Press
Woodiwiss, A. 1993 *Postmodernity USA*, London, Sage
Worsley, P. 1984 *The Three Worlds: Culture and World Development*, London, Weidenfeld
Wright, P. 1985 *On Living in an Old Country*, London, Verso
Young, J. 1997 *Heidegger, Philosophy and Nazism*, Cambridge University Press